This Book Will Be Helpful And Of Interest To:

1. Men and women who speak in public, conduct classes, or address their business associates or neighbors

2. Toastmasters and chairmen of meetings and committees

3. General readers who enjoy humorous stories, epigrams, and actual illustrations of speeches

. . . Among the topics covered in this invaluable book are:

EVERYDAY SPEAKING

WHAT TO TALK ABOUT

DEVELOPING YOUR SPEECH PLAN

HOW TO USE ANECDOTES AND STORIES EFFECTIVELY

HUMOROUS STORIES FOR ALL OCCASIONS

For a complete summary of topics turn immediately to the table of contents!

Material for this book was taken from three of Mr. Prochnow's best-selling guides to public speaking, published originally by Prentice-Hall, Inc. They are *The Speaker's Treasury of Stories For All Occasions, The Successful Speaker's Handbook,* and *The Toastmaster's Handbook.*

THE

TOASTMASTER'S AND SPEAKER'S HANDBOOK

•

by Herbert V. Prochnow

WILDSIDE PRESS

CONTENTS

v

PREFACE

This book is planned to be helpful and of interest to three groups: (1) toastmasters and chairmen of meetings; (2) persons who speak in public, conduct classes, or address committees or conferences; and (3) general readers who enjoy humorous stories, epigrams, and illustrations of actual speeches.

Every month many thousands of luncheons, dinners, conventions, discussion groups, and other types of meetings are held in this country. Some one person, whether he is called the chairman, president, or toastmaster, is responsible for every meeting, and particularly for the program.

This book aims to bring to the person in charge of a meeting a great wealth of useful material to assure the success of his work and the capable discharge of his important responsibilities. For the responsibilities of the chairman or toastmaster are extremely important. Consider the thousands of community organizations, church groups, chambers of commerce, Rotary, Kiwanis, Lions and Optimists Clubs, parent-teacher associations, conventions, and many other groups which hold meetings attended by millions of persons every year. Many individuals attend forty or fifty luncheon discussions each year. The number of hours spent in these meetings approaches fantastic figures. If the plans for the meetings are slipshod and careless, the waste of time in these vast audiences is certain to be as great as it is inexcusable.

The author believes that nothing should be left undone by the chairman or toastmaster which will assure those attending that they will be well rewarded for the time spent at any meeting. Time is one of the most precious assets each of us possesses. It is the responsibility of the chairman or toastmaster to see that not one minute of it is wasted. That requires preparation. To paraphrase Emerson: There is no such thing as competent performance without complete preparation. There is nothing better than a well-prepared and planned "impromptu" introduction!

This book also aims to help those who would like to learn how to speak well, and to assist those who have some experience in public speaking to speak even more effectively.

About the year 1800, David Everett, who apparently was young and inexperienced in public speaking, and who was about to make a speech, said:

"If I chance to fall below Demosthenes or Cicero,
Don't view me with a critic's eye,
But pass my imperfections by.
Large streams from little fountains flow,
Tall oaks from little acorns grow."

Mr. Everett must have uttered these words with his tongue in his cheek. One's best efforts after years of experience at public speaking will quite likely fall below the speeches of the great Demosthenes and Cicero. One's first efforts certainly will. But if one follows the concise and simple instructions which are presented here, the fundamentals of good public speaking should be readily acquired and should give one confidence and reasonable competency in public speaking.

Few persons are called upon without experience or practice to give speeches on national coast-to-coast radio networks. However, millions of persons have occasions to speak for three, five, or ten minutes in their businesses, clubs, associations, churches, unions, neighborhood groups, and other organizations. These speeches may be quite informal, but they may play a very important part in one's advancement in business and in the professions, and in directing the affairs of clubs, associations, and all types of organizations.

The ability to speak effectively and to the point can be acquired, and it can become an instrument of power and usefulness. It can be invaluable in many ways in business, in the professions, and in one's social and personal life. Public speaking is not only a practical and constructive tool in life, but there is a great deal of personal satisfaction in being able to present one's ideas clearly, concisely, and forcefully.

It is believed that this book presents a great deal of material never before included and so presented in any book for toastmasters and public speakers. It is obviously a handbook not only for toastmasters, but also for all public speakers, ministers, attorneys, teachers, salesmen, and others who have opportunities to use a practical, helpful work of this character. The general reader will likewise find entertaining stories in a number of chapters.

H. V. P.

Chapter 1

RESPONSIBILITIES OF THE TOASTMASTER

In 1891, I. H. Browley said that—

"These dinner speeches tire me; they are tedious, flat and
stale;
From a hundred thousand tables comes a melancholy wail,
As a hundred thousand banqueters sit up in evening dress
And salute each moldy chestnut with a signal of distress."

It is the specific responsibility of the toastmaster to see
that the speeches are not tedious, flat and stale and that
there is no reason for a melancholy wail from a hundred
thousand banqueters. A thoroughly competent toastmaster
assumes charge of everything from the arrangement of the
program to the ventilation of the room.

Plan the Complete Program

Sometimes the chairman of a meeting has complete charge
of the program and assigns to the toastmaster simply the responsibility of introducing the speaker. However, for purposes of this book, and in order to make the discussion comprehensive and thorough, we shall assume that one person,
whether he has the title of chairman, president, master of
ceremonies or toastmaster, has complete charge of every detail of the program. The responsibilities may be divided
among several persons but this discussion will cover all of
them.

Someone has said that if you sit in one of the great sidewalk cafés of Paris long enough, everyone in the world will pass your table. It may also be said that if you will take an active part in your community in the parent-teacher association, church work, the Rotary, Kiwanis, Lions, Toastmasters, Optimists, university club, trade and professional associations, the association of commerce, the country club, the women's club, Red Cross, Boy Scouts or any one of a thousand worthwhile community activities, you will be called upon to plan a program, introduce speakers, and conduct a meeting. Each one of us finds that sooner or later—for better or for worse—he is called upon to serve as chairman or toastmaster of a meeting.

In Shakespeare's *Midsummer Night's Dream* Quince says to Snug, who was given the part of the lion in the play, "You may do it extempore, for it is nothing but roaring." And roaring may be all right for an audience which is satisfied with noise. But what audience is satisfied simply with noise, and who wants simply to be a lion? The person who conducts a program may do it extemporaneously. He may handle the meeting in an off-the-cuff manner, hoping that everything will go well. However, managing a program for an intelligent audience in this way is to invite disaster.

Moreover, any chairman who will bring together one hundred persons, for example, for a luncheon for an hour and a half and fail to prepare for that hour and a half by checking every detail—the luncheon, the speaker, the introduction, the comfort of the audience and the speaker—has simply robbed, the word is robbed, one hundred persons of one hundred and fifty hours of time. There is a colossal waste of time in luncheons, dinners, conventions and meetings of all kinds because of inefficient and incompetent management, and because of inadequate preparation by program chairmen and program committees. Ten hours of thorough, hard work by a program chairman may make ten hundred worthwhile hours for an audience of a thousand men, each of whom gives one hour of precious time. A person who wastes the time of others robs them of a portion of life itself.

Cicero said regarding Antonius, "All his speeches were, in appearance, the unpremeditated effusion of an honest heart; and yet, in reality, they were preconceived with so much skill that the judges were not so well prepared as they should have been to withstand the force of them!" In the same manner a program may proceed so smoothly and efficiently that it appears wholly extemporaneous; and yet, in reality, it has been prepared with so much skill that the audience is almost unaware of the reasons for its effectiveness.

Subjects for the Program

The chairman must assume responsibility for the complete program. Nothing short of this is adequate. One of the first requirements is to determine the nature of the subjects which the organization wishes discussed. This will necessarily depend largely upon the particular interests of those composing the group. Business, economic, social and political conditions may all be factors influencing the choice of subjects for discussion.

Members of organizations are often asked to express their opinions verbally or in answer to written questionnaires regarding the types of programs they desire, such as travel and illustrated lectures, political discussions, scientific addresses and humorous speeches. They are also asked to submit names of possible speakers, preferably persons they have heard. In some cases there will be a wide range of possible acceptable subjects. Some speakers also will be permitted to select their own subjects within broad fields, such as medicine, law, banking, accounting, journalism and engineering.

How and Where to Secure Good Speakers

A far more difficult problem in planning the program is the question of how and where to secure good speakers. Members of any organization will ordinarily have friendships extending over a relatively wide area which will enable them to suggest good speakers about whom they have heard others comment or actually have heard themselves. Newspaper accounts of speeches which have been given before other groups will provide clues of possible speakers. Individuals who have achieved some particular distinction in a community or who have returned from trips abroad are prospective speakers.

Sometimes it is desirable also to write to distinguished persons asking them if they contemplate visiting in or near your city in the months immediately ahead. Anyone who expects to make such a visit may be willing to give an address at that time. Large business concerns may have men who visit certain cities or states with regularity and have a worthwhile message they are willing to present. When United States Senator Roe and Representative Doe come back to your state between sessions of Congress, they may welcome an opportunity to speak to your club. When a local doctor returns from the convention of the American Medical Association, he may be induced to talk on the latest studies of heart disease or arthritis.

Professor Brown is a distinguished scientist of the faculty of Keene University. His old home is in your city, and he visits there once each year. The chances are that he would be flattered by an invitation to speak in his old home town. The governor of the state and prominent state officials are definite possibilities for programs.

The opportunities for uncovering unusual speaking talent and for learning about situations that will make excellent speakers available are unlimited. The wide-awake program chairman will use them.

Current subjects of widespread public interest will automatically suggest the names of persons competent in those fields or already in the public eye because of their discussions of these subjects. Local judges, ministers, attorneys, businessmen and educators are all possibilities. Finding topnotch speakers is largely a matter of alertness, imagination and aggressiveness on the part of the chairman.

A Time Schedule for the Meeting

After obtaining the speaker the chairman should work out a schedule of the meeting in detail, indicating exactly how it will be conducted. No chairman should take the chance of conducting a meeting with nothing more than a hazy conception of the time each part of the program will require. He may have a luncheon program for the Mudville Club scheduled from 12:15 to 1:45 P.M. He hopes the luncheon will be over at 1:05 P.M. so he can have five minutes for announcements and the introduction of guests, five minutes to introduce the speaker and thirty minutes—the period from 1:15 P.M. to 1:45 P.M.—for the speaker. But the chairman has failed to inform the hotel of his schedule and the luncheon itself takes until 1:15 P.M. Moreover, he has failed to check carefully the time required for announcements and the introduction of guests, with the result that fifteen more minutes elapse. At 1:30 P.M. he makes his introduction of the speaker which is completed at 1:35 P.M. leaving the speaker ten minutes instead of thirty minutes. While this is going on the audience becomes aware of the situation, as most of those in attendance have appointments and responsibilities in their businesses and professions shortly after 1:45 P.M. There is an air of restlessness in the audience and some persons whose appointments are particularly pressing leave rather than having to get up and go during the speech. In the meantime, beginning about 1:15 P.M., the speaker senses the situation and starts mentally cutting his speech. First, he takes out a humorous story or two. Time keeps running against him, so he cuts out an interesting illustration. Then another. He wishes to make three points in his address. At 1:25 P.M. he knows that is impossible. Out goes one point. At 1:30 P.M. out goes the second point. At 1:35 P.M. he is a nervous wreck in a cold sweat. How in the world did he ever agree to address this audience anyhow? He has a kind of sickly inner laugh when he remembers how the program chairman urged him by letter to accept. He would be the principal feature; they all wanted to hear him, the chairman had said.

The speaker accepted, worked twelve hours to prepare the speech and traveled sixty miles to make it.

Now he hears the chairman apologizing to the audience for the "unavoidable" reduction in the time for the address, but "we are certain our distinguished speaker will give us something worthwhile in the time remaining." And so he gets up and presents a disjointed and rambling speech that lacks almost everything he had planned to give it. There is no joy in the Mudville Club—mighty Casey has struck out.

How many speakers have had precisely the foregoing experience? Scheduled to speak thirty minutes at a luncheon, they are given ten minutes. A speaker agrees to address a dinner meeting. The dinner starts forty-five minutes late; the treasurer's report, the minutes of the last meeting and a discussion of the annual ladies' night take forty minutes; the high school glee club sings an hour instead of thirty minutes. When everyone is ready to go home, the address of the evening is announced. It does not make sense, and yet that is the manner in which hundreds of meetings are conducted. Sometimes a member of a club will bring a previously unannounced guest from Korea, China or Timbuktu, who is asked to say just a word. The guest traces the history of his country, its present problems and future promise for twenty-five minutes while the invited speaker and audience sit by helplessly. It doesn't make any difference whether the invited speaker is important or not important. There is no way to get back the time which was rightfully his and of which he has been robbed. To paraphrase a quotation from *The New England Primer* of 1688,

> The uninvited guest cuts down all,
> Both great and small.

There is practically no way for an invited guest to insist on his rights during a program that is obviously being badly managed. As Nicholas Murray Butler said, "One of the embarrassments of being a gentleman is that you are not permitted to be violent in asserting your rights." The chairman might well follow Bacon's advice, "Be sure to leave other men their turns to speak."

The person who wishes to conduct a meeting with efficiency and in a manner to win the praise of the audience and those who participate in the program will prepare a simple memorandum for himself carefully scheduling the time to be given each part of the program. Sometimes the time schedule for a meeting is even given in the printed program for the benefit of the entire audience and the program participants. For example, the Rotary Club of Chicago often uses a schedule similar to the following in its printed program:

> 12:30—Silent Invocation
> 12:31—"The Star-Spangled Banner"
> 12:33–1:10—Luncheon and Fellowship
>   1:10—Announcements and Introductions
>   1:27—Introduction of the Speaker
>   1:30—Address
>   2:00—Adjourn

Courtesies Shown the Speaker

No program chairman should expect a speaker to prepare a speech conscientiously and take the time necessary to attend a meeting to deliver it without showing the speaker even the most ordinary courtesies. A well-known businessman told the author, "Many clubs and business associations will importune you strongly to come to their communities perhaps fifty, one hundred or five hundred miles away to give an address. You dislike greatly to take the time and effort evenings after your work in the office to prepare it. But you finally agree to do it. Your audience expects a masterpiece. You do your best to deliver it. The audience is on its way out of the room before the chairman gives a ten word sentence of brief appreciation. No one took care of your hotel reservation. Sometimes you even buy your own luncheon or dinner ticket. The only time you get a word of appreciation is a year or two later when the program again requires a businessman as a speaker. Then they call you long-distance to extend the invitation and express appreciation for your address given months ago."

This businessman may have been too critical of program chairmen as a group, but there is no good excuse for a program chairman or committee overlooking any of the little courtesies that really reward a speaker, particularly the speaker who comes to a club without accepting any remuneration whatsoever.

In the first place a good hotel room should be reserved for the speaker if he is to stay overnight. Even if he is in the city only during the day, a hotel room reserved for him for the day is a splendid way to give him the proper attention and perhaps the short rest he deserves. He may find it helpful to go over his notes or manuscript alone before the program. If the speaker has work he wishes to do or desires privacy, respect his wishes.

It is a mark of real courtesy if a member of the organization which the speaker is to address meets him at the train and takes him to the hotel. It may also be possible to take him on a short drive around the city or have a meal with him. The author remembers some unusual and unexpected courtesies shown him in Salt Lake City where he was to address the annual convention of the Utah Bankers Association. Shortly after his arrival at the Hotel Utah a beautiful basket of fruit was delivered to his room through the kindness of one of the officials of a local bank. At noon the president of another bank invited the speaker to luncheon. The local bankers and the Utah Bankers Association showed a thoughtfulness for the speaker which was almost embarrassing in the many ways in which it found expression. Courtesy is a language everyone understands.

Publicity for the Speaker and the Meeting

Prior to the meeting the proper person in the organization, perhaps the program chairman, will have obtained information and perhaps a glossy photograph of the speaker for use by local newspapers for advance publicity. Copies of the speech or excerpts from it may also be obtained and sent to the newspapers for release at the time the speech is delivered. Advance copies of a speech make it easier for a reporter to make a good summary of the speech, and they give the speaker greater assurance that he will be accurately quoted.

Copies of newspaper clippings announcing the speaker, as well as news items printed about his speech itself, will be welcomed by him. The speaker may never have an opportunity to see the local newspaper and thoughtfulness in sending publicity material of interest to him will be greatly appreciated.

The president or program chairman of the organization holding the meeting may wish to write the speaker expressing gratitude for his address and commending it. If the speech shows conscientious preparation and contains a worthwhile message, he may write in addition to the speaker's superior. For example, let us assume that Professor Jones makes an excellent address before the annual convention of the state bar association. The best way to express gratitude is to write the president of the university in which Professor Jones teaches, perhaps sending a copy of the letter to Professor Jones. It is not imperative that a copy of the letter be sent to Professor Jones, as the president of the university will certainly tell the professor about it. Professor Jones being a modest, conscientious person will prepare an able address, but will never tell his superior, the president, about the success of the meeting. In the business world, too, almost invariably the best reward for speakers is a strong word of commendation to their superiors. Top officials of most businesses welcome letters indicating that members of their organizations have earned the appreciation and good will of audiences.

In some instances organizations furnish a modest gift for the speaker, such as a book, a box of candy or some local product. One credit men's association in Indiana sent the wife of a speaker a large bouquet of roses on the Christmas following a speech that had been given in November. A large corporation in Chicago selling electrical appliances gave an economist whose speech had greatly impressed them an attractive table radio. Gifts of this kind are rare instances of thoughtfulness and courtesy, but they do show what some organizations do for good speakers. A bit of appreciation—a spoken word, a letter, a small gift—may be the means of showing speakers who do conscientious, hard work on their addresses that audiences are really grateful for superior achievement.

Rotary International has given careful consideration to this whole matter of expressing appreciation to speakers and has distributed the suggestions which follow to each one of its more than 8,000 clubs:

An Obligation Due Speakers

Is your club considerate of its out-of-town speakers?

Among other courtesies extended to the club program speaker—such as meeting him at the station, introducing him to club members, giving him all of his agreed-upon time to speak, thanking him for his talk—does the president or chairman remember to offer to reimburse the out-of-town speaker for expenses he may have incurred in making the trip to your community?

The latter is not only a courtesy but an obligation that is due the invited speaker. It can be handled in a way that need cause no embarrassment to anyone.

Recently, when a Rotarian accepted an invitation to address a certain Rotary club seventy-five miles distant, he was met at the train and conducted to the meeting place. After the meeting the guest was quietly handed an envelope containing a thank-you note and money adequate to cover his expenses. Such procedure is routine in this club.

Even though the speaker may live only a few miles away, it may take four or five hours out of his day to deliver a twenty-five-minute talk to your club. This he may be glad to do without any honorarium, but the club does have an obligation to make sure that he is reimbursed for all out-of-pocket expenses.

The guest may good-naturedly refuse to accept anything, but the club secretary or other officer should tactfully persuade him to accept—and thus the club will feel free to call again upon him, or some other member of his club, for a talk.

Before the Meeting Starts

Some time in advance inform the speaker of the exact time and place of the meeting, and make arrangements to meet him beforehand. For example, you may tell him that the program will start at the Community Hall at eight o'clock, and you or someone you designate will call for him at his hotel at 7:40 P.M. Sometimes the speaker and the guests at the speaker's table are asked to assemble in a special room near the meeting place in order to become acquainted and to march in to the speaker's table in some definite order. In that event tell each person, in writing as a rule, about the arrangements.

It is good policy to have the speaker and the guests at the speaker's table meet each other prior to the beginning of the meeting. Sometimes it is possible also to introduce the speaker to other members of the audience before the meeting.

If some special seating arrangement is planned for the speaker's table, each guest should be informed in advance of his place. At any event, the speaker should always be advised of his place at the table.

Members of the Audience Are Guests

A toastmaster who aims at perfection in the discharge of his duties considers that the members of the audience are his guests. From the time the first person arrives until the last one leaves a competent toastmaster will do everything possible for the best interests of his guests.

A Program That Is Too Long

Sooner or later, and generally sooner, every chairman finds himself with a program that is too long. The program may have too many speakers. It may have too much entertainment, or there may be too much business to be conducted. As that eminent philosopher, the television comedian Jimmy Durante, has said, "Everybody wants to get into the act." This is too often true.

The problem should be considered from two viewpoints: (1) how to prevent this situation from arising, and (2) what to do if it has arisen.

The program chairman must never lose sight of the simple fact that he will be held responsible for a program that is too long. It is his job, ruthlessly if necessary, to insist on a program that can be presented properly within the necessary time limits. Under no condition should he permit himself to be a party to plans that result in too long a program—a program that is distinctly unfair to the participants and a headache to the audience. To paraphrase Gertrude Stein: A chairman is a chairman is a chairman. Whatever meaning Gertrude Stein would have attached to this statement, it certainly means that a chairman is meant to be chairman, exactly that.

Just plain sense will tell the chairman how much time he can allot for the program. If the program includes dinner, for example, and is scheduled to begin at 6:30 P.M. and be over at 9:00 P.M., there are exactly 150 minutes available. If the dinner requires 75 minutes, then 75 minutes remain for announcements, introductions of guests at the speaker's table, business matters, introduction of the speakers, their speeches and entertainment. Deduct 5 minutes for announcements, 5 minutes for the introduction of guests, 10 minutes for business matters, and 15 minutes for entertainment—then 40 minutes remain. Five minutes may be needed to introduce a speaker and 5 minutes may well be set up for some delay in the program, or in case some parts of it run over a minute or two. Approximately 30 minutes remain for a speaker.

There is no method by which 30 minutes can be divided to include two speeches of 25 minutes each. Thirty minutes will also not include one 45-minute speech. It is the job of the chairman to hold the nonessentials to an absolute minimum and reserve every possible minute for his entertainment and speaker, particularly the latter, if the speaker is considered the main part of the program.

Once the schedule is fixed, every part of the program must conform to it and nothing should be added which throws the program and the time schedule clear out of balance. Inserting twice as much entertainment as the time will permit, arranging for two speakers when the time will only permit one, or arranging for three speakers when the time will only permit two—these are all cases of incompetent program management. If the toastmaster is to err on the number of speakers, it is better to err on the side of having too few on the program. It has been said that intelligent people express themselves briefly and say at once whatever is to be said. Likewise, intelligent chairmen build programs which are not too long and which move with dispatch.

Order of the Speeches

If there are several speakers on a program, it is probably best as a rule to have the principal speaker last, assuming that one speaker is considered the main speaker. If this speaker is scheduled earlier, some members of an audience may walk out after this speech and not hear a very good speaker who is less well-known.

Where a convention, for example, is particularly desirous of having its delegates hear the message of a particular speaker, he may be given a place on the program at a time when the convention has its peak attendance at the sessions.

Once in a while there is a speaker who wishes unusual privileges. He may ask to speak ahead of others so he can leave for a train. This may be a very good reason for giving him a special position on the program. However, this does not entitle a speaker to take more time than has been set aside for his speech, thereby reducing the time available for others.

A speaker may also ask to be moved ahead or after other speakers in order to get what he believes is a preferential position on the program. It is the responsibility of the chairman to be fair and completely impartial in dealing with responsibilities of this character.

Time Allotted Each Speaker

Earlier in this chapter we have indicated how important it is to conduct a meeting on schedule. Each speaker should be advised in advance exactly how much time will be given to him. This information can be included in the original invitation. When the day for the meeting comes, he can be shown the schedule for the meeting so he understands clearly the time set aside for him. The speaker is justified in expecting the chairman to adhere conscientiously to the schedule throughout the program. A time schedule is not something to which the speaker is to be held rigidly at all events while the chairman does as he pleases, even taking time of the speaker.

Publicity for the Meeting

Reference has already been made to the possibility of obtaining glossy photographs of the speaker and copies of his speech, or excerpts from it, for the press. In addition, this material may be sent to trade papers and magazines. If the speaker is nationally known, and particularly if he occupies a position where his views make news, publicity can also be sent to national news magazines. The speaker himself may be associated with a business concern or other type of organization which has a publicity department that will send out news releases about him. Occasionally the organization conducting the program can arrange for the speaker to receive the press personally before or after the meeting. This may give a program the type of publicity which builds prestige for the organization conducting the meeting.

Organizing Panel Discussions

A panel discussion is ordinarily one in which two or more persons, generally with a chairman, discuss a subject which has previously been selected. For example, four persons with a chairman or moderator may discuss some phase of American foreign policy which is debatable. Two of the speakers may take the affirmative and two the negative. At the conclusion of the more formal discussion, the speakers may ask each other questions. The audience may also be permitted to ask questions. At other times each participant will simply present the part of a particular subject regarding which he is especially qualified. There may be no attempt to take affirmative and negative sides. To illustrate, a panel of businessmen may be asked to present, in a January meeting of an association of commerce, their views on business conditions for the coming year. A banker may express his views on the financial outlook, a department store president on retail prospects and problems, a manufacturer of steel on the outlook for his industry, and a construction authority on public and private construction. This type of panel and symposium, especially if questions are permitted, can be very effective. Each speaker will ordinarily be sufficiently different from the others, if the program is well planned, with sufficient variety so that it appeals to audiences with widely divergent interests.

When the Speaker Fails to Arrive

If a speaker advises the program chairman a week or more before the date he is to speak that he will not be able to fulfill his engagement, there may still be time to obtain someone in his place without too much trouble.

A more difficult situation arises if a speaker fails to appear at the last minute because of illness or another emergency. When it becomes necessary to obtain a substitute speaker upon short notice, it is always best to tell the person invited exactly the reasons for his being asked to speak at so late a date. He will wonder just what happened which resulted in an invitation that afforded so little time for preparation. If a prospective substitute is given all the facts, there is a possibility that he will accept in a spirit of good sportsmanship. In a predicament of this character it is often possible to find some highly qualified speaker who has a speech available which he has prepared for some other occasion and who will welcome an opportunity to deliver his talk before a different audience.

A farsighted program chairman should keep a list of several persons who may be called on to speak in emergencies. In small communities, for example, a local minister, or high-school superintendent, or an attorney may be willing to speak on short notice. The chairman may also prepare a list of subjects which would be suitable for discussion by the audience. The chairman can then announce that the speaker has suddenly found it necessary to cancel his speech, and that he himself, or some other person, will lead a discussion in which the audience is to participate. Possible subjects for discussion might be: (1) the question of how to promote a local improvement involving the addition of a park and baseball field for the young people, (2) the enlargement of the local public library, (3) what policies the community could pursue to induce new industries to locate in the city. Many other possibilities will occur to the chairman. In fact the scheduled speaker's absence may turn out to be a blessing. A meeting of this kind may be tremendously successful as each person present has a chance to participate in the discussion. Open discussions dealing with vital local issues should prove especially successful for clubs like Rotary, Kiwanis and the Lions and for organizations of businessmen and civic-minded citizens.

Chapter 2

TECHNIQUES OF THE TOASTMASTER

Someone in good humor once said of an eminent American statesman that he was certain the statesman was not a Baptist as he would never agree to submerge himself that long. The competent toastmaster submerges himself to give the speaker prominence. No person is a good toastmaster who is unwilling to make the speaker rather than himself the center of attention.

Length of the Introduction

It is clearly not the business of the toastmaster to be so incredibly dull that the speaker will seem to be a genius by contrast. But neither is it the toastmaster's business to speak at such length and with so elaborate an analysis of the speaker's subject that the speaker is left with the responsibility of saying nothing briefly.

There is an old story that when William Jennings Bryan was at the height of his power as a speaker he arrived in one city where he had an engagement to speak but had only a very limited time between trains. The chairman of the meeting felt called upon, not only to introduce Mr. Bryan at length, but also to extend his remarks to include other subjects. When he had finished his introduction, only ten minutes remained for Mr. Bryan's speech. As Mr. Bryan was hurrying down the aisle out of the auditorium after his address, he heard one member of the audience say to another, "That man Bryan certainly is a great speaker." "Yes," said

17

the other person, "he is an excellent speaker, and that fellow who followed him for ten minutes wasn't so bad either."

There is no excuse for the chairman to make so long an introduction that the audience rightly has some doubt as to who was to make the principal speech. The toastmaster is the starter for the engine, and not the engine. Consequently, the toastmaster must keep clearly in mind at all times his particular function in the meeting itself.

The average introduction need not take more than two or three minutes. If the biographical information about the speaker is lengthy, it is best to pick the most essential points and those of interest to the particular audience. The most distinguished persons may be presented effectively with short introductions. For example, in introducing the President of the United States, it is the custom merely to say, "Ladies and gentlemen, the President of the United States."

Announcements, Entertainment and Other Parts of the Program

It is to be expected that there will be announcements of some kind in every type of program, but the announcements must be subordinated to the main part of the program. No effort is ever made to have the celery, olives and relishes at the beginning of a dinner substitute for the filet mignon, potatoes and peas. Likewise, the announcements should be announcements—not speeches. Bill Jones who has charge of the annual club golf tournament may feel that his announcement is the most important part of the program. He may use far more time than is allotted to him as he urges attendance and describes the tournament. Sam Smith is supposed to take five minutes to call attention to the ladies' night, but he appropriates fifteen minutes, and so announcements devour the time of a program. All of the announcements must be carefully planned for time and must be held to schedule.

Ventilation and Other Arrangements

It may seem unnecessary to comment on ventilation, but too many speakers have had to face audiences which were gradually being anesthetized by poor ventilation. Anyone who prepares a speech carefully, so that it merits the best thinking of an audience, deserves physical conditions in the room which will help to make the audience receptive rather than drowsy. The author has found sometimes when he has spoken near the end of a long program that the members of an audience greatly appreciated being invited to stand and stretch for a moment while the windows were opened. It is better for a speaker to lose two or three minutes of his speaking time, if necessary, to assure himself of an alert audience. Check the ventilation and temperature in the room before the meeting starts and have someone at the back of the room watch the ventilation during the program.

Arrangements should always be made with the hotel or other meeting place to provide a lectern. Never wait for a speaker to request one. As presiding officer, the chairman will find a lectern helpful and convenient for notes and papers. Even if the speaker does not use a manuscript or notes, a lectern serves as a pulpit, and provides a place for the speaker's hands, giving him greater ease as he speaks. *Always* arrange for a lectern.

The chairman should have enough helpers and committees to take all details of the meeting off his mind so that he can concentrate on his job of presiding. Committees should be appointed to handle reception, fellowship, table arrangements and any other matters that may be complicated.

Brief Opening Comments

The objective toward which we are aiming is perfection in conducting a program. Consequently, it is suggested that any announcements or brief comments which the toastmaster makes before presenting the principal speaker should be carefully prepared. There must be no stumbling in making the simplest announcements, no seeming unfamiliarity with the pronunciation of persons' names or geographical locations. The small parts of the program as well as the major parts must move smoothly.

Prepare Introductions in Advance

Place cards should be used so the guests can readily find their places at the speaker's table. If there are a number of guests, the chairman should have before him a list of the guests as they are seated to his left and right. The guest list may also have information about each guest. This avoids embarrassment by keeping the chairman posted on important names or facts that may come up in the conversation.

In introducing guests remember always to give the guest's name last. To illustrate, "Starting at my extreme right, I am pleased to present the executive vice president of the Johnson Iron Corporation, a past president of the Augusta Association of Commerce, and now vice president of the Economic Club of Augusta—Mr. Richard D. Johnson." Always speak loudly and plainly so the audience hears each name clearly.

Sometimes a chairman may forget what he is going to say, like the Dutch gentleman acting as toastmaster in the old story who announced, "Chentlemen, dis is der distinguished chentleman who is going to address you dis evening. I have been selected to interduce him. I have done so, and he will do so." The story is also told of the Southerner who got so excited at the prospect of introducing Jefferson Davis, president of the Confederacy, that all he could say was, "Here he is!" It is best generally for the chairman to have a written memorandum of the comments to be made.

Getting the Good Will of the Audience

The chairman who has prepared in advance the various announcements, scheduled the meeting to run on time, advised the guests of their places at the speaker's table and arranged for the ventilation to be properly regulated has already earned the good will of an audience. He may say as he introduces the speaker that "this audience is representative of the leading business and professional interests of our city—men and women who are vitally interested in the important problem our speaker is to discuss." Honest praise of the good qualities of an audience is permissible and is appreciated. As Cicero has said, "We are all excited by the love of praise, and it is the noblest spirits that feel it most."

Commending the Speaker

However, far more important than praising the audience is the whole subject of using praise or commendation in introducing the speaker. The chairman's praise of the speaker may be so faint that it appears the chairman is uninformed and is speaking with caution, or knows the speaker so well he dreads what the audience is about to experience (after all, the chairman may have to live with the audience for years after the speaker has left town). On the other hand, the praise of the speaker by the chairman may be so strong that no speaker can live up to the reputation the chairman has given him. Chauncey M. Depew, who was a great speaker, is reported once to have said that he preferred the taffy now rather than the epitaphy later.

Nevertheless, an introduction can be so extravagant in its commendation that even if the speaker is excellent, he never can reach the heights of the introduction. A great many American audiences believe Tom Collins of Kansas City, Missouri, is one of the best humorous lecturers of our time. He has told the author that he hoped this book would make it "clear that it is fatal to a speaker who intends to be humorous to promise his audience they soon will be rolling in the aisles with uncontrollable mirth. When a toastmaster begins to mumble about Will Rogers, you know you might just as well cut your wrists and go home, because you are ruined.

"Humor is not an exact science and it is dangerous to overpromise and build a hurdle no one can clear. I believe as cute an introduction as I have had in many a year came recently when a chairman said, 'Our speaker is a veteran of two wars and has gone through hell for you. It is no more than right that you should now go through hell for him, and listen to what he has to say.' Certainly that is a lot better type of introduction than one in which the audience is promised one hour of uninterrupted laughter which, of course, they never get." No introduction should be so extravagant the speaker cannot live up to it.

After a member of one audience had listened to a long and highly commendatory introduction in which the chairman had given all the excellent business positions the speaker had held previously, the member said, "That speaker lost more good jobs than anyone I ever knew." It is advisable not to make it too difficult for the speaker by presenting what may sound like an obituary of him.

Good-Natured "Kidding" of the Speaker

On some occasions it is possible for the chairman to "kid" the speaker and to make remarks which seem to reflect unfavorably upon him. Ordinarily this type of introduction should be reserved by the chairman for those occasions where he knows the speaker very well or knows beyond doubt that no offense will be taken. In fact there are situations where the chairman and speaker may arrange between themselves for an introduction of this character with a suitable response.

Phil Hanna, financial columnist of the *Chicago Daily News,* once began an introduction of his friend Bob Casey, ace war correspondent, as follows: "When the committee asked me to introduce our emaciated [Casey is a large person] speaker, I had no idea how interesting a job it would be." He then described, in good humor, Casey's automatic system for filing all his correspondence unopened in his coat pocket instead of answering it promptly. Ordinarily no chairman would make such a pointed reference to the speaker's waistline. But in this introduction it was all good fun. Mr. Hanna went on at length to tell the story of Mr. Casey's excellence as a reporter. Mr. Casey began his response as follows: "I don't know what I'm doing here—I'd much rather hear Phil Hanna talk (about Casey)."

Sometimes a chairman will make an unfortunate statement through a blunder in language or pronunciation, or in comments regarding the meeting or the speaker. To illustrate, De Witt M. Emery, president of the National Small Business Men's Association, tells of an experience he had as a speaker.

"I have in mind one experience which I shall never forget, and I hope that I may still have the opportunity of introducing the gentleman of whom I am to speak. He was chairman of a Town Hall Club in the Far West. They had seven programs on their schedule for that year, and I was the seventh one. They had been having an attendance, they told me, of around 250 per meeting. For the seventh meeting, they had an attendance of, I should say, around forty.

"The chairman devoted fully ten minutes to telling all of the things he had done in trying to get out a crowd for that meeting, and then he turned the meeting over to me with this comment: 'Anyway, we have had six good meetings!' And I assure you, his statement was one hundred per cent correct."

Channing Pollock, author, playwright and dramatic critic, was once introduced to an audience with these words, "Now I am pleased to present Channing Pollock, author, playwright and distinguished dramatic critter." It was one of those unexplainable twists of the tongue for which both the chairman and speaker were unprepared. Only good luck or some quick wit by the chairman or speaker will help a situation of that kind. The chairman might have said, "I assure you that, like the radio program 'Information Please,' that comment was spontaneous and completely unrehearsed, but it was unintended."

A chairman should check himself on the pronunciation of all names, and the correctness of initials, titles and business or professional affiliations. Mr. Johnson is not Mr. Johnston. Mr. R. V. Smith is not Mr. R. D. Smith. The Old National Bank is not The Old National Trust Company.

Former Senator Owen Brewster of Maine states: "I had an introduction in Syracuse in which the chairman said he was now going to 'give the biology of the speaker.' I got a little worried about that. It worked out all right when he finally concluded by saying that they asked me because I came from Maine. They considered that it was a safe thing to have a person from Maine, because when he reached the Senate he reached the summit of all Maine men's ambitions, since they couldn't go any farther; so he thought a politician like that was likely to come nearer telling the truth. There is some advantage in having a fellow who arrives in the Senate and can 'put behind all hope ye who enter here.'" In this illustration the word "biology" was undoubtedly used deliberately and in good humor by the chairman.

Dr. Harold Moulton, former president of the Brookings Institution of Washington, D.C., tells of a chairman without a sense of humor who introduced him as follows: "Inasmuch as there are no reporters present, Dr. Moulton is going to take his hair down and give us the real inside." (Dr. Moulton is bald.)

Good-natured fun is permissible, in fact frequently desirable, but the audience and chairman must never forget that the speaker for any occasion is an invited guest. No rudeness should ever be shown to the speaker in introducing him. Poking fun at the speaker is permissible if the speaker is fully at home with his audience and the chairman, and understands it is wholly fun. Politeness and courtesy are essentials in conducting any program.

At the conclusion of the introduction the chairman gives the speaker's name in a loud and clear voice, turns toward the speaker, and waits until the speaker has risen to his feet before sitting down.

After the Speaker Is Introduced

The question of what to do after the speaker is introduced is simple. Unless it is absolutely imperative that the chairman leave the platform, he should remain in his chair until the program is completed and the audience has departed. Further, he should pay strict attention to the speaker, incidentally setting a good example for the audience.

After the Speaker Has Completed His Address

If the speaker makes a good speech, the chairman obviously should express his appreciation in the strongest terms. In Chapter 1 we have indicated other ways in which appreciation can be shown to a speaker.

If the speech was a poor one, the chairman can still thank the speaker but in less lavish terms. After all, the club is partly responsible, for the speaker was invited by the club.

Many audiences, particularly luncheon groups or those whose members must catch suburban trains home after an evening program, get up and leave the moment the speaker finishes and before the chairman can say even a sentence of appreciation. If the club publishes a bulletin, sometimes a line is included urging the audience to remain for just a moment as a courtesy to the speaker while the chairman thanks him.

Introducing Several Speakers

It should be said again and again that it is better to err in having too few speakers and entertainment features on a program rather than too many. This is particularly true if one speaker, or one entertainment feature, is to be the principal event. A program which is too crowded is unfair to the participants and to the audience as well. It is simply disaster by plan. There is no good excuse for it.

As a rule, the principal feature is the last one—the grand finale. Exceptions may sometimes be made, for example, in political meetings where a governor or United States senator may be compelled to make appearances before several groups in the same evening; obviously all of the appearances cannot come last on each program.

In some cases a subject for discussion may be divided into two or three parts with one part assigned to each speaker. The speakers then will speak in the order which will permit the best development of the subject.

Whenever there is any danger that the program may be

crowded, the speakers must be held rigidly to schedule and the introductions must be correspondingly brief. Any chairman who fails in that situation has not done his duty either to the speakers or to the audience.

In conducting a program that is a bit crowded, the chairman can only hope that he does not have a speaker who begins by addressing his audience as follows: "How do I know what I'm going to say until I open my mouth and get going?" The chairman can say to himself, "You may not know what you are going to say until you open your mouth, but I know when you are going to close your mouth and permit other speakers to have their fair time."

W. B. Rogers, president and general manager of The Bond Hotels of Hartford, Connecticut, is an exceptionally able chairman. He is a strong believer in brevity as a general principle in presiding. He has told the author, "I once heard that if all toastmasters were laid end to end across the country, it would be a good thing. For that reason I have always believed that in presiding—brevity is next to godliness."

In presiding at a meeting where there are several speakers, good sense is the best indication of what the length of the introductions should be. When in doubt, it is probably better to be brief rather than long. However, an introduction may be so brief that it fails utterly to do justice to the speaker or the audience. No introduction should fail to identify the speaker properly and give the audience sufficient information to establish him as one competent to speak on the subject. Thus the chairman should describe the background of the speaker, state, if desirable, the reason for his appearance and give the subject to be discussed.

A toastmaster's remarks may be as Lowell once said, "a platitude, a quotation and an anecdote," but his comments definitely must identify and establish the speaker in the minds of the audience.

Incidentally, in establishing the speaker's position in the field in which he is to speak, the competent chairman never tries to tell the audience what the speaker will say. If the chairman does make this error, he runs in danger, first, of making the speaker's speech and, second, of expressing opinions which the speaker later may be compelled to correct with considerable embarrassment to everyone.

It is an ironic fact that as a toastmaster becomes more competent he is more tempted to add to the length of his introductions and announcements. There is a danger that he will come to know that he is good, particularly after he has listened to the commendation of his friends. Under the spur of flattery he will lengthen his remarks until he not only begins to infringe on the speaker's time but also makes a speech of his own with each introduction. Eventually this type of toastmaster will lose the good will it may have taken him a long time to establish. He will then find that nothing recedes like success.

Handling the Heckler

As a rule it is best to ignore a person who interrupts the meeting, particularly if the interruption is of a minor character and is not repeated. If the person has asked an intelligent question, but is one of those individuals who is such an enthusiast that he cannot ask the question in its proper place at the end of the speaker's address, then the chairman or speaker should merely say that he will be pleased to consider the question at the conclusion of the address. If the speaker has not agreed to answer questions in an open discussion at the end of his address, he may be willing later to talk personally with those who would like to ask questions.

If a heckler is really rude, however, the audience ordinarily will resent his interruptions and will favor the speaker or chairman in any reasonable response made to the situation. The chairman may also state that the subject being discussed is highly controversial, but everyone will agree that in a spirit of fairness the speaker should be entitled to express his viewpoint. The chairman may add that questions will be permitted after the speaker concludes or that a speaker with a different viewpoint will address the club at a later date.

A heckler who continually disturbs a meeting must necessarily be requested to leave. However, it never pays to make a major issue out of an insignificant disturbance. Some members of the club sitting near the offender, or one of his friends, will ordinarily handle any unnecessary interruptions with little or no fuss.

Some time ago a candidate for the nomination for the presidency of the United States was addressing an audience consisting in part of students. Some of the students in the front row came to the meeting with identical magazines, all of which had large pictures of one of the opposing candidates for the presidential nomination. Each student held his magazine so the picture was prominently displayed in a manner intended to disconcert the speaker. The candidate whose picture was displayed was a man of intelligence and of broad tolerance for the viewpoints of others. He would undoubtedly have disapproved of this display of discourtesy.

A demonstration of this kind is childish. Students who had reached any kind of maturity in their thinking would have no part in the pranks of children. Intelligent persons are always desirous of hearing both sides of issues that affect the national welfare discussed by those in positions of leadership in our national life.

By and large, no speaker or chairman ever has any serious problem with anyone wishing to heckle or interrupt a speaker. The good chairman, no matter what the situation, never loses his temper, has a sense of humor and uses good sense.

Last-Minute Changes in the Program

If the program is carefully planned, the probability that changes will be needed is unlikely. However, it may be necessary, as previously indicated, to shift speakers to accommodate a speaker who must catch a train or some other form of transportation. In the event a speaker becomes ill and is compelled to cancel his engagement, a local speaker may be obtained. It is best not to make too much of the absence of a speaker as it seems to imply that other speakers on the program are less important. Moreover, a substitute speaker, knowing the difficult situation he occupies, may make an extraordinary effort to do an outstanding job. The chairman should give him every consideration in introducing him. The audience knows the substitute is in a difficult spot, and if he does well they will give him a great deal of credit.

Use of Humor

A toastmaster tells a humorous story or uses an epigram or witticism to excite mirth or laughter. Washington Irving once said that "Honest good humor is the oil and wine of a merry meeting, and there is no jovial companionship equal to that where the jokes are rather small and the laughter abundant." And it was Joseph Addison who said, "If we consider the frequent reliefs we receive from laughter, and how often it breaks the gloom which is apt to depress the mind, one would take care not to grow too wise for so great a pleasure of life." A toastmaster who is able to use humor well has an extremely effective speech instrument at his command.

Not to tell a humorous story well is a serious handicap in those situations where humor could serve to highlight an introduction. Chapter 11 contains many illustrations of how toastmasters have used humor to make interesting and entertaining introductions. Practice and careful study are required to make the best use of humor.

Chapter 10 explains how to use anecdotes and stories effectively.

A toastmaster will find it an asset to have a few extra anecdotes and epigrams ready for an emergency. Knowing the subjects to be discussed and the speakers, he can arrange to have pertinent extra material on a card available on a moment's notice.

The epigram, witticism and humorous definition are terse comments that may be of great assistance in making a toastmaster's remarks colorful. Samuel Taylor Coleridge has given a good epigrammatic definition of an epigram as follows:

What is an Epigram? A dwarfish whole,
Its body brevity, and wit its soul.

Chapter 14 contains hundreds of epigrams and witticisms
suitable for use on many different occasions.

Chapter 13 has dozens of stories taken from actual
speeches or introductions. Many of these stories are humorous. The source of each story is given so a toastmaster can
say, "As Governor Brown of [name of state] once said," or
"United States Senator Smith once told an interesting story
on this point. Senator Smith said . . ." and the toastmaster
tells the story. Chapter 15 has hundreds of quotations suitable
for use in introducing men in various professions and occupations, and for use on various occasions. Many of these quotations are humorous. Chapter 16 has scores of humorous
stories and anecdotes. Thus the chairman will find a great
many items, both serious and humorous, in this volume which
he can incorporate in his introductions and speeches.

At the Close of the Meeting

At the close of the meeting, it should be emphasized again,
do not forget to thank the speakers. The audience should not
be allowed to start for the door until this is done. It does not
call for a speech. It can be done in a minute. As the last
speaker finishes and sits down, the chairman should rise immediately so there is no lapse in the program and no period
during which there is no one at the lectern. Close the meeting rapidly, once it is over.

One Last Word

As we conclude these two chapters on the work of the
toastmaster, we stress again the subject which has been re-
emphasized repeatedly in these pages—careful preparation
for every meeting. The author of this volume was given an
interesting story on the importance of preparation by a man
who had the unusual privilege of serving as president both
of the Rotary Club of New York City and the Rotary Club

of Chicago. This club president said, "The Rotary Club of Chicago met on Tuesday. Therefore I had a standing appointment at four-thirty Monday afternoon with the secretary of the club. We spent from thirty minutes to an hour and a half in planning and timing. Then with the biographical data on the speaker and any others who were to participate in the meeting, I spent such time as was necessary at home Monday evening preparing my introductions—actually writing them out in detail—then studying them. My notes were used only as a guide, and were not to be read. On Tuesday noon, fifteen minutes before the meeting, the secretary and I would double-check to determine any last-minute changes." Note how thoroughly this club president prepared for a meeting.

The chairman should be fully prepared for his part of the program. He should have a working familiarity also with the rules of parliamentary procedure so he will conduct every meeting fairly and with complete confidence in himself.

Chapter 3

TEN FUNDAMENTALS FOR THE TOASTMASTER

1. Work out carefully every program for which you are toastmaster. You are responsible for seeing that the audience is fully rewarded for its time.

2. Conduct the meeting on schedule. Don't let it drag.

3. Give the speaker the opportunity to make the speech. That's what he is there for. The audience should never be in doubt as to whether the toastmaster or speaker made the speech.

4. Give the speaker every opportunity to succeed—a good audience, a quiet, well-ventilated room and a carefully prepared introduction.

5. Give the speaker his full time. Don't cut him short or let him run way over the schedule.

6. Make the introductions brief if the list of speakers is long.

7. Express real appreciation to the speaker who has made a conscientious effort to do a good job.

8. Give the audience a chance to stand up and stretch during a long meeting. Then you know they are all awake.

9. Refuse to act as toastmaster for any meeting that is of no value or is obviously too long. Why should you help to inflict mass boredom?

10. Make no apologies for your own unpreparedness. You have no right to be unprepared.

Chapter 4

EFFECTIVE PUBLIC SPEAKING
AND LEADERSHIP TRAINING

This book deals not only with the responsibilities of the toast-master, but also with effective public speaking and training for leadership—activities that can help you attain greater satisfaction and success in business or professional work and more complete enjoyment of the opportunities of social life.

In our complex and interrelated world with its stream-line trains, jet airplanes and television, the Biblical quotation "No man liveth to himself," has acquired an even broader significance. A successful and happy life depends more than ever before upon one's relations with other people. No matter how intelligent you are, or how hard you work, you may at any time be blocked or hampered in achieving the purposes which you desire by misunderstanding or a lack of sympathetic cooperation on the part of other people. To secure the ready cooperation of others you often need a command of effective speech. You need skill in conveying your ideas and wishes to them accurately, quickly and tactfully, so you will obtain from them the right reaction and response. It is not a question of whether you personally enjoy having the ability to present ideas effectively to others; if you do not have this ability, you are seriously handicapped.

A Powerful Instrument to Help You

This study aims at the heart of the problem of leadership with which so many are confronted. It considers primarily one very important phase of the subject which is often neglected, namely, how to acquire the ability to speak in public. Specifically, how can you train yourself to address a group of listeners of any size with assurance? If you work faithfully through the instructions given here, reading a few pages each day, you will find yourself possessed of a new and powerful instrument which you can employ profitably on a great many occasions whether speaking to one person or to thousands. In addition, the instructions in this book should be helpful in many other ways in your business, social and personal life and in developing your leadership qualities.

Instructions You Can Apply at Once

We do not intend in this book to devote our attention merely to broad generalities. We propose to present as simply and clearly as possible practical principles and useful material that will help you. Full mastery of the art of public speaking will come gradually with experience. Men of great ability in public speaking give to it a lifetime of study, developing year by year added power and finesse. Here we discuss simply and briefly those fundamentals the intelligent man or woman should know in order to develop his own ability. Anyone who has intelligence, genuine interest in other people and a general store of information can grasp these instructions easily and begin to put them to use almost immediately even though he has given no previous attention to public speaking. What you learn, moreover, you will not have to unlearn later on. The treatment is basic and comprehensive. It gives you the fundamental principles of the art of leadership through public speaking.

Motives for Study—Necessity, Enjoyment

There are two main reasons for systematic study of public speaking. The first is necessity. The need to speak clearly and forcefully is invaluable in achieving success in your business or professional work. The second reason is enjoyment. Intelligent study of public speaking for use in business, professional, and social life brings pleasures of various kinds which constantly increase as you become more expert.

Public Speaking in Business Life

If you are active in your business, your profession or your social circle, occasions frequently develop when you are called on to stand up and express your mind to a group of listeners. As you progress in business or professional work, you find yourself involved in an increasing number of meetings. There may be conferences, sales meetings and conventions in your own business when plans are presented and policies discussed, when committee reports are offered and considered, and instructions explained to subordinates. In many large organizations, participation in conferences and meetings constitutes a very important duty for almost everyone holding a position of responsibility.

For the business executive, whether he is president, sales manager or personnel director, the ability to stand up and tell others what he means, clearly, concisely, logically and forcefully, is imperative. Anyone in business upon whom the responsibility of guiding others depends must be able to talk clearly and to the point if he wishes his management of a business to be productive. Only those who can express themselves effectively and tactfully can obtain the willing and intelligent cooperation of the individuals for whose guidance management is responsible.

There are also the meetings of business or professional associations and groups to which you belong (either from personal interest or as a representative of your business or your friends and associates) and in which every member is expected to share in the discussion. Participation in this discussion is often a helpful and speedy road to advancement. It makes you known to people of influence in your field and gives you opportunities of demonstrating your competence as a leader and executive. This in turn increases your value to your own business or to those with whom you are associated in a profession.

In Social Affairs

This is only one side of the picture. Outside of business hours much of the time of the active man or woman of today is occupied with meetings of community and civic organizations, fraternal or religious bodies and social groups. Here also there is business to be transacted in which, as a member of the organization, he has an interest. Frequently some issue arises whose decision is of great importance to him. In social activities, the man who can express himself on his feet, as officer, member or guest of an organization, will be sought after. He will stand out from the crowd. Furthermore, upon the person who is not afraid to voice his sentiments will depend in considerable measure the repute in which that organization is held by people in general and its members in particular.

The truth is that for anyone who means to be a leader in business, professional or social life, a reasonable command of the technique of public speaking is almost as necessary as a command of effective conversation with individuals.

Neglected Responsibilities

There is a surprising difference in the attitude taken by most persons toward their responsibilities for conversation in contrast to public speaking. Almost everyone feels that he must hold up his end of a conversation. From childhood on, he takes part in conversation as a matter of course, and as a rule gives some thought to improving his ability to converse. Although one may at first be diffident or tongue-tied in conversations, he watches others and tries more or less consciously to imitate them, and through repeated practice to develop a degree of skill. But many persons never think of developing a similar skill in addressing groups of listeners. Perhaps we should say that many persons never think they can develop the ability to speak well. Public speaking, we should remember, is an activity of adult life, to which very few persons are "broken in" in youth. Too many men and women simply do not think of it as an accomplishment within their reach. They hold back, hesitant to try. Before long they come to believe that they have no ability in that direction.

Neglect Is a Handicap to Success

Such an attitude is most unwise. If you are unable to take your part in public discussion, you will almost certainly come short of meeting your business and social responsibilities. If you fail to get up and speak when a matter in which you are concerned is under discussion, you not only miss opportunities, but you may incur criticism. In fact, you may be considered either not interested or not informed.

As one result, you are almost certain to be passed over for many offices or functions, because you are presumed to be unable to meet the modest public speaking requirements of the position. You may resent it but at the same time have inward doubts of your ability. Everyone can think of instances in which men and women deeply interested in the work of an organization and well qualified for leadership have remained privates in the ranks merely because they so often insisted they could not "make a speech" that their associates finally took them at their word.

Rewards for Those Who Speak Well

On the other hand, if you come forward and take your part in the discussions of groups to which you belong, your rewards (if you do well) are immediate and very considerable. Many persons who speak on such occasions do it only passably. They escape criticism and put themselves on record, but no more. If you will give attention to the practical techniques of effective public speaking, you can learn with surprisingly little effort to do it very well. Then you may win attention and distinction.

In every field of work in every town, there are men and women who are looked to as leaders. Nine times out of ten these are the persons who have demonstrated the ability to express themselves well. They have taken an active part where matters of general interest were discussed. People have become accustomed to looking to them for thoughtful opinions and suggestions. Thus they are able to make their abilities, information and convictions count to a maximum degree. Every opportunity which such an occasion brings helps to develop their powers further and to broaden their knowledge of affairs and of people. Gradually, but surely, they come to handle still large responsibilities. They capitalize on the opportunities before them for progress. In fact, they create such opportunities.

Self-Expression a Duty

You have a responsibility for making known your ideas. As a member of your business or social circle you have convictions which ought to be placed at the service of your associates. If you are inexpert in public speaking, you are likely to fail in the full discharge of this duty. To illustrate, if you are in charge of a department in a business concern, at every department conference you will probably have to speak, whether you are an expert at public speaking or not. You will find it necessary to declare your views on matters under discussion or perhaps to present information relating to subjects on which you are especially informed. If you are attending a meeting of an industry as one of the representatives of your organization, and if you sit still and say nothing, through fear of making a poor appearance, it may prove to be greatly to the disadvantage of yourself and your organization. There may also be some topic that has failed to receive intelligent discussion and on which you have highly specialized knowledge which would enable you to make a real contribution. If you keep still, because you feel you are inexpert at public speaking, you are in a sense failing to meet your responsibilities.

A New Source of Pleasure

The ability to talk clearly and forcefully to groups is not only useful but also a source of personal satisfaction. It opens a new world of experience. You should enjoy the study of public speaking. There is pleasure in working with others for constructive and worthwhile purposes. There is satisfaction in knowing that one has the ability to present ideas to others effectively.

You are aware of the pleasure derived from a satisfactory conversation, in a business interview, for instance, when you present an idea you have thoughtfully developed and see it gradually find acceptance by the person with whom you are talking. It is gratifying to have a meritorious idea of yours gradually accepted by an associate until it becomes a part of his own thinking. You experience this sort of satisfaction in a much greater degree when you present your thoughts to an audience. You have an opportunity to develop your idea adequately without interruptions by the listeners' comments and replies. However, an opportunity of this character demands that one do his very best to present ideas of real value to listeners. It is a privilege which should never, never be abused by half-baked preparation and presentation.

For the same effort and time you can produce a much greater result by addressing a group than by conversing with the same number of persons one by one. The saving in time is obvious. The saving of effort is due in part to the fact that what you say makes a stronger impression upon each individual because of the silent influence of the group. When the audience as a whole is favorably impressed with your presentation, each individual is influenced that way. The judgment of the audience reinforces his own convictions.

Orderly Presentation of Ideas

Studying public speaking in the way that is outlined here brings an indirect benefit of great importance which at first may not be recognized. It improves your effectiveness in other relationships with your associates and friends. The training it gives you in organizing and uttering your ideas develops a readiness in adapting your conversation to listeners, which is useful many times. Good public speaking trains you to analyze beforehand the ideas you wish to present, to think them through clearly from the viewpoint of the persons you are addressing, and to formulate them in a way that is logical and convincing. In conversation there is a constant temptation to utter ideas in a disconnected form and to assume that the listener will somehow piece them together. Practice in effective public speaking tends to safeguard you against that fault in conversation. Practice in public speaking also develops a fluency of language which is of use in conversation. Furthermore, the practice of public speaking develops greater variety in your delivery, in your manner of uttering your remarks. In the conversation of persons who have never developed the extra sensitiveness to their own manner of utterance which the right sort of public speaking brings, there may be a tendency toward monotony in the way the sentences are sounded.

A Power for Everyday Use

A thoughtful and conscientious study of public speaking and the possibilities it affords for developing leadership should help you to make greater use of opportunities for advancement in your business or professional work. It should enrich and enlarge your social life. It should assist you in the more orderly presentation of your thoughts and in their clear and effective utterance. It makes you more sensitive to human relationships and contacts, and better able to adapt yourself to them.

Chapter 5

EVERYDAY SPEAKING IS NOT
DIFFICULT TO LEARN

The speeches required in professional, political and business life are not too difficult to prepare. They are entirely within the capacity of an intelligent person's thought upon matters in which he is interested.

No Special "Gift" Required

You may, however, be harboring another misunderstanding with regard to the procedure itself, the act of making and delivering the speech. Very often a person who has never faced an audience looks upon the act of addressing a group of listeners as something requiring special powers or "gifts," powers which most persons do not possess. This notion is as erroneous as the one about subject matter. You can learn to make a speech as surely as you can learn to write a letter, drive a car or handle a sales interview. You will be surprised, indeed, at the ease with which you can pick up the necessary technique if you go about it in the right way.

Expert Versus Beginner

At first, it is true, you may be dismayed by the expertness in public speaking of some of the people in your own circle of acquaintances. As you listen to the representative of a rival concern in your trade association or to a fellow member of a civic organization, or even to a ready talker among your own subordinates at a conference within your own company, you may be tempted to think that these persons have some special endowment which you lack. Their thoughts, it may seem to you, run on so smoothly; their delivery is so easy and impressive; they seem never to hesitate for words, so that you wonder how they do it. You say to yourself, "I could never talk like that!" Naturally, you shrink from getting up and inviting comparison with them.

This feeling may be even stronger if you realize that they have no actual advantage over you in understanding of the matters under discussion, or in general mental ability. Someone gets up—someone who really knows less of the situation than you and whom you could easily equal in effective conversation. He carries the group successfully with him to a decision that you feel is wrong. You are inclined to attribute his success to some mysterious personal "gift" which makes you feel impotent beside him.

Then some other acquaintance, perhaps much more capable and experienced than the first person, but without that strange "gift" of speech—as you suppose it to be—will get up and try to answer him and do a very poor job. His looks and manner reveal intense nervousness; he hesitates for words; perhaps he even gets his ideas twisted; and he sits down in obvious discomfiture. Watching such a performance may prompt you to a determination not to cut such a sorry figure yourself, to keep still even though it means remaining in the background, rather than attempt something you feel you cannot do successfully.

Expertness a Matter of Practice

But you would be in danger of making a serious mistake. You have no reason whatever to be dismayed by the performance of these persons in your own circle of friends and acquaintances. Actually, what produces the impression upon you and the others who listen to them is not, in most cases, any exceptional or unusual power. It is merely the expertness that comes from practice. These persons have given intelligent practice to an activity which the others, who make a poor impression by comparison, have never studied. The right kind of practice will enable you to develop similar skill for yourself. The chances are that the first attempts of these men whom you admire, when they began earnestly to practice public speaking, were just about as faltering and ineffective as those of the beginners for whom you feel sorry and with whom you may now classify yourself.

You Have the Ability

You have as much ability as those persons whose ease and readiness before the group so impresses you. They are not geniuses. They are merely competent persons with normal ability. Indeed, it is *that* fact which wins them a hearing. They are putting into words ideas which seem to their listeners sensible and sound, which come as the opinions and suggestions of people like the listeners, whom the listeners can trust. You simply need good common sense and normal ability. Therefore, you also can make yourself an impressive and influential speaker if you will take the trouble to learn the simple techniques of addressing a group. In fact, it is entirely possible that when you in turn have had the advantages of practice, you will be even more effective in the public speaking of daily life than some of these persons whose performance now appears so remarkable to you.

No Mysterious Procedure Involved

In the first place, there is nothing essentially strange or mysterious in the procedure involved when you stand up to address a group of persons. You do not need to learn to do something different from anything you have done before. It is merely a matter of employing in a somewhat modified way the techniques you have acquired in conversation, and you have been practicing conversation your entire life.

Let us suppose you are conversing with a few friends in the front of an auditorium. You are telling them about an experience you had on a recent trip to another city. Your story is very interesting. Some other friends of yours come along and stop to listen. Gradually the group becomes larger and as it does, those on the edge of the group are unable to hear ·you. They suggest that everyone in the group sit down so they can all hear you as you stand and continue telling of your experience.

Now at what point did your conversation change to a speech? Was it when the group grew larger? Was it when everyone else sat down? You were telling the same story after your listeners were seated and you were standing alone. If, when you stood alone, you suddenly realized you were about to make a speech, you might have lost your nerve and the story would not have been finished. But you just kept on conversing and, therefore, held your listeners. It is that simple.

Public Speaking Is Enlarged Conversation

There is no major difference between conversation with a few friends and conversation with an audience, except of course that we must use our voices to a little better advantage; we must speak a little louder and more distinctly when talking to an audience. We get some of the same help from an audience that we get from our friends in a conversation. Of course, John, Henry and Mary do not break into our speech by asking a question or by objecting to this or that statement. They do not give voice to their thoughts, but we find that they do take part in our speech by their general attitude, their facial expressions, a shake of the head or a nod, the attention they give. All these take the place of the verbal agreement, disagreement or question which is given in conversation with a small group. Therefore, the public speaking that we wish to use in meetings and before public groups is *merely enlarged conversation.*

No Special Vocabulary Required

Perhaps you think that your command of language is not adequate for public speaking. Men and women may say that they cannot address an audience because they do not have sufficient education. Those very same persons have no hesitancy in expressing their ideas to their friends and associates and they can often be exceptionally interesting in conversation. They imagine that their language is not good enough for making a speech to these same friends and associates.

What words do we need in order to express our ideas to others? There are many persons who go through life, express their ideas, make known their wants, get the results they desire, and have only rather limited vocabularies. Your vocabulary is probably much larger than the meager stock of these individuals. You have no hesitancy in taking part in conversation. You should not hesitate to get up on your feet for the "enlarged conversation" with an audience.

Listen carefully to the speeches and sermons you hear. You will be surprised how few words you hear in them that are not in your own everyday vocabulary. In many speeches you may hear no words at all which would not come to your own lips in careful conversation.

The words that will express your ideas in conversation are the same words that you should use on your feet. Simplicity of expression makes for ease in understanding. The simpler you can make the talk—that is, in the words you use—the more assurance you have that everyone in your audience will be able to follow you. You will know that the least educated will understand what you are saying, and you cannot offend the most educated, because he, too, will know what you mean and will have your idea vividly impressed upon his mind.

Sure Rewards from Careful Effort

After all, the question of whether or not you develop skill in public speaking depends on whether you have anything to say. That thought bears repetition—it depends on whether you have anything to say. If you have, you can learn to say it effectively. That is only a matter of following certain simple directions that have been developed by ages of experience. You can make speeches—when the occasion calls for them—if you will invest in your own future to the extent of careful and systematic practice. You can progress, if you continue your experimental study of this practical art, until you are able to meet with ease the responsibilities of any occasion that may come to you.

Learning to make full use of your power will of course require care and attention on your part. It will require acquisition of habits of steady self-control with respect to some things which in the past you have done on impulse, or even automatically. But the benefits you will receive for such effort and care should be rewarding to you. The work itself will be interesting from the start because at every moment you are studying people and their reactions, which is one of the most interesting of all human activities. And you will be able to put your efforts to practical and worthwhile use.

Chapter 6

TAKING THE FIRST STEPS

Merely thinking about the matter will not achieve what you are seeking—the ability to think on your feet and express your thoughts. Action is necessary. Prove to yourself that you *can* do it in the only way possible—that is, by actually making the attempt.

Therefore, make an opportunity to stand up and talk. Get up at a conference of your business associates. Say something at the lodge or club. Do not try to make a speech at first; merely stand up and say something. Make a motion, object to something with which you do not fully agree or ask a question. Make it as short as you like, but say something. You will have started. Putting off the trial until some other occasion will not help you.

A Good Way to Begin—Asking Questions

Probably the best of all ways of making the first plunge is by asking a question. Or rather, to begin by asking a question enables you to slip into the speaker's attitude by easy stages, and without ever having to make a sudden plunge.

Accordingly, at the next meeting of your club, civic or church group, in a business conference or trade gathering, watch the discussion and when something is said that is not entirely clear to you stand up and ask a question. Do not break into a speech by someone else, but wait until the speaker has finished. Interrupting a speaker is permissible in conversation but not, as a rule, in a group discussion.

Address the Chairman

There are two points of technique to bear in mind. The first has to do with observance of the rules of group discussion, or what is called parliamentary practice. In group discussion all questions and remarks are supposed to be addressed to the presiding officer. Therefore, remember to "address the chair" and direct your question to him and not to the person who has been speaking. The correct form to employ is, "Mr. Chairman, may I ask the last speaker a question?" or, "Mr. Chairman, I should like to ask a question." The chairman will answer, "State your question," and then you may proceed.

Expand Your Question

The second point of technique concerns only yourself. In order to obtain full benefit from your first practice step in public speaking, do not compress your inquiry merely into three or four words, as you would do in conversation. Instead, expand it a little, into three steps, as follows:

1. State your question briefly.
2. State briefly the reason for the question. Indicate the point which you find obscure or inconsistent.
3. Repeat the question.

AN EXAMPLE

Suppose, for example, that your club is considering a report from the entertainment committee, and certain figures seem to you indefinite. You might say something like this, "Mr. Chairman, I should like to ask a question on an item in this report."

The chairman will say, "State your question," and you will proceed. "Does the figure given by the committee for the price of the hall represent the total cost? The reason I ask is that on such occasions we have found previously that there are usually a number of service items, such as janitor's fees, that have to be covered. Sometimes these are included in the charge for the hall and sometimes they are not. I should like to know whether the figure we have been given includes all expense items connected with the use of the hall."

Do the same thing at the following meeting, and so on for a while. It will break the ice for you. Many persons who are now expert speakers began by thus asking questions, in that way becoming accustomed to standing up and hearing their own voices.

Offering a Brief "Remark"

Another way of getting started is to get up, in the course of a discussion, to utter a brief remark, just two or three sentences. In a courteous manner, challenge some statement made by one of the speakers, or add a brief expression of your own view. Some of those present have given their ideas in regard to the subject. You have some feeling on the matter. You have some thoughts relative to this topic. Because of what the others have said, you will have no difficulty in expressing yourself regarding it. You may elaborate on what they have said, or you may disagree with them and give your own ideas.

As a matter of fact, you may already be saying to yourself what you feel should be said, even if you do not get up; you are making a *mental* speech. The trouble with that kind of speech is that no one will hear it and have the benefit of your constructive ideas. Make yourself heard; get up and tell the others what you are thinking.

Do not elaborate your statements, but merely utter two or three sentences, as you would in conversation, taking care to speak somewhat louder, so that you may be heard. After resuming your seat, watch the effect of your remarks. Listen closely to any replies or comments made by other speakers. That will show you whether you made your point clear, and whether you expressed it effectively.

Only you can help yourself. The first time you rise in this way, you may feel like the man who said, "I do my hardest work before breakfast." "What is that?" asked his friend.

"Getting up," he said. Getting up may seem, the first time, a severe task, but make the attempt and you will find that it was easier than you thought.

Acquiring the "Speaker's Attitude"

Repeat these exercises—asking questions or injecting brief remarks—in every meeting in which you take part, for several weeks. Every time you get an opportunity to join in a discussion, seize it. It is good practice, and practice is what is necessary. Practice to give yourself self-confidence. Practice to prove to yourself that you can talk standing up.

Gradually you will get used to hearing your own voice in public. This will gradually beget a freedom of expression. You will come to feel as easy and composed when expressing your thoughts to a group of listeners as you do in conversation. Then, on some occasion, you will undoubtedly have the impulse to extend your remarks on a subject that interests you particularly, and you will find yourself making your first little speech.

The Question of Stage Fright

If you set about the study of public speaking in the systematic way just described, you are likely to escape altogether those queer panicky sensations which come to most persons when they first face an audience, and to which the name "stage fright" has been given. It may be, however, that you will find yourself called upon for a regular "speech," a connected talk of several minutes, without having put yourself through the preliminary breaking-in process of questions and remarks. In that case, when for the first time you rise to speak, you may be assailed by a sudden feeling of extreme nervousness.

You see all those pairs of eyes fixed upon you; you start to speak and your voice sounds strange in your ears. You are struck with a sudden thrill of fear, fear lest you may say or do something inappropriate or ridiculous, or may forget entirely what you want to say.

Its Cause

Consider the nature and cause of this feeling. Then we shall find that the cure is not difficult. It is a combination of two main elements. Although you may have no fear in speaking to individuals separately, there is, first, a natural excitement, a heightened sensitiveness, which is involved for you in the act of standing up before a group. It is entirely natural. A person who has this extra nervous energy will probably make a better speech because he is "keyed up." If you did not have it at all, you would be abnormal. In substance, it is not different from the feeling you experience when you are introduced to some distinguished individual. In an inexperienced speaker there is, second, a feeling of self-distrust, lest he may not be able to meet the demand—whatever it may be—that will be laid on him as he talks. With some persons this distrust amounts almost to panic. In some cases the unhappy speaker pictures himself making some stupid blunder. In other cases everything seems to go blank for him. Sometimes the panic-stricken individual halts, hesitates, mumbles some inane remark, and sits down in confusion. This is a wretched experience, like seasickness. People who have had a serious case of it often have a permanently timid attitude toward any effort to address an audience.

A Natural Result of Excitement

Now we should understand that this particular feeling is practically universal. Almost everyone who rises to address a group of people experiences it at first. Many expert public speakers continue to experience these sensations, to a degree, all their lives. The fact that you do experience it is some evidence that you possess the responsiveness which is essential for effective transmission of your message to other people. Do not worry over the fact that you have these sensations. Just consider what to do to tone them down so that they do not hinder the effectiveness of your talk. That can be done.

A Simple Remedy

In the first place, the purely physical sensations, the pumping of the heart and the trembling of limbs, can be at least partially overcome by merely remembering to stop and take a few deep breaths before beginning to talk. That will temper your excitement and will help you to restore your ordinary self-control. Do not rush in to your remarks. Just stand still, look steadily at your audience, and take two or three good deep inhalations of breath. You will find that the deep breathing will help to allay the feeling of oppression. Your nervousness will in some degree disappear as soon as you hear your own voice at the beginning of your talk.

Incidentally, the fact that you stand there a moment, quietly looking at the audience, will help to make them think of you as composed, self-possessed, probably an experienced speaker—which will tend to make them listen respectfully.

Useful Mental Treatment

The procedure which has just been described should assist in overcoming any stage fright. You will start on your talk and then your interest in making your point will help you forget about your own nervousness. With some individuals it is true the sensations of nervousness are so strong as to persist in spite of the practical first-aid remedy just mentioned. The reason is, almost always, that these people cannot get over the feeling of strangeness, unusualness, in the situation. If you are one of these extra-sensitive people, give yourself some mental treatment.

Conversing with the Audience

As already noted, you have no fear of the individuals in that audience. It is the act of standing up and addressing them as a group which you feel to be unusual. But is talking before a group really unusual? After luncheon the other day, you and a number of friends and acquaintances stood in a group and discussed some subject in which you were mutually interested. There may have been ten in the group. There was nothing unusual about talking with them. Suppose the ten had been casually seated around and you had been standing in the room? Could you not have discussed the same subject without feeling that you were doing something out of the ordinary? Convince yourself that talking before any group is merely an enlarged conversation.

Do not talk *to* them, *at* them, or over their heads. Talk *with* them and they will, in effect, take part in the conversation. Though they will not speak, they will manifest their interest on their faces and in their appearance.

If you "converse" with your audience in this way, the unusual aspect of public address will be eliminated. The chief difference between everyday conversation with one or more individuals and conversation with an audience is a mental one. You have been led to believe that public speaking is entirely different from what you ordinarily do when you talk. It is not. Once you realize that your relation with your audience is a normal and natural one, fear, doubt and worry can more easily be dissipated. When you stand up to present your thoughts to a group, do so with courage, confidence and faith in yourself.

Challenge Boldly Your Timidity

Challenge boldly the feeling of being the target of the unspoken critical thoughts of your listeners. Not everyone who hears you will agree with all that you say. It is not necessary that they do so. The disagreement they may manifest may come from misunderstanding, and in that case you can remove it. It may come from a conviction which you cannot overcome. But it does not come from an attitude of attempting to embarrass you. On the contrary, all of us like to hear men express themselves. Not only do we like to hear them, but we applaud those who do it fearlessly.

Therefore, if you express your thoughts boldly, even those who disagree will respect you and admire you. Train yourself to look directly at your listeners. Looking squarely into their eyes will give you confidence. You will perceive and interpret rightly the response they are silently making to your remarks.

And remember, finally, that normal listeners are not seeking things to criticize. They want to be interested in what you say. They are not expecting you to say anything out of the ordinary. If you have made careful preparation of your comments, you may be able to contribute some worthwhile ideas to your listeners. They will appreciate them and will value your remarks.

Chapter 7

WHAT TO TALK ABOUT

Success in addressing an audience depends first of all upon having something to say, having a message. We talk for the purpose of conveying ideas. Unless we have worthwhile ideas to present to listeners, we cannot expect to retain their attention and support, for we have no right to take up their time. There is no excuse for making a public speech unless one has conscientiously prepared worthwhile ideas to give his audience.

Always Have a Message

You should apply this principle also as a matter of course in conversation. Sensible men and women do not just chatter. What you say in conversation bears upon the subject under consideration or opens another subject which you believe your companion will be interested in when he hears of it. Everyone feels embarrassed, awkward and ill at ease when he has to "make conversation" or talk just to fill time, for example, with a stranger at dinner. If you will remember always to make a worthwhile contribution when you address an audience, your progress in public speaking will be rapid. You will have accomplished the most important objective in public speaking: presenting something of value to an audience. The fact that you have something worthwhile to give will affect both your audience and yourself. It will show in your own manner, giving it an impressive, composed, businesslike character. This in turn will impress your listen-

55

ers and dispose them to pay respectful attention to what you have to say.

This, therefore, is the first rule for success in public speaking: Always have something to say that you feel certain is worth saying. That involves thorough and conscientious preparation.

What the Rule Means

This rule may not at first seem very helpful to one who has shied away from opportunities to speak in public and who has been told that he must now take every opportunity for *practice*. For you say, "I don't often have a real message for an audience. It is rare, indeed, that I have anything in mind which I feel might be a worthwhile contribution to a group of listeners. If I speak only when I have something which I very much desire to convey to the group in which I find myself, my speeches will be few and far between."

Well, let us see. Is this really the situation? Perhaps you have misconstrued the expressions "message" and "worthwhile." Perhaps you are making the error noted in Chapter 4 with respect to the *nature* of the speaking in business, professional and social life and assume that you must champion some great cause or attempt the explanation of some intricate idea. It is not necessary that your message be mighty or momentous. It need not sway nations! If you have some contribution to make to subjects under discussion among your business or professional friends and associates, the members of your Rotary, Kiwanis, Lions or Optimists club, the social groups of your church or your chamber of commerce, you can make a worthwhile speech.

The Impulse to Speak

Perhaps the desire to present an idea to an audience, with definiteness although not in a life-or-death attitude, comes to you more often than you realize. However, because public speaking is now an unfamiliar activity, you do not try to carry out the desire. You are by no means mentally passive, uninterested in other people and their affairs and ideas, and in their reaction to your opinions and purposes. If you were thus lacking in responsiveness to what goes on around you, you would not be reading about public speaking. In conversation, certainly, you do not sit mute and tongue-tied until one of the great dominating interests of your life comes up; instead you take an interest in whatever topic is under discussion and participate to the best of your ability. Do the same thing when participating in group discussions.

What Can You Talk About?

What are the matters regarding which you desire to convey your thoughts to others? The natural answer will be: Matters which you think are important for the other people to know—useful, instructive, profitable, beneficial or entertaining to them. The question becomes finally: What material of this character is there in your own mind, either impressed on it by your daily experience or developed through your private observation and reflection? With the answer to that question we shall begin to get somewhere.

Talk of What You Know

This is the answer: You will talk about matters with which you are intimately acquainted, those which pertain to your business, your occupation or your personal life. If you want to get helpful practice in public speaking, utilize subjects related to your business, your profession, your work.

Do you think there is little about such topics that would interest others? Let us see. You are so close to your work that everything about it is familiar to you. It is not familiar, however, to other people. Some aspects of it are not familiar even to fellow members within your organization. It does not matter what your business is, whether it is operating a railroad or raising oranges, inventing electrical devices or selling shoes, plumbing or trucking. The story can be made interesting. There are all around you men and women who do not know how your business is run, what is necessary to carry it on, the future which might be in store for anyone entering your field of endeavor.

Never forget that public speaking is merely conversation —enlarged conversation, carried on with more than one individual, but still conversation. You can interest your friend in a conversation on almost any subject if you are really interested in it yourself. You can interest also the composite individual constituting your audience.

Opening Up the Subject

But remember to *open up* the subject. Otherwise you will merely scratch the surface of your topic and fail to tell the things about the subject that are really significant and worthwhile. For instance, suppose that your subject was matches and that you were "merely talking." You might simply state what a match is, and where it can be purchased, and then conclude with, "I think that's all that can be said on the subject." Why should that be all? Because you had not really thought about the subject from the standpoint of attempting to pass on to listeners really significant facts or comments with reference to it. You did not develop your ideas.

That is not the way to make an interesting *speech* on the subject. If your business was matches, and you were to try really to make a speech about matches, you would very likely take an encyclopedia and read something regarding matches. You would familiarize yourself with the whole history of matches and perhaps the part fire played in the development of modern civilization. A little reading would enable you to give a very interesting talk.

The Question of Cleverness

Someone may object that the subject of matches would not be a worthwhile topic. "A talk about matches could not be clever." This comment, which might be made by one who has not given much thought to the question, needs to be considered. Let us see what truth there is in it, and how far it is justified. It may be conceded at once that almost everyone likes to be considered "clever."

At the last banquet you attended, one of the speakers may have been applauded because of his clever address. Everyone commented upon it. Many of those present, perhaps you among them, thought, "I wish I could talk like that." Cleverness, we feel, always receives the approbation and acclaim of others.

When we call a speaker clever, we may mean one of two different things. We may mean that he expresses his thoughts in a surprising form. When a person deliberately sets himself to make his talk "clever" in this sense, there is great danger that his talk will be amusing momentarily, but will leave no worthwhile ideas.

The Essential—Knowing Your Subject

The other meaning of clever is that the speaker gave an able talk; he proved himself a talented speaker. Now who is the able speaker? The man who knows his subject, who handles it in such a way that he interests and convinces us. The word "talented" should not lead you to believe that public speaking is an *unusual* talent. Any average person can be an able talented speaker. There are certain subjects on which you are an able conversationalist—subjects concerning which you would be called talented, subjects which you know thoroughly, subjects about which you are thoroughly informed and enthusiastic.

A Golfer

To illustrate, there is a quiet individual who belongs to your organization. It is hard to draw him out. His only sociability seems to be that he plays golf. He is not an expert, just a fair golf player. The other day he made a hole in one. Did you hear him telling about it? If he can buttonhole you, he will tell you the next time you meet. He has something that he is interested in; he is enthusiastic; he is overjoyed. He wants the world to share in his excitement, in his enthusiasm, in his joy. He becomes on that one subject, an able, talented conversationalist.

All Have the Power

We are all talented with the power of speech and expression. We should use that gift and obtain the most from it. The talented man makes an able speech, because he knows what he is talking about, has put thought on it and developed it. Because he is convinced of the value of his subject, it necessarily follows that he will paint mental pictures with power, force, interest. He must and does dominate. Unless you are extremely timid, unless you fear, unless you are worrying about the outcome, unless you lack self-confidence, you can do the same with a subject in which you are interested. You can get a reputation for being a talented speaker.

A Speech About Packing Cases

A very interesting speech was delivered in a debating club by a young man who worked in the receiving department of a big retail store. A member of the club who was a golf enthusiast had given a vivid and instructive description of the way to make certain golf strokes, using a golf club to illustrate the proper stance and swing. Later in the evening the man in the delivery department, who was a quiet chap weighing perhaps 130 pounds, borrowed the golfer's club and described the way to handle big packing cases weighing up to 350 pounds. He held the club like a box-hook and illustrated the stance and movements by which a slender man is able to handle boxes more than twice his own weight.

No one would have supposed that an interesting speech could be made on that subject. But when he finished he had given his listeners some unusual ideas. He brought out points of human dynamics which his audience had never considered.

Therefore, talk about ordinary things, but think them

through. Talk about the things you know, but develop your knowledge so it is unusually complete. Make yourself the master of your subject.

Subjects Familiar to Others

Do not be afraid to talk about subjects regarding which your hearers also are informed, even if they know more about the subject than you do. No man knows everything on any one topic. The learned man will tell you that the longer he lives, the more he realizes how little he knows. We can all learn from the college professor, from the professional writer and from the laborer. The man digging the ditch that you passed this morning knows more than you do on some topic, if you could get him to discuss it.

There may be, therefore, people in your audience who know more about the subject than you do. Still there may be just one phase of the subject, one point about it that they have not observed as you have. There may be just one side of it on which you can give them a new viewpoint. We all have ideas which, if communicated, would help others.

Your Thoughts Are Different

"Oh, but my thoughts on that subject are obvious. Everybody must know them." That is just the point! *They do not.* You are so well acquainted with your business, are so close to it, that there does not seem to be anything out of the ordinary in it. Your ideas, your thoughts, being yours, seem obvious to you. You assume that everybody must have the same thoughts and you think that there is no use discussing what everybody knows. You want to be able to say something new, something that is startling.

Remember, however, that people are not always interested in things about which they know nothing at all. In your conversation with friends, you discuss matters that are of mutual interest. You do not talk about things your friend does not understand.

Courage to Utter the Obvious

Have the courage to express what you think. Express it even if you think it is obvious. If others have the same idea, they will agree with you. We all like to be able to sit back and hear a speaker give opinions or enunciate thoughts which agree with ours. When his ideas agree with ours, we feel he is right. For that reason we tend to agree with his subsequent statements. So what seems obvious to you may be the means of winning your audience.

Have the courage, therefore, to give voice to your opinions. Think them through carefully, and if, in your good judgment, they are correct, then have the courage to express them.

Believe In Your Own Mind

Believe in your own thoughts. Express what you think without fearing that it is commonplace. Think—then say what you have to say with courage, conviction and enthusiasm. Subjects on which you can speak effectively to audiences should not be hard to find. They may or may not be connected directly with the subjects that are being discussed at the time by others. *Pick your subject and stick to it.* Think it out. Make your decision and then hold to that decision.

Chapter 8

DETERMINING WHAT YOU WANT
TO SAY

When asked the secret of success, Chauncey M. Depew once replied, "There is no secret about it. Just dig, dig, dig."

What is the secret of effective speaking? There is no secret about it. It is just *practice, practice, practice.*

A Gift to Be Developed

Public speaking is a gift, but it is a gift that is yours and mine. We do not call walking—the power to walk—a gift. Yet it is just as much of a gift as effective speaking. You had to learn to walk. So also you learned to talk. If you can talk in conversation, you can just as easily talk standing up before a group. You probably could not win a walking or running race without training, but training and practice at accelerated walking or running would help make you an athlete. Training and practice in accelerated thinking and speaking will help make you effective when you stand up to talk. While age may hinder one from becoming an athlete, age will help one to be effective as a speaker. The older the person, the longer has experience been his tutor. Because of your experience you have the foundation for talking interestingly. What you need is to add sufficient preparation to the knowledge gained by experience.

Preparation—Various Meanings

There are various methods of preparation for effective public speaking. Some instructors lay special stress upon the importance of detailed and elaborate preparation before mak-

63

ing a speech. "Know your subject," they repeat again and again. This sort of preparation is necessary for many types of speeches. You cannot talk on anything about which you have no knowledge, but sometimes you have no opportunity to prepare a speech before you are asked to talk briefly on a subject.

To speak extemporaneously does not mean speaking without preparation. You may not prepare a written speech for a talk, but you will still be prepared. You are prepared by your knowledge of the subject, by your life's experience. While you may not write the words for a particular talk that you will give, back of every talk is the experience of years.

What, then, do we mean by talking in this instance without preparation? We mean that you do not prepare the words. The subject will be related to matters with which you are already familiar, and therefore you will be ready to speak. The subject which may be given you will be in the field in which you are prepared to talk from your experience and knowledge. In this sense, your "extemporaneous" talks, as well as the "extemporaneous" talks of every worthwhile speaker, have taken a long time to prepare. The preparation has been going on for years.

Subjects on Which You Are Prepared

Whether or not you are aware of the fact, you have made preparation for effective public speaking of this character. There are topics on which you are able right now to talk convincingly even without further study. In fact, the type of subject that you, as a businessman or officer of a fraternal or service organization, will be called upon to discuss is almost certain to be one of which you have definite knowledge. You obtained that knowledge from observation, from experience, from conversation, from reading.

It should be emphasized that with respect to these subjects your preparation has been going on for a long time. Your experience, which is your preparation, is so close to you that it may not seem to you an adequate foundation for presenting trustworthy material, but in reality it is a very good foundation. It will take practice, of course, to attain the readiness and fluency for which well-known speakers are notable, but practice will bring this also in sufficient degree.

Subjects That Call For Study

You may be asked, however, to talk on some subject for which experience has not thoroughly prepared you, or on an occasion when a more formal address is imperative. In that case it is necessary to make definite preparation by means of reflection, reading and conversation. You may make a detailed outline and write the complete speech. You may speak from written notes or from mental notes. Public officials sometimes feel it necessary to read a speech because of the danger on an important public issue of not expressing exactly the thoughts they have in mind. They wish to be quoted in the press just as they have carefully set down the words in writing. Ordinarily it is not as effective to read a speech as it is to speak from mental or written notes one has made in advance of a speech. Sometimes one may also have a speech fully written, keeping it before him as he speaks merely to remind him of major thoughts and of the sequence of his ideas. The written manuscript is also available for publicity releases.

Your Idea Versus Its Presentation

The specific preparation required before you can work up an effective speech includes two different lines of activity. There is your own *mental* preparation, which is requisite before you can determine what you want to say. There is also the preparation required for determining how to present your ideas to the listeners you are to address. In the case of an experienced speaker both processes may be carried on very rapidly—almost instantaneously. For the inexperienced speaker, on the other hand, both aspects require careful attention.

Preparation in its second aspect—that is, determining how you will present your ideas to your listeners—will be taken up later. Here we must consider your mental preparation, the preparation required in determining what you desire to say.

Reflect, Read, Consult

With regard to your personal preparation, which is certainly necessary when you have to talk on a subject not wholly familiar to you, or when you are given time to prepare a more formal address for some special occasion, the formula to follow may be summed up in three words: *Reflect, Read, Consult.* That is to say: Turn the subject over carefully in your mind, to make sure of just what you actually think about it at present. Then read books, magazines and other written matter, to see what others have said about it. Finally, make opportunities of conversing upon the subject with other persons, as often as time permits, to discover how it appears to people who are probably somewhat like those you are to address.

Using the Thoughts of Others

Do not fear to use ideas that have been expressed by others, but put those thoughts, unless you are quoting, in your own words. Elaborate them as you see fit. Draw your own conclusions from them. Make them your own. Your ideas will then be augmented and clarified by the ideas of others.

This use of other persons' ideas as a basis for your own is a perfectly legitimate practice. It has been followed in all ages. With respect to ideas, thoughts and reflections which grow out of observing life, there may be only a little that is new. Many of the ideas that we call new and modern are merely a restatement of ideas that were first conceived ages ago. Many of your own thoughts which you regard as completely original have undoubtedly been expressed before. You have a right to utilize any idea, provided that you do not merely "parrot" it but give it an original application.

Shakespeare

The great master writer of all time, Shakespeare, did not hesitate to take the ideas, the plays, of others. He used their plots, and some of their scenes, and from them developed his great dramatic masterpieces. But remember, he made the thoughts, the plots, his own.

Lincoln's Gettysburg Address

Lincoln's Gettysburg speech will live while the English language exists. His great conclusion is quoted in patriotic speeches on many occasions. Was the wording, "government of the people, by the people, for the people," original? No. Lincoln had a copy of Theodore Parker's speeches. Parker had used the words, "A Government of all the people, by all the people, for all the people," in a speech at Boston in 1850. In 1795, Thomas Cooper had said, "Government of the people and for the people." Years before Lincoln's address John Marshall had stated, "Government over all, by all, and for the sake of all." Webster had used almost the same sentiment in his reply to Hayne in 1830, when he said, "The people's government made for the people, made by the people, and answerable to the people."

Some of your thought combinations may never have been expressed until now. Those that have been voiced differed in the manner of expression from the form and language you will use. While there is little new under the sun, by taking the old, dressing it in a new garb of language, you can interest others. Because it seems new it will have a freshness of appeal.

The Value of Consultation

In addition to reflecting upon the subject, and reading widely and attentively, discuss it with other persons of your acquaintance, or with strangers when you have an opportunity. Ask questions. Find out what others know about the subject. Conversation with others is a most valuable element in preparing your own thought.

Alertness Finds Material

Suppose, then, that you have selected your topic. It is being held before your mind, and you are actively examining it, thinking through it. You will be amazed to find how material will collect. To your surprise, when reading your morning newspaper, you will find a paragraph or comment that bears on your subject. In casual conversation a remark will be made that will help you in developing it. A lecture, a sermon, a book, will give you a suggestion that will aid you. Why? Because your mind is awake, alert. It is receptive on the subject. It is eager to grasp whatever will help in making the topic clear. Bryan defined "eloquence" as: "The speech of one who knows what he is talking about and means what he says." An unknown author once said, "Eloquence is logic on fire."

Chapter 9

DEVELOPING THE PLAN
OF YOUR SPEECH

A capable speaker not only has something to say, but he must also know how to say it effectively. The great speakers, such as Winston Churchill, have had something to say, but, in addition, they have recognized that careful study must be given to the manner of presenting a speech.

The first step in preparing your speech for the audience consists in determining carefully your central idea, your main thought, just what it is you wish to say. This is an important step in preparation. It is one which the beginner almost always neglects but to which the experienced speaker has learned to give close attention.

Always an Idea, When You Talk

When we talk about a subject either to another person or to a group, it is always for the purpose of making some statement, expressing some comment, view or opinion. For example, the subject which you talk about in conversation with a friend may be a topic like one of the following:

Reducing city taxes

Your company's new promotion campaign

The coming Red Cross drive

Determine the Idea Beforehand

In conversation you do not stop and explicitly consider what this central idea of your remarks is to be. You "just know" what you wish to say; your thought comes to you in a flash—automatically, subconsciously. You utter it with almost as little conscious reflection as moving your legs when you walk. But when you make a speech, it is different. When you have to go into a matter in detail before a group of people, it is wise to consider definitely beforehand just what it is that you intend to say—in other words, to determine the central idea of your speech.

If you are urged to go to the Town Improvement Association meeting and give them the views which you have expressed to your friends on reducing the local budget, you will have to think over your case and make up your mind as to what you will recommend. For you will be challenged, you will have to support your statements. Or, if you are asked to tell about your fishing trip in Canada at the monthly meeting of your club, you will also find it wise to determine carefully the central idea of your remarks. Otherwise, you may run on indefinitely and weary your listeners.

An Orderly Sequence of Points

After determining the central idea of your speech, you must consider how to present it fully and with effect to the group of different individuals who constitute your audience. The minds of these different individuals work at different speeds. To make sure that they all grasp your central idea, and at the same time, you need to break it down into steps or sections, which can be presented to the audience one by one in orderly sequence. If you do this skillfully, you can render even an extensive or intricate idea understandable and really interesting.

Always Plan Your Talk

Even when you speak on the spur of the moment you need a plan, sometimes framed quickly but carefully in the few moments between the time you are summoned to the platform and the time you begin to talk. When you have time for systematic preparation, you will of course work out a plan carefully. Some speakers will tell you they never make a plan for a speech, but the statement is hardly valid. The truth is that the *effective* speaker who says he speaks without formally making a plan actually knows his subject so well he has unconsciously planned his remarks. Having talked on the subject many times, he has a mental plan which serves to make his talk a cohesive, logical treatment of the subject. Without a plan you are in great danger of rambling. You may entertain for a while. You may even interest an audience for a short time. But you are not at all likely to cause people to think, or to rouse them to action and get results. The plan will make your talk logical. You will know what you want to say, and you will be able to say it effectively because of your plan. The definite arrangement of your plan will help you to remember.

Stick To the Plan

When you stand up to talk, ideas may come to your mind which seemed to elude you during your preparation. It would be easy to make use of these ideas, but do not succumb to the temptation. If you do, you may find yourself off on a tangent. You may wander away from the subject. In all probability, when you have exhausted the thought that momentarily attracted you, you will experience great difficulty in getting back to your subject. Therefore, always prepare the plan of your talk and stick to it. Your talk will be more forceful and more interesting, which means more effective.

Three Functions of the Plan

The plan is really the skeleton of your talk. The headings of topics which make it up should be in logical sequence. You will divide the material and arrange the portions so that your thought proceeds by a clearly followed line of march. The plan should fulfill the following functions or duties:

1. Convey your central idea fully, giving all that is necessary. This includes allowing for and answering by anticipation the questions that may be asked.

2. Give the central idea in the proper perspective, the proper proportion.

3. Present it in a way that will be easy, pleasing, interesting to your listeners.

Three Main Stages

In accomplishing these purposes, you will find that your development of the central idea falls into the following three distinct main stages or steps:
1. The introduction
2. The body, or discussion
3. The conclusion

The Introduction

It would be unwise for you to launch immediately into the body of the talk, for you would probably not get satisfactory results. You must first strive to win the attention of your hearers. You desire not their passive attention, but their active interest. Therefore, your speech needs an introduction.

In building this introduction, remember the advice of the poet Alexander Pope:

> Men must be taught as if you taught them not,
> And things unknown proposed as things forgot.

Do not let your introduction give the impression that you are the teacher and the audience is about to be taught something. Make it fit your particular audience. Use it to awaken their interest and gradually lead into your subject. If you do this skillfully it goes far toward insuring success to your speech.

Personal Introduction

Various methods may be used to introduce your talk, depending on the occasion. One method is the *personal introduction*. Carl A. Gray, president of the Grenby Manufacturing Company of Plainville, Connecticut, began an address before the Economic Club of Detroit as follows:

I come to Detroit today in humble admiration for the city and you people, who have built so much and do such remarkable things. It is a real pleasure and privilege, I assure you, to talk to you.

I want you to know me, however, in my own guise. I am just a small manufacturer from the little town of Plainville, Connecticut, operating an electro-mechanical factory. I believe in the profit-and-loss system and want to see it maintained. I am no specialist and haven't any particular brand of economic salvation, except sweating, striving and producing. . . .

I like to be known as a representative of little business, because small business has always been and still is the biggest employer of labor. Two out of three people employed in manufacturing are employed in shops of less than one hundred persons. When you add to this the many small enterprises in other fields, you have eight out of ten people employed in companies of less than one hundred personnel.

I do not minimize the importance to our economy of large companies. Your big companies were once little fellows like myself. They have grown up. Our country would suffer without them. There is no question about it—and I am not just trying to make kind remarks because I'm here in Detroit.

In this instance the personal introduction has a human quality and a frankness which must have won the attention of the audience and prompted them to listen closely.

One other illustration of the personal introduction to a speech is from a significant address on " 'American,' the Meaning of the Word," by Herbert Hoover, former president of the United States, at a celebration of his birthday at West Branch, Iowa:

Introduction to an Address by Herbert Hoover

I am glad to have your invitation to come again to this Iowa village where I was born. Here I spent the

first ten years of my boyhood. My parents and grand-
parents came to this village in the covered wagon—pio-
neers in this community. They lie buried over the hill.
They broke the prairie into homes of independent living.
They worshiped God; they did their duty to their neighbors. They toiled to bring to their children greater comfort, better education, and to open to them wider opportunity than had been theirs.

I am proud to have been born in Iowa. As I have said
before, through the eyes of a ten-year-old boy it was a
place of adventure and daily discoveries. The wonder of
the growing crops, the excitements of the harvest, the
journeys to the woods for nuts and hunting, the joys of
snowy winters, the comfort of the family fireside, of
good food and tender care.

And out of the excessive energy of all small boys, the
evenings were filled with accounts of defeat and victory
over animate and inanimate things—so far as they were
permitted in a Quaker community.

Indelible in those recollections was a widowed mother, sitting with her needle, cheerfully supporting three
children and at the same time ministering to her neighbors. After that came life with Uncle Allan on his farm
near this village, with the joys and sorrows which come
to every small boy en route to life's disciplines by way
of farm chores. And among them was the unending making of provisions for the next winter. But in those primi-
tive days, social security was had from the cellar, not
from the federal government.

A Caution

The introduction to Herbert Hoover's address is an excellent illustration of the effective use of the personal introduction. As a rule, however, the personal introduction should be
used with great care. Talking about yourself may encourage
apologies, and it is difficult to apologize at length successfully. Attention should rather be directed to the subject. It
is not necessary to avoid entirely the use of the pronoun "I."

The proper use of the pronoun "I" is not a fault. Merely remember not to overuse the pronoun and never use it in a boastful manner. An audience, like an individual, resents boasting. Modesty on the part of a speaker is an asset. The tone of Herbert Hoover's introduction commands respect for this reason among many others. It is not only earnest, but also genuinely modest, with a touch of humor—an almost unbeatable combination.

Reference to the Occasion

Reference to the occasion is an easy and spontaneous method for introducing a speech. It should be used especially on dignified occasions. Lincoln's Gettysburg speech is a classic example of the introduction which has reference to the occasion. President McKinley, delivering the address at the dedication of the Grant monument in New York City, began as follows:

A great life, dedicated to the welfare of the nation, here finds its earthly coronation. Even if this day lacked the impressiveness of ceremony and was devoid of pageantry, it would still be memorable, because it is the anniversary of the birth of one of the most famous and best-loved of American soldiers.

The author used the following reference to the occasion to begin an address on "World Trade and World Stability" at Notre Dame University:

This first World Trade Conference at Notre Dame University opens in a strangely distraught world. Men everywhere are struggling with new and powerful forces, for the world is economically and politically disheveled. It has threatened to ride to its doom in a powder cart, as nations have engaged in the cooperative suicide of two world wars. The economic machinery has run down in many nations, and sound business and financial traditions have been destroyed in various parts of the world. Unless there is a release again in these nations of the great fountain of private and free enterprise, the progress of decades may be lost.

It is gratifying that this university has organized this conference to examine one of the most important aspects of contemporary international economic life. Thoughtful men have come increasingly to recognize that in a well-balanced economic order experience must be combined with education. The realism of the market place and the idealism of the classroom must join hands. Education must relate itself intelligently to the fundamental needs of the everyday life of the community and the nation. Out of this union there will come to education, on the one hand, a still richer and more rigid training for young men and women so they may play productive roles in a complex economic order. And to business, on the other hand, there will come that broad education which will steadily raise it to even greater levels of constructive achievement.

It is a privilege, therefore, to participate in this important conference.

Statement of the Topic

The most logical and the most common type of introduction is that which states the topic to be discussed. It calls the attention of the audience to the subject. It establishes the importance of the topic. You may use this form of introduction with good results on almost any occasion. A notable example of this form of introduction is the beginning of an address in Chicago by Theodore Roosevelt on "The Strenuous Life."

In speaking to you, men of the greatest city of the West, men of the State which gave to the country Lincoln and Grant, men who pre-eminently and distinctly embody all that is most American in the American character, I wish to preach, not the doctrine of ignoble ease, but the doctrine of the strenuous life, the life of toil and effort, of labor and strife; to preach that the highest form of success comes, not to the man who desires more easy peace, but to the man who does not shrink from danger, from hardship, or from bitter toil, and who out of these wins the splendid ultimate triumph.

Erwin D. Canham, editor of the *Christian Science Monitor*, began a lecture at Yale University with the following brief statement of his subject:

> Let me tell you my thesis bluntly at the outset. It is that the struggle for the salvation of society in our time will be lost unless we in the West—and particularly we in the United States—awaken to and project the fact that we are the great revolutionaries in world history, and that our revolution is basically a spiritual one which we have already proved in action.

The Humorous Introduction

The humorous introduction is much used. It is good for informal, friendly and festive occasions. It is particularly apropos for after-dinner speeches.

The following examples illustrate the use of the humorous introduction:

From an extemporaneous address delivered at an Associated Press luncheon by General Dwight D. Eisenhower, then president of Columbia University:

> Mr. McLean, my many, many good friends that I am privileged again to meet, and all those others here that I should so like to meet personally, to all of you, greetings.
>
> My first word must be one of apology because, whenever before any professional group a layman is called to speak or to make an appearance, he certainly must do a bit of soul-searching to determine some reasonable excuse. As I see it, the invitation by itself is not enough.

Once in a little Kansas town a Californian was coming through and he found it convenient to spend the evening. There was a funeral service going on in the village church and he entered. At one place in this very informal ceremony the minister asked whether there was anyone present who should like to get up and to pay a tribute to the dear departed, and, no one speaking, the Californian took advantage of the opportunity to get up and say:

"Well, I didn't know the deceased and I have never been in the town before. Still I thought it was a good opportunity to describe something of the beauty and the wonderful climate of California."

I am not here, I hope, with such a complete ignorance of your profession as this man exposed as to the town and to the guest of honor at that particular ceremony. I also can claim no possible professional connection with such a distinguished body, a connection which I must admit I think I should rather envy because of the very deep respect that I have for the press and the very deep conviction I have of its responsibilities and its opportunities in the world of today.

Shortly after Alben W. Barkley was elected Vice President of the United States, he made an address in Chicago in which he used the following humorous story in his introduction:

Now I was under some disturbance mentally as to what I should talk about here today. I am not going to make a political speech. I have never made one here, although it is impossible to discuss anything these days without it having some political implications, in the sense that politics is the science of government; and if I should accidentally or unintentionally trespass upon any political expressions or sentiments, you will understand that I am not talking politics but I am talking about the science of government.

I have not entirely become accustomed to being Vice President of the United States. I don't think the country has either. I always feel some embarrassment in speaking in that capacity because I recall a very, very witty and yet I think sincere remark made to me many years ago by Vice President Dawes when he was vice president of the United States. You know, he made a great effort to institute some reforms in the rules of the Senate. We have been trying it ever since with not much more success than he had.

But one day he called me up to the Vice President's desk, and he said, "Barkley, this is an awful job I've got."

I said, "What's the matter with it? You still have it. I haven't noticed that you have resigned."

He said, "I can't do but two things."

I said, "What are they?"

He said, "One of them is to sit up here and listen to you birds talk, and I can't reply. And the other is to look at the papers every morning to see how the President's health is."

Care in Planning the Introduction

Make your introduction suit your audience and your subject. You are conversing with them. You desire to have them give credence to what you say. Your introduction should lead them to listen with respect and liking. If it reflects your feeling and attitude sincerely and earnestly, it will arouse the interest and attention of your hearers, and lead them to your subject matter.

When preparing a speech beforehand, you may find it best to prepare the introduction *last*. The reason is evident. It is only after you know definitely what the course of your speech is to be, that you determine just how to set the stage and lead up to your central idea.

The Body or Discussion

The body, or discussion, is the principal part of your talk. It is here that you bring out plainly the central idea, the real meat of your address. It is here that you prove your contention, give information or entertain your listeners. In prepar-

ing your speech you may prepare this section of it before you
work out the introduction. The procedure on this section is
optional. But your first step will probably be to determine
your central idea and principal subdivisions.

Planning the Body of a Speech

Let us take a subject and make a plan for the body of a
speech. Take, for example, this title:
"America's Pride in her Public Schools."
This phrase would provide a topic for a talk. One need not
grope in the dark to find reasons why we may have pride in
our public schools. The plan for a speech on this topic might
be:

1. The American government is founded upon the principle of equal opportunity.
2. Equal opportunity necessitates education.
3. Education must be universal among the citizenry.
4. Education must be available to all.
5. America has tried to live up to its ideal of education.
6. The accomplishments of our public schools may be
measured in part by the crowded conditions in our colleges.
7. There is much still to be accomplished.
8. Our educators realize their responsibilities and the needs
of our public schools.
9. A good foundation has been laid.
10. Our school system is among the best in the world.

Here we have in rough form a plan for the body or discussion of our subject.
When we examine these ten points more closely, we see
that their logical relation is shown more clearly if we group
them again into four points, as follows:

1. The American principle of equal opportunity demands
education.
2. Equal opportunity calls for universal, free educational

facilities. The amount of money spent by the various states each year shows to what extent the nation is taking care of the demand.

3. Colleges are demanding higher standards from applicants since they cannot accommodate all who seek to enter. We cannot rest on what we have accomplished. Our educators know that much needs to be done, especially in rural communities and in the consolidation of school districts. Efforts must be made constantly to raise the educational standards of teachers.

4. Our educational system is merely a foundation, and we cannot rest until every child in this country has a place in a conveniently located competent public school. Our public school system is among the best in the world.

In this grouping, you notice, the first and second of the ten points go into our new first point; the third, fourth and fifth into our new second point; the sixth, seventh and eighth into our new third point; and the ninth and tenth into our new fourth point.

Later in the process of preparing the speech, these four points would be filled out with facts and detail ideas. These would have been gathered, of course, from experience, reading and conversation. It is imperative that you thoughtfully and conscientiously work to obtain facts, illustrations and figures that will make clear your central idea, give your audience new information and buttress your conclusions. You can obtain facts and information of this kind on this subject from your local public library and from the school system in your community. Very few persons will have taken the time to obtain such facts and figures, and you should not find it too difficult to give an informative and worthwhile speech.

The Conclusion

At the end of the body of the speech you need a conclusion. This should be brief, but it has an important function.

To stop short at the end of a detailed discussion which fills the body of your speech would be too abrupt. Good speakers never end their remarks with the bald statement: "That is all I have to say on the matter," or, "I think that's all." Instead they add a brief summary of what they have said, or a brief conclusion, or a stirring appeal.

Summary or Restatement

Here are two passages which illustrate the use of a summary or restatement of the chief points that have been presented. The first is the conclusion of an address on "Thrift and Citizenship," by Judge George F. Eyrich, Jr., of Cincinnati.

> . . . . This country, in order to continue its matchless progress, must preserve the quality of its citizenship.
> The men, or organizations, who develop thrift among the people and give that thrift expression in the form of progress in the community, through the building of homes, are performing a real service to the nation. We believe that our institution is developing stability and love for country among our people and contributing to the happiness of our citizenship. This is a practice of true Americanism in which we find much pleasure in being engaged. It gives us hope for and confidence in the future of our country. No more important or happier service can come to any individual or institution.

Another example of restatement of the main idea is illustrated by the conclusion of an address by John D. Rockefeller, Jr., on "The Personal Relation in Industry."

> . . . . If I were to sum up in a few words what I have been endeavoring to say to you in regard to the personal relation in industry, I should say, apply the Golden Rule.
> Every human being responds more quickly to love and sympathy than to the exercise of authority and the display of distrust. If in the days to come, as you have

to do with labor, you will put yourself in the other
man's place and govern your actions by what you would
wish done to you, were you the employee instead of the
employer, the problem of the establishment of the personal relation in industry will be largely solved, strife
and discord as between labor and capital will give place
to cooperation and harmony, the interests of both will
be greatly furthered, the public will be better served,
and through the establishment of industrial peace, a
great stride will have been taken toward the establishment of peace among nations.

Quotation

A very effective form of conclusion for a speech of serious
or impassioned character is a quotation. Charles L. Anspach,
president of Central Michigan College of Education, closed
an address at the annual swingout of the college with quotations as follows from Henry Van Dyke and James Russell
Lowell:

> As a working creed basic to such faith I give you the
> statement of Henry Van Dyke, "Be glad of life because
> it gives you the chance to love and to work and to play
> and to look up at the stars; to be satisfied with your pos-
> sessions but not content with yourself until you have
> made the best of them; to despise nothing in the world
> except falsehood and meanness, and to fear nothing ex-
> cept cowardice; to be governed by your admirations
> rather than by your disgusts; to covet nothing that is
> your neighbor's except his kindness of heart and gentle-
> ness of manner; to think seldom of your enemies, often
> of your friends, and every day of Christ; and to spend
> as much time as you can with body and spirit in God's
> out-of-doors—these are little guidepaths to peace."
> Tonight we toast the future. May you be successful
> in claiming its promises and in establishing a firm path-
> way for those who follow. Tomorrow in the words of
> James Russell Lowell you say:

My golden spurs now bring to me,
And bring to me my richest mail,
For tomorrow I go over land and sea,
In search of the Holy Grail.

Appeal to Feelings

Perhaps the most impressive type of conclusion, when the occasion is important enough to justify it, is the impassioned appeal to the listeners' feelings. Outstanding among the great speeches of the world is the conclusion of Patrick Henry's speech in the Virginia Convention:

It is in vain, sir, to extenuate the matter. Gentlemen may cry, Peace, peace—but there is no peace. The war is actually begun! The next gale that sweeps from the North will bring to our ears the clash of resounding arms! Our brethren are already in the field! Why stand we here idle? What is it that gentlemen wish? What would they have? Is life so dear, or peace so sweet, as to be purchased at the price of chains and slavery? Forbid it, Almighty God! I know not what course others may take; but as for me, give me liberty, or give me death!

By the side of this we may place, as an appeal no less powerful although of a different character, the conclusion of Lincoln's second Inaugural Address:

With malice toward none; with charity for all; with firmness in the right, as God gives us to see the right, let us strive on to finish the work we are in, to bind up the Nation's wounds, to care for him who shall have borne the battle and for his widow and his orphan, to do all which may achieve and cherish a just and lasting peace among ourselves and with all nations.

Chapter 10

HOW TO USE ANECDOTES AND
STORIES EFFECTIVELY

Almost all of us will agree that good stories and anecdotes are interesting to hear and entertaining to read.

But can such stories and anecdotes be helpful to us in a practical way from day to day? The answer is yes. They can assist us practically in dozens of ways. In fact, they can give encouragement and inspiration.

An anecdote is a narrative, or story, ordinarily brief, of an incident or event of unusual interest. It is often from biography. It may come also from history, autobiography, philosophy, one's experience or from other sources.

In this book there are scores of such stories and illustrations. In addition, there are humorous, serious and inspiring observations on life taken from many sources and embracing a great diversity of subjects. Many of these stories are included for entertainment and for their humor. Some are included for meditation and reflection; others are a part of this anthology for the intellectual and emotional inspiration they may provide. All of them may, on the proper occasion, be used to make clear some observation to another person, to emphasize a viewpoint, to strengthen a speech, to enliven conversation. We use illustrations and stories in our conversation, in letters, in speeches and in writing of all kinds. The stories of Lincoln and the parables of Christ were illustrations used to present great ideas effectively.

Basic Rules for Telling Stories

There are certain basic rules with which we should be familiar if we are to make the best use of anecdotes and stories. Twenty of them are here summarized.

1. Do not overemphasize to the listener or reader that the story you are about to relate is an extraordinarily good one. Your praise may be too lavish. Let him judge the merit of your story.

2. You must sincerely feel that the story is a good one, and worth telling, or you cannot use it effectively. If you have any doubts, skip it.

3. The length of a story is not too important. If it is a long story, it must have interesting points as you proceed, and the climax at the end must be good enough to justify the length. If the anecdote is long, it is especially important not to have a single unnecessary word. If it is short, it must be sufficiently complete so the listener does not fail to understand the anecdote.

4. Do not add a great deal of unnecessary material that has no close relationship to the story.

5. The story must be closely connected with your subject of discussion or the point you are trying to make in your comments or writing. It must fit snugly into your comments if it is to accomplish your purpose.

6. You should not applaud your own story. If you tell a story you think is humorous, the listener either thinks it is or thinks it is not. You cannot make it funny with your laughter. If you tell a story you think is inspiring, you should permit the listener to judge for himself. You cannot give a signal for the listener to look inspired. Once told, your anecdote must stand without your support. To paraphrase Shakespeare in his *Love's Labour's Lost*:

> An anecdote's prosperity lies in the ear
> Of him that hears it, never in the tongue
> Of him that makes it.

In relation to humorous stories, Keith Preston in *The Humorist* stated it a little differently, but with the same conclusion:

> He must not laugh at his own wheezes
> The snuff box has no right to sneeze.

7. Your story must be related to subjects which are of interest to the listener. A golf player is interested in stories about golfers. He is probably not interested in soccer or diversified farming. A farmer is more interested in anecdotes about farming than about bookkeeping procedures. To be most effective, anecdotes must touch the fields in which the listener has some interest.

8. If the story you have told has made no impression on the listener, do not repeat it in a vain effort to get some response. Never waste time trying to salvage or explain an anecdote that has died. A boring person is one who is constantly explaining the obvious.

9. A story is always told because you believe it will interest the listener. It should never be told because you like it or your Uncle Bill thinks it is good.

10. There are some persons who apparently seek attention by off-color anecdotes. They remind one of the lines in William Cowper's translation of the *Iliad:*

> Might he but set the rabble in a roar
> He cared not with what jest.

Jonathan Swift's comment that wit "disdains to serve ignoble ends" describes the proper use of stories precisely. The person loses who gets the reputation for telling anecdotes which are off-color, of double meaning or filthy. There are stories of this kind in biography, history and other fields. It pays to forget them and to gain a reputation for colorful expression of one's ideas with the help of interesting, unusual and clean anecdotes.

11. Read widely. As Thomas Carlyle said, "All that mankind has done, thought, gained or been: it is lying as in magic preservation in the pages of books." If you are well-read, you will acquire many stories which you can use profitably. Hundreds are to be found in this book. You may classify some anecdotes in this book as old, including some of

those Lincoln told and which have often been repeated. But when an anecdote fits an occasion exactly, even if you think it is old, it may often be used effectively.

12. It is especially important that the listener hear clearly the opening sentences of your story or the whole point may be lost.

13. If you use a story to criticize some type of conduct, it is a good idea to tell it in reference to yourself if you can. Most listeners grow tired quickly of the person who makes himself the hero of his own stories. People like the person who tells a story on himself. He seems more human. Even in the use of anecdotes, humility is "that low, sweet root from which all heavenly virtues shoot."

14. Unless you are very good at it, never use a dialect in telling an anecdote.

15. Unless it is a common form of physical ailment, such as nearsightedness which millions of us have and can often find occasions to laugh about, it is never good to use a story to make fun of persons with serious physical troubles. For example, it is not funny to laugh at people who lisp or stutter or who have lost an arm or an eye. However, anecdotes which tell of achievement in the face of hardship are often inspiring and encourage us to greater accomplishment.

16. If your story was originally told by or about some distinguished person, for example, an author, statesman or artist, it is highly desirable to associate the story with that person. Any story takes on additional interest if you can associate a name with it.

17. If you tell a humorous anecdote and there is laughter, never repeat the line that brought the laughter. Adults are not little children who cry, "Daddy, do it again." That can become very boresome. Let the listener repeat the humorous line if he wishes, but do not do it yourself.

18. Many anecdotes and stories have a definite point or climax. Decide exactly how that climax should be worded. Tell the story so it builds up interest to this point. The major emphasis should be on this point. No other secondary points should be added after the big point or climax. The story

should end precisely at the climax. That's all; there isn't any more.

19. Always be certain you have a story clearly in mind before you try to use it. You will be in trouble if you have to say, "I'm not certain just how the story goes." "No, that wasn't it." "There is something I missed. But anyway, you get some idea of the story." If you do not have the story well in mind, you will probably waste both your time and the listener's. If one does it often, he may get the reputation of being a bore.

20. Remember, people like a good anecdote or story. They like to be inspired. They like to have their hearts touched. They like to be encouraged. They like to laugh. They like stories that deal with other human beings, their hardships, their struggles to overcome difficulties, their sorrows and their triumphs.

Chapter 11

ILLUSTRATIONS OF ACTUAL
INTRODUCTIONS

This chapter contains dozens of actual introductions which have been used at meetings of many types, many of them to present nationally known and distinguished speakers. Anyone who is to act as the chairman or toastmaster of a meeting will find these illustrations of great practical assistance to him in preparing his introductions. The use of humorous stories and epigrams and the exact techniques followed by some of the ablest chairmen are fully illustrated here, so the reader should find much material of value to him.

In some cases where the speaker made an unusual and interesting response to the introduction it is also given.

In addition, this chapter contains invocations, speeches made when gifts were presented to officers of clubs, remarks for beginning a discussion period, comments made in presenting a mayor to open a convention, a mayor's welcoming speech, brief remarks at the time of the death of a member of an organization and other practical material for the chairman.

      *   *   *

Harry L. Stone, manager of bank relations, International Harvester Company, Chicago, introduces James Conzelman, well-known football coach.

Most Chicagoans identify the name of Jimmy Conzelman with football. His first experience as a college football coach was at Washington University in St. Louis, where he developed a team which had been in the doldrums for years into a three-time winner in the Missouri Valley conference. Ordinarily a coach's principal responsibility is to instruct his squad in football strategy and incidentally throw in a little character-building along with it, but with Jimmy Conzelman the multiplicity of duties was almost interminable. He discovered that one of his duties was to speak before high-school students, alumni groups, civic clubs and university gatherings, and it was this which kindled Conzelman's determination to become a successful public speaker.

Jimmy Conzelman has had an amazing career and is a man of many accomplishments. He is an author, commencement orator, after-dinner speaker, radio commentator, actor, sculptor, band leader, piano player, song writer, champion boxer, football player and coach.

Since the golf season is just beginning, it is interesting to note that mention of his golfing ability is conspicuous by its absence, but a man who has been so prominent in the field of sports couldn't help but excel in this pastime. He most assuredly would not be classed as a Civil War golfer—out in 61 and back in 65. Perhaps the following recitation entitled "The Dissatisfied Golfer" would apply to his prowess on the links. Here it is:

> Unto a golfer sick with shame
> Late one evening the devil came,
> And the Old Boy said with his oily leer,
> "Why are you sitting grieving here,
> What on earth do you want to do
> Would you sell your soul for a seventy-two?"
> The golfer cried to the grinning Nick,
> "For a seventy-two I'd sell it quick."
> "Done," said the devil, "put her thar!
> Tomorrow you'll shoot the course in par.
> Now get to your bed and rest content,
> I'll see you later"—and out he went.
> True to his bargain the devil kept,
> From tee to tee that golfer stepped
> Making the short holes and the far
> As had been promised to him, in par.

Twice he had putts for a birdie three,
But more than he asked for could not be.
His friends rejoiced, as good friends do
But he shook his head at that seventy-two.
"Once I was stymied by a tree,
There were two short putts I missed," said he,
"And but for the rotten luck that's mine
I'd have shot that course in sixty-nine."
All that is left to be paragraphed
Is that deep in Hàdes the devil laughed!

When the St. Louis Browns Baseball Team won the American League pennant in 1944, there were comparatively few people who realized that Jimmy Conzelman was in the background casting his magic spell. He modestly disclaims all credit for the Browns' accomplishments, but those who know his capacity for laughing off his serious achievements were not deceived.

I have gone on at length and will now terminate with a story about a wife whose husband was ailing. The doctor in attendance advised the spouse that her husband was seriously ill and needed a good rest, and to accomplish this he left some sleeping powders. The wife inquired when she should give them to her husband, and the doctor replied, "Give them, nothing. You take them!"

It is now your pleasure to see me take a powder and present to you one of the most colorful figures in the sports world—Jimmy Conzelman.

❋   ❋   ❋

M. Glen Miller of the M. Glen Miller advertising firm of Chicago, who is a past president of the Chicago Federated Advertising Club, introduces Arthur H. (Red) Motley, vice president and a director of the Crowell-Collier Publishing Company and publisher of The American Magazine. *Following Mr. Miller's interesting introduction, Mr. Motley responds with a humorous comment. (This was much enjoyed by the audience.)*

Distinguished guests and members: It is a considerable honor for me to have this little task today, because, for a long time I have been a great admirer of Red Motley's. He is the kind of man to whom the people in the advertising business look up. In the advertising business we like to think of Red Motley as one of our sacred cows. I use that term in the more affectionate meaning, rather than that used by agronomists or in animal husbandry. I don't mean to imply, however, that he isn't sometimes referred to by the name of some other wild or domestic animal or its offspring. But he is the kind of man that we like to point out as an example of Horatio Alger success. He is the kind of man who has made his own way by hard work and perseverance and by knowing the right people.

Red Motley has done quite well for a boy. He has just turned forty, and if any of you think life has just begun for him, you have something to hear a little later on.

He will undoubtedly tell you something about his religion and his political beliefs and his predilection for blondes. That probably is due to the fact that he came from Minnesota, where blondes are thick—I mean numerically thick.

He went to the University of Minnesota and later took law at Columbia, but this peculiar episode was brought to a quick finish when he got his first client. It seems he took a case for a merchant who had had an altercation with one of his customers, and the case came up in court just at a time this merchant had to go out of town. So he left word with his fiery young attorney to let him know just as soon as the case had been decided. After it was over, Motley sent a telegram to his client, which read: "Right has triumphed." Shortly thereafter, he got a return telegram from his client, and it said: "Appeal the case."

Red Motley doesn't mince words. He cuts right through to the core of things, and I think his forthrightness and honesty are probably responsible in a great degree for his success. When he was made publisher of *The American Magazine,* I wrote him a little note of congratulations. It was a pleasure for me to have had such a thing happen to someone I knew, and I wrote a very nice affectionate piece of copy. It was a masterpiece of copywriting, to tell you the truth. After an appropriate interval, an envelope came back with the Crowell-Collier mark on it, and I opened it and inside was a little slip of scratchpad paper and across it was scrawled, with a red pencil, "Thanks. Red."

You will hear a talk today that I guarantee will grip you from beginning to end. Red is in very fine fettle today. I know from talking with him briefly before the meeting. I might tell you about one meeting that he addressed. During the course of the long and arduous talk, Red had become a little hoarse, and after it was over and the people began to come up and talk to him, there was a man with a little boy and Red said to him, "Well, how did you like it?" The boy looked up at him and said, "You need a new needle."

I think it's no more than right for Red to stand on his own feet from now on, and it is a good deal of pleasure for me to introduce to you Mr. Arthur H. Motley, vice president and director of the Crowell-Collier Publishing Company and publisher of *The American Magazine*.

Mr. Motley began as follows:

Well, I made it. There was a minute there that I thought I was not going to get a chance to make the speech. I thought Miller was going to make it.

*   *   *

Even the introduction to club members, perhaps at an annual meeting, of persons who may be employed in the club office can be done in an interesting manner. Thomas R. Mulroy, Chicago attorney, made the following brief but clever introduction:

First, may I present Miss Moore, that lovely and gracious lady who, at this very moment, is transcribing my poor words on the right here. Miss Moore is a skillful secretary, court reporter, stenotypist and ticket seller. Verily, she is the quintessence of an amanuensis. And since you may not have the time to look up those words as I did, I would tell you that they simply mean, in the current slang of our children, that Miss Moore is on the beam, she's in the groove, and she's cooking with gas!

*   *   *

The same Mr. Mulroy, past president of the Executives' Club of Chicago, introduces Ilka Chase, radio, stage and screen star.

It is a tradition of this club, Miss Chase, that the president in introducing an *artiste*, such as you, must attempt to be satiric and sardonic—but not today! You, my dear lady, are a dangerous woman, and I would not think of letting you have the last laugh.

You know there is an old adage that God made women without a sense of humor so that they could love men instead of laughing at them. Our guest is a devastating exception to that rule.

Anyway, it is too hard to introduce women. You have to select your words with such infinite care. For example, you may call a woman a kitten, but you must not call her a cat.

You may call a woman a mouse, but definitely not a rat!

You may call a woman, as a term of endearment, "duck," but you simply must avoid "goose!"

You may, and I recommend it to you gentlemen, greet your wife in the morning with a cheery: "My dear, you certainly are a vision," but, please, oh, please, never say, "My dear, you certainly are a sight!"

But men are queer, too. They say the main difference between man and beast is man's brains, but there the difference ends, because man is lionhearted, chicken-livered, pigeon-toed, busy as a bee, sly as a fox, blind as a bat, gentle as a lamb, drunk as a hoot owl, stubborn as a mule, strong as an ox, vain as a peacock, happy as a lark, or crazy as a loon —depending upon your particular point of view.

Miss Chase gained stage fame on Broadway by her portrayal of the part of the brazen cat, and I don't mean kitten, in the play entitled *The Women*. She is now a scintillating movie star.

Miss Chase is the author of two successive best sellers, *Past Imperfect* and *In Bed We Cry*. I read *Past Imperfect* and liked it very much. I read *In Bed We Cry* . . . period!!

Abraham Lincoln once wrote a review of a book—not Miss Chase's, of course—from which I wonder if I might adopt his comments as my own view of *In Bed We Cry*. Mr. Lincoln wrote:

"For those who like this kind of book, this is the kind of a book they will like."

Miss Chase has always been years ahead of her time, a genuine prodigy.

At the tender age of fourteen, she was valedictorian of her graduating class in a secluded convent school, and on the occasion of her address she delivered this sweet, idealistic and unsophisticated philosophy of true love (with my own apologies to Dorothy Parker):

"Dear fathers, mothers and classmates, I would like to recite a poem about true love:

"When you finally swear you're his,
Shivering and sighing.
And he vows his passion is
Infinite, undying—
Classmates, make a note of this:
One of you is lying!"

Here is indeed the truly soft-spoken woman's woman, incorrigible romanticist, shy rosebud, as we next find her at the age of twenty-five. One evening an old friend of the family rushed in to her and said, sobbing: "Ilka, some man has taken my car and run away with my wife!"

"No! No!" exclaimed Ilka. "Not your *new* car!"

Now that all my bad jokes are concluded let me say in all earnestness that this huge gathering today is a dramatic tribute to Ilka Chase, one of America's brilliant women.

I do now present to you with a genuine feeling of privilege the one and only Ilka Chase.

       ❀   ❀   ❀

Edwin B. Moran, secretary of the National Association of Credit Men and author of The Credit Side of Selling, *introduces E. N. Ronnau, assistant vice president and general credit manager of the Cook Paint and Varnish Company of Kansas City, Missouri.*

When our next speaker was asked for biographical data, and told not to be modest, he wrote:

"When modesty was made a virtue, it was a great day for fools, for it brings the genius and the fool down to the same denomination."

It was really difficult to trace this speaker's "Who's Who" but the Credit Interchange Department of the Credit Men's Association never fails—we got all the dirt.

He was born in the state of Kansas, but you can't hold that against the state.

After the usual growing pains of youth, St. Mary's College gave him a B.A. degree, but shortly after he left there, the school closed.

He has a charming and smart wife, from whom his three sons and one daughter inherited their good looks and intellect.

He has five grandchildren, and from his bragging, we know they are chips off the old block, with all modern improvements.

While not advertising it, he admits he has all known vices, but tries to keep them under control.

His hobby is hunting. He has just returned from a pheasant-hunting trip in South Dakota, and if you believe him there is no need for any of you to plan a trip there because he got all there were.

He has been active in the Credit Men's Association at Kansas City for more years than he admits his age to be; he has served as chairman of too many committees to enumerate, as director, vice president and then president, during which term he brought the membership to its all-time high.

He is now a director of the National Association of Credit Men and in his spare time serves as assistant vice president and general credit manager of the Cook Paint and Varnish Company.

A fellow who does a grand job of being a true friend.

He will represent the credit man's point of view in this forum discussion on "Sales and Credit Methods in Promoting Distribution and Profits."

My very good friend—Ed N. Ronnau.

*   *   *

Harold O. McLain, past president of the Executives' Club of Chicago, introduces Thomas R. Mulroy, attorney.

It is a great pleasure to be here today, but I at once admit that I realize it is exceedingly hazardous for me to attempt to be either fatuous or facetious with Mr. Tom Mulroy. To attempt verbal jousting or repartee with him is, of course, to court the whirlwind, and, on the other hand, to phrase his serious qualities too patently is to emphasize the obvious to you fellows who have known him so long and are already his admirers and friends.

In spite of these difficulties of approach, however, I suppose I should accord some compliance with the traditions of this rostrum, and so, as the fellow said in the Turkish bath, "Won't you please bear with me," while I follow the plan of the Texas steer, with a point here and a point there, and a lot of bull in between.

Now you know that Tom, even as a youth, and as a child, indicated remarkable precocity and sagacity and erudition. That was evidenced when he was just a little fellow in a primary class—and under the tutelage of a very stout schoolmistress. The teacher was emphasizing to the children that animals have capacities that sometimes physically exceed those of men, and she told them of the little yellow canary she had at home, how it could sing, and she propounded this question to the children: "Can you tell me what my little canary, at home in his cage, can do that I can't do?" Tom, who was of a practical turn of mind, volunteered, raised his hand, and said, "Teacher, I know what he can do that you can't do—he can take a bath in a saucer."

A little later, one day, one of the school trustees visited the room. He mounted the teacher's platform, and, to test the children on their powers of observation, he moved from one side of the platform to the other, meanwhile taking a pencil out of one vest pocket and putting it into another. Then he turned to the children and said, "Can anybody tell me what I have just done?" Again Tom volunteered. "I know what you did, sir," said Tom, "you walked in front of our teacher without saying 'Excuse me.' " He was very bright.

Advancing in his school work, he was one day asked in an economics class to explain some of the uses of cowhide. Tom had ready answers. "The main use of the cowhide," he said, "is that it helps to hold the cow together."

In a class on anatomy, he was once asked to define the word "anatomy." Tom said, "It consists of three parts—the head, the chest and the stomach. The head contains the brains, if any," which showed that he was perspicacious, even in those days. "Then," he said, "the chest contains the liver and the lungs. The stomach contains the bowels, of which there are five—a, e, i, o, u."

As he progressed a little higher in his school work, one day they were discussing inflation. Tom volunteered the information that inflation was a bad thing, in that it caused two to live more steeply than one, but in one way, inflation had its virtues, because, said Tom, "under inflation, when you forget your change, you don't lose so much."

Then, as he got a little older, he finally very zealously began the pursuit of real knowledge. Sometimes it was diurnal, sometimes matutinal, and very often nocturnal.

Tom is a great host. He entertains people hospitably and bounteously. Recently I was at a stag poker party in his home. We sat down at the table at eight o'clock in the evening. We were just starting to play when we heard the patter of little feet and the chatter of little voices up above.

Tom said, "Just a minute, fellows. Those are my little children, and at this time they always come to bring me a goodnight message. It makes me feel very humble and reverent to have those little folks come and talk to me at night. Let's listen."

We listened, and a small voice piped up and said, "Daddy." Tom said, "Yes, Mary, dear, what is it?" Mary replied, "Daddy, I wanted to tell you that little Willie found another bedbug in his bed."

Of course Tom's drive and energy and vitality often make him a little hectic. I commented on it and sympathized with his wife, Dorothy, one time, on that problem. She said, "I'll tell you, Harold. Tom means well, and I try, always, to be patient and philosophical with him, and I always try to remember, too, that it is better to have loved and lost than never to have loved at all."

Away from his home, Tom is primarily an athlete, and a man among men. I love to play golf with him. His innate ability as a golfer and his capacity for sharp and dishonest trading for strokes on the first tee is outstanding.

Recently I had a game of golf with him at Exmoor. As he came in and sat down in the locker room and disrobed to put on golf clothes, I noticed some big numbers tattooed on a certain portion of his anatomy. I said, "Tom, why do you have those numbers tattooed on you?" He said, "Those numbers aren't tattooed on me; that's where Dorothy hit me with the license plate when I held the door open for her to drive the car in the garage."

Now, isn't that just like a woman? A woman can go through an eighteen-inch aisle in a Walgreen store and never knock a thing off the counter, and then go home and drive the car into a twenty-foot door and knock both fenders off both sides of the car.

Well, as I said, we started to play golf. We got around to about the third hole when a dog ran out from under a fence and attacked Tom. The dog snapped at his heels and then at Tom's legs. In self-protection Tom pulled his niblick out of his golf bag and made a pass at the dog with the steel head of the club. The club hit the dog back of the ear and knocked him out.

The dog's owner came over the fence just then, picked up the dog, and said to Tom, "That was a dirty trick, knocking out my dog."

Tom said, "Well, what did you expect me to do? The dog was trying to bite me; I had to defend myself."

The dog's owner said, "Why didn't you use the handle end of the club? Why did you have to hit him with the head?"

Tom said, "I would have used the other end of the club, if it had been the other end of the dog that was attacking me."

Going on with our game, we got around to the eleventh hole, when Tom sliced a long ball over into the rough. He went over there, found the ball and stooped down and picked up a few leaves. Then he took a club out of his bag, put it back of the ball and picked up some more stuff. Finally my partner, Harry Stone, said, "What are you trying to do, Tom? I thought you might possibly have a spoon lie here, but if you keep on with that, you'll soon be able to hit with your driver."

Well, we had a fine game, and Tom enjoyed himself, and, as usual, he insisted on keeping the score. He won $3.75. After the game he drank five old-fashioneds, ate a double order of rare roast beef with two pieces of pie à la mode, and then climbed into his car, completely happy, and drove away smiling, all set for another week of hard work in his law office.

I know I'm taking a lot of time here, but I'm doing that purposely. I propose to take so much time that when it comes Tom's turn, he will either have to give up his speech or else abandon those insidious and castigating sarcasms he is prepared to heap on me. He won't even have time to take a bow.

But let's take up where I left off with Tom, back in his

office. You know, gentlemen, when you get Tom in his law office, it is time to abandon these stupid inanities and be serious about him.

Tom Mulroy is a conscientious, indefatigably industrious and serious student of the law. He is one of the youngest lawyers with high rank in his profession, or, if you prefer, he is one of the highest ranking lawyers who is young in his profession, in this Chicago area.

He is to tell us today about a subject which is significant to all of us; he is to describe and talk about a legislative enactment which is perhaps one of the major enactments since the beginning of the war.

The Taft-Hartley Act is the most discussed, cussed and praised act in many moons. Tom is going to tell us about it, and I guarantee to you that no lawyer in the United States could bring to you a more thoroughgoing and yet common-sense and understanding analysis of that act than it will be your privilege to hear today in this place.

I think Thomas Mulroy is exactly the right man, at exactly the right time, with exactly the right subject, and I think you will all agree with me that Tom Mulroy also is in exactly the right place when he is here today at the Executives' Club, among his admirers and friends and wellwishers.

I hope you will all indicate to Tom how grateful we are to have him here to speak to us on the subject of the Taft-Hartley Act. Thank you very much.

*   *   *

M. Glen Miller of the M. Glen Miller Advertising firm of Chicago presents Edward J. Jeffries, Jr., then mayor of Detroit.

Mr. Chairman, gentlemen, and you in the cheaper seats: It has always been my assumption that an introduction was intended to identify a speaker, to qualify him on his authority or to apologize for the poor cuss.

As one of the country's outstanding politicians and municipal planners, Mayor Jeffries needs no identification. As mayor of America's fourth largest city, he needs no apology as an authority on municipal government. And that leaves me with but one alternative.

Now, I cannot apologize for a man who was elected to the Detroit City Council at the ripe old age of 31, who was elected to the office of mayor at the age of 39, and who, after three terms, is still only 44 years old.

I cannot apologize for a man whose favorite vegetable is spinach, who, although a promising young son-of-a-judge of Detroit, went to work as a boy, cutting lawns, cleaning sidewalks and running errands for neighbors, and who, when he was old enough, worked in theaters, the post office, and in Henry Ford's atelier of automobile production.

Matriculating at the University of Michigan when only 16, Mayor Jeffries took his A.B. and LL.B. degrees and then went bounding off to jolly old prewar London, where he spent four delightful terms of study on the exhilarating and fascinating subject of Roman and British constitutional law.

A great high-school football player, Mayor Jeffries now would rather play golf, in which he is good enough to have won the championship of his own club.

An excellent bowler, he slings a mean bridge hand, is a formidable opponent at any kind of card game, and if his purpose was not so serious today, could regale you with a variety of ingenious card tricks from this platform.

His Honor smokes a pipe, and his wife objects to it no more than most wives do. He drinks only enough to escape solicitation for membership by the W.C.T.U.

Married to a musician, he loathes concerts, but obediently accompanies his spouse, sits quietly and awake during the program, and reaches home without making any nasty remarks.

Now, I ask you, how can I apologize for a guy like that?

I don't want to tell you about his municipal administration. I hope he will do that. But I do want to remind you that shortly after taking office he was able to reduce his city's financial indebtedness to a point where he saved some forty-two million dollars in interest charges.

I don't think it is seemly for me to apologize more for Mayor Jeffries. I feel that he should be presented to you in person and apologize for himself.

Gentlemen, Mayor Edward J. Jeffries, of Detroit, Michigan.

*   *   *

Chancey I. Weaver, past president of the Rotary Club of Columbus, Ohio, introduces Dr. Rees Edgar Tuloss, president of Wittenberg College, to the Columbus Rotary Club.

Because I live in Springfield, Ohio, I was tendered the honor of introducing my distinguished fellow townsman, the president of Wittenberg College, to this club, composed about one half of the garden variety of businessmen and the other half of president and members of the faculty of Ohio State University. To prepare this introduction, I read a number of books, including one by Emily Post. In her book, she says, "An introduction should do several things: first, quiet the audience; second, qualify the speaker as having sufficient information adequately to cover his subject; third, to warm the speaker to the audience and create a friendly atmosphere for his message." I also noticed a footnote, which said, "It is considered good form to leave a little time for the speaker."

This man is distinguished for his work in the Lutheran Church, for his long and capable service in education and for his business accomplishments, including a bank presidency, the operation of his own private business and his able speaking and writing in this country and abroad.

To those members of this club, who, like myself, mingle in the lowly marts of trade, Dr. Rees Edgar Tuloss is a man of parts, to those of you who tread softly in the halls of higher learning, this man is an intrepid and untrammelled exegete.

*   *   *

John C. Lewe, Judge of the Appellate Court of Illinois, introduces Dr. Norman Vincent Peale, minister of the Marble Collegiate Church of New York City and author of A Guide to Confident Living *and* The Power of Positive Thinking.

Our speaker is the minister of the Marble Collegiate Church of New York City. This is the oldest Protestant church in America, now in the three hundred twelfth year of its history. Every Sunday morning and evening, I am informed, it is filled to capacity, which suggests a story that my father once told me about an elderly Christian lady who was dissatisfied with her pastor. In recounting his many failings, she said, "Six days a week he is invisible and on the seventh day he is incomprehensible."

For almost a decade, Dr. Peale has been speaking on a nationwide radio hookup over the National Broadcasting System, on the radio program known as "The Art of Living." To his parishioners, and millions of listeners throughout the land, this crusader of modern Christianity is both visible and comprehensible.

Dr. Peale is active in many civic and church organizations. He has written two excellent and well-known books, *The Art of Living* and *You Can Win.* Our speaker was graduated in 1920 from Ohio Wesleyan University. He has honorary degrees conferred upon him by Syracuse University, Ohio Wesleyan University and Duke University. It is indeed a high privilege to present to you Dr. Norman Vincent Peale, whose subject is "The Art of Living in America Today"—Dr. Peale.

❈   ❈   ❈

Frank Spencer, department manager of Socony-Vacuum Oil Company, introduces James A. Farley, chairman of the board of the Coca-Cola Export Corporation and American statesman.

First of all, I want to say that after our guest speaker has made his address, there will be a short period during which you may ask some questions, and Mr. Farley has agreed to answer them.

Less than sixty years ago, down in a place in New York called "Glassy Point" or "Stony Point"—I can't get it quite clear—the Irish parents of our speaker today, who christened their son James A. Farley, decided right off the bat that their son was going to be a Democrat. How did they decide that? Well, the facts are these.

There was a Republican politician in that neighborhood who was looking about, casting about to get some Farley votes, so he went around and in order to develop a little favor with the Farley family, he tried to kiss little Jim, but little Jim bit him on the nose. In a recent nationwide broadcast, Mr. Farley admitted that was his first real public service to the Democratic party.

When I assumed this job of introducing Mr. Farley, the first thing I did was to get a book: *Jim Farley's Story of the Roosevelt Years.*

This book has interested me very, very much indeed because it disclosed a lot of things that I and a lot of other Republicans have suspected for many years and never knew.

I have been advised by some of my friends what I should do and what I shouldn't do in connection with making this speech or should say in this introduction.

James Farley has been one of the wheelhorses of the Democratic party over a period of thirty-five years. It was he who contributed more than anyone else to the political campaign which elected the first Democratic president since Woodrow Wilson. His party loyalty has been unparalleled. He loyally and consistently supported his chief year after year, frequently under difficult circumstances, until the time came when he felt that "the boss," as he always referred to President Roosevelt, had departed from those party principles in which James A. Farley believed.

Mr. Farley's thirty-five years of political service to the Democratic party have given him the intimate close contact with people of all walks of life which has contributed tremendously to his present-day success in the status of a businessman. As chairman of the board of the Coca-Cola Export Corporation, he has helped spread the gospel, even into foreign fields, of indulging frequently in "the pause that refreshes."

It has been sixteen years since Mr. Farley was elected chairman of the National Committee of the Democratic party and that election took place right here in Chicago. Since that time, Mr. Farley has been in and out of Chicago hundreds of times, but this is our very first chance to welcome him here as a business executive. As such, he is naturally interested in his subject today, "World Conditions," from an economic view. But as a man who will always live with at least a corner of his heart belonging to the Democratic party, he is vitally interested in world conditions as they will affect national policy. It is therefore with great pleasure that I present our guest speaker of today, the Honorable James A. Farley.

* * *

Portion of the humor in an introduction used by Thomas R. Mulroy, Chicago attorney, when he introduced Miss Sylvia Porter, financial editor of the New York Post *and economist Leon Henderson, of the Research Institute of America, who were to debate before the Executives' Club of Chicago:*

I have talked privately with each of our two debaters, as to what each thought of the other, and I got quite an earful because they have been fighting over economics for years. For example, when I asked Miss Porter what she really thought of Leon Henderson she said, "In any list of the ten best economists in America, Leon Henderson would rank eleventh."

I asked Mr. Henderson if he reads the brilliant daily column that Miss Porter writes in the *New York Post*, of which she is financial editor. He said yes he does. I said, "How do you like her as an economic writer?" He said, "Well, in my judgment Miss Porter either ought to put some fire into her writing or vice versa."

*   *   *

> *T. Louis Chess, past president of the Lions' Club of San Francisco, presents the following introduction which he used at a meeting of the American Legion, as an illustration of a concise introduction. Ordinarily it is necessary to give a more detailed introduction in order clearly to establish the speaker's authority to discuss the subject and to give the audience the proper background.*

My comrades: Our speaker today has a message of great importance and of interest to every good American. It is my pleasure to present Admiral _____, Chief of Operations of the United States Navy, whose subject will be "American Defense on the High Seas."

*   *   *

> *Thomas Robert Mulroy, Chicago attorney and past president of the Executives' Club of Chicago, introduces Harold O. McLain, president of the Railways Ice Company and past president of the Executives' Club of Chicago.*

Harold McLain is such a beloved and brilliant personality that I thought you would like me to tell you today something of his background so that you might better understand his climb up the ladder of life.

May I say at the outset that—if I may coin a phrase—Harold was born. He did not exactly come from a good family—he was sent. In the Chicago public schools he pursued his studies, never quite overtaking them.

Harold was graduated from the University of Michigan, and then went on to Columbia University Law School in New York, where, as a result of Broadway's bright lights, he was as broke as the Ten Commandments.

After leaving law school Harold did a short term in the Army with Teddy Roosevelt at San Juan Hill.

Out of the Army, Harold took a short fling as a pioneer radio announcer, and I am delighted to find from extensive research that his idea of a proper and effective commercial was considerably different from what is considered effective today. His first commercial went like this:

"Mothers, go now to your nearest store and buy Quaker Oats.

"Are Quaker Oats shot out of a gun? Do Quaker Oats greet you with vibrant freshness? No! They just sit and sneer at you!"

He left radio and then spent fourteen years as a practicing lawyer in Chicago, and I say to you that Harold McLain wrested from reluctant juries triumphant verdicts of acquittal in every case in which his clients were clearly and unmistakably innocent.

Yes, Harold McLain was a fighting lawyer who gave no quarter—as any bellboy will tell you.

Since 1926, Harold has been president of the Railways Ice Company and a leader in the ice industry in this country and Canada.

About a year ago, alas! Harold entered politics—politics, ah! sweet politics—where they pat you on the back so they'll know where to stick the knife.

Harold was elected president of the Highland Park Republican Club and campaigned very vigorously for Tom Dewey in 1944. Yes, in October, 1944, Harold entered politics; the day after election day Harold gave up politics!

As a matter of fact, he really did a good job for Tom Dewey. Dewey ran very well in Highland Park; he placed.

Chairman Brownell of the Republican National Committee, in speaking of the effective work Harold did for Dewey in 1944 in Highland Park, said, "Quote (pause) unquote!"

That concludes my thumbnose sketch of Harold McLain.

Now that my poor jokes are finished, may I express, with deep sincerity, the profound affection and respect which every one of the fourteen hundred members of this club shares for Harold McLain. As our president for two years, Harold, in his weekly introductions, was invariably a great attraction and certainly a better orator than the speaker of the day.

In any discussion of Harold McLain I hold these truths to be self-evident: that he is an outstanding business executive, that he is a public-spirited citizen, that he is a gentleman rich in character and charm, but this above all, that he is constructively articulate.

In these times that try men's souls, here is no summer soldier or sunshine patriot who shirks from the service of his country; here is a man with the courage to stand up and be counted on the contentious issues of the day, a man who has a genius—and this I stress—for espousing with powerful force and clarity the aims, the ideals, and the record of American industry.

I know no more persuasive advocate at the bar of public thought than our great and good friend; I know no more dynamic exponent of the American system of free enterprise; I know of no more winsome fireside philosopher.

Gentlemen, I give you the "favorite son" of this great club, Harold McLain.

*   *   *

A portion of Mr. McLain's response to the above introduction by Mr. Mulroy:

I tried so hard to get a chance to see what Tom's jokes were and to see his script. He told me that he would have nothing to say about me except serious, well-intentioned stuff, that he wouldn't think of making any jokes about me. So I am really in a spot that deserves your complete sympathy.

I am highly appreciative, of course, of this honor and privilege of coming before you because all of us who are in the Executives' Club understand and appreciate deeply what an honor it is to occupy this forum. I am very grateful for the things Tom Mulroy said.

For perhaps the past ten years since we became acquainted in this organization, and even before, Tom and I have been very close friends, and we have had a good many business transactions together. In those transactions I have always tried to be friendly with Tom, and certainly he has been exceedingly close with me.

Seriously, I am glad to have this chance to declare there just isn't anything I wouldn't do for Tom Mulroy, and I am encouraged to believe, too, that there just isn't anything he wouldn't do for me. That is the way it has been with us in the past ten years: There just isn't anything we have done for each other.

Of course, we have a good deal in common because we have both occupied this rostrum here. We both have used this same springboard, but he has been making swan dives, and I have been making belly-flops. That is because he is a top, first-class presiding officer. He is the best.

There isn't anything second-class about Tom. He is really first-class. He is the top at this kind of thing. You know, ordinarily a chairman or a toastmaster is supposed to be sort of the punk that starts off the fire, but on the contrary, Tom is the luminous incandescence that contributes a scintillating sparkle and brilliance to these otherwise drab programs.

He is articulate, erudite and oracular. He is prophetic, provocative and vocal. He is ubiquitous, vehement and loquacious. He is indeed an orator, and he is a raconteur. He is the embodiment and the epitome of *cacoëthes loquendi*.

He is just a top guy at this kind of thing, and I am not going to waste any more time trying to live up to the stuff he handed me.

I have a rather heavy subject here today that is certainly by every test a contrast to this persiflage in which we have been indulging here, and as Alderman Kenna used to say when he would get up in the city council to discuss an important subject, "Leave us face it."

✻   ✻   ✻

Dr. Franklyn B. Snyder, then president of Northwestern University, introduces Dr. Alfred P. Haake, economist and economic consultant, and Professor Harold J.

Laski, British economist, who debated the subject, "Socialism Versus Free Enterprise."

We are here today to listen while representatives of two branches of the English-speaking family of nations discuss a question of great and timely interest. Whatever you may think of the merits of the two philosophies which will be expounded, we all agree on this: It is good to meet in this way and to talk together and think together on controversial and important matters. We are grateful to the Executives' Club of Chicago for having given us this occasion.

The privilege of free assembly and of free discussion is very precious to the Englishman and to the American, and we agree that there must be no curtailment of this privilege —no censorship, no thought police. I add, to preserve this privilege, we must use it as we are proposing to do today.

The two contestants who are going to take part are experienced battlers in the ring. I might call them intellectual "Golden Glovers" and of the heavyweight class.

In this corner, the representative of the United States and in this corner that of Great Britain.

The story of Dr. Alfred P. Haake's life is a typical American story of hard work, of ambition, of the ability to find in this new world satisfying opportunities of many sorts. He was a boy who worked his way through college, too, and claims the University of Wisconsin as his alma mater.

He tells me he has been a truck driver, a grocery clerk, a journalist, a businessman; he must be something of a politician to have gotten himself elected mayor of Park Ridge, and we know he has an interesting and honorable relationship to General Motors. He is widely known for his ability to make men listen and make them think about important questions.

Professor Harold J. Laski, as you know, is a subject of his Britannic Majesty and an eloquent advocate of those policies which we Americans associate with the present government of England.

A graduate of New College, Oxford—it was new in the

year it was established, the year 1379—where he took a "first" in modern history, a man who, even as an undergraduate, was recognized as a man of unusual intellectual power even in the Oxford environment. He soon became an influence in the thinking of his own country and of the United States by virtue of his eloquent and cogent writings and addresses.

He has had many contacts with American universities. He, too, makes people think and in academic parlance some people who listen to him give him an "A," some people give him an "F," but nobody gives him a "C—."

You might have expected the boy who worked his way through a Midwestern institution to represent the point of view of labor—of socialism. You might have expected the graduate of an Oxford college, traditionally associated with the old way of doing things, to represent capitalism and free industry. But both of them, gentlemen, have reversed their fields and Dr. Haake speaks, as you know, for free enterprise and Professor Laski for socialism.

The rules of the contest which have been handed to me are very simple and both contestants profess to know them. Dr. Haake will speak first, Professor Laski second; then each will be given two brief periods in which to say, in simple and understandable English, what he really thinks of his opponent's arguments.

One last word before we call these men into the ring. This contest is conducted strictly under Marquis of Queensberry rules—no hitting below the belt, no rabbit punches, break clean if I tell you to, don't hit after the bell and go to the neutral corner if the other man hits the canvas. And may the best man win!

*   *   *

The chairman frequently is called upon to introduce guests at the speaker's table. Edwin B. Moran, secretary of the National Association of Credit Men, once told the following interesting story prior to introductions he was called upon to make.

The president of this club at each and every meeting, as he comes to the presentation of the speaker's table, has a very delightful privilege.

He can say anything he wants to about these distinguished gentlemen arranged on his right and left, and they can do nothing about it. Thus, he may give expression to suppressed desires long lurking in his system.

You know, the other evening one of the grand ladies of the city, renowned for her elaborate dinners, discovered just before the guests were expected that her butler was ill, and therefore unable to perform his usual duty.

So in the emergency she summoned from her staff of servants Mrs. O'Brien, a trusted employee in the family for many years, and she said to her: "Now, Nora, you stand at the drawing-room door and call the guests' names as they arrive."

Nora's face lit up at the very prospect of such a privilege, and she said: "Thank you, ma'am, I have been wanting to do just that to some of your friends for the last twenty years."

❊   ❊   ❊

J. L. Hemery, assistant to the general manager of the Clearing Manufacturing District of Chicago, introduces Lynn Saylor, advertising manager of the Ingersoll Steel Division of the Borg-Warner Corporation.

Our speaker, in addition to being a past president of the Magic Carpet Luncheon Club of Chicago, is one of our founders. He hails from the beautiful state of Iowa. Lynn has a prolific imagination. He injects his energetic personality into strange things. He dreams up and brings out of them practical realities. His outstanding ability has attracted the attention of such concerns as Certain-Teed Products, Warwick Manufacturing Company and the Ingersoll Steel Division of the Borg-Warner Corporation. Of course, as the demand for Lynn's services grew, Lynn's demand for remuneration increased so that now he is the high-salaried advertising manager of the Ingersoll Steel Division.

The other day I called at Lynn's office and while waiting for this busy executive I overheard two of his young lady employees discussing his eligibility. Miss Green said, "I know he is rich, but isn't he too old to be considered eligible?" Miss Brown replied, "My dear, he is too eligible to be considered old." Lynn grows younger every day. He has been a power behind our club since its inception. His subject is "Advertising for Prosperity." I present Lynn Saylor.

*   *   *

Harold O. McLain, president of the Railways Ice Company of Chicago, speaks on the occasion of the retirement of a club president from office.

The retiring president evidences the poise of Pericles, the power of Daniel Webster, the humor of a Bill Nye, the delicate imagery of a Thomas Moore and the magnetism and lure of a Lauren Bacall! He is as adamant as John L. Lewis, and his voice is as mellifluous as the limpid notes of the sweet wind, and as persuasive as the dulcet strains of the Oriental flageolet. As he approaches a myopic and melon-shaped forty, he bursts like a lovely, incandescent rocket on the scene, which, under his guidance, has run the gamut of variety from a Babylonian weenie roast to a Guy Fawkes Day in Cheapside.

*   *   *

Edwin B. Moran, secretary of the National Association of Credit Men, introduces Louis Ruthenburg, president of Servel, Inc.

Our speaker admits his hobbies are horseback riding, fishing, agriculture and armchair farming, which one might understand if he looks at "Who's Who" and sees that the speaker is a member of the Engineers' Club in New York City, the Wall Street Club in New York City, the Metropolitan Club in Washington, D.C., and the Evansville, Indiana, Country Club.

He was born in Louisville, Kentucky. He studied mechanical engineering at Purdue University, which gave him a degree in 1907.

He has had an interesting and broad industrial background, which included a year of engineering work in Europe.

He has been associated with such organizations as:

The E. C. Walker Manufacturing Company
The Kentucky Wagon Works
The Dayton Engineering Laboratories Company
General Motors Research Laboratories
General Motors Truck Corporation
Yellow Sleeve Valve Engine Works

In 1929 he became president of the Copeland Products, Inc., and at the same time, chairman of the refrigeration division of the National Electrical Manufacturers' Association.

He was given an honorary M.E. degree from the University of Detroit.

The speaker is:

President of the Indiana State Chamber of Commerce
Member of the executive board of the American Gas Association
Member of the board of trustees of Purdue University
Director of the National Association of Manufacturers
Director of the Mississippi Valley Association
The Indiana chairman of the Committee for Economic Development

All this would cause you to believe he is very busy, but he has another main sideline at the present time which provides him with spending money. He is president and general manager of Servel, Inc., of Evansville, Indiana.

Our guest and speaker, Louis Ruthenburg.

*　　　*　　　*

Opening remarks of an introduction for a ladies' day meeting of the Executives' Club of Chicago by Harry L. Stone, manager of bank relations of International Harvester Company.

This is the first occasion I have had of addressing this club at a time when the audience is graced with the presence of the fair sex. We must admit it takes the women to add the sparkle, the warmth and the proper balance to these affairs. And so, ladies, we extend you a very cordial welcome.

I believe it was man that first described woman as nothing but "a rag, a bone and a hank of hair." And I am certain it was woman who termed man as nothing but "a brag, a groan and a tank of air."

* * *

Sometimes a chairman is called upon to open a discussion after an address. Paul A. Mertz, director of company training of Sears, Roebuck & Company and past president of the Industrial Relations Association of Chicago, opens a discussion meeting with the following pertinent story.

We hope this is only the beginning—that this is really going to be an industrial conference.

I attempted the difficult task myself when addressing the National Association of Cost Accountants at their Southern Division convention in Nashville, Tennessee, of trying to prove to them that they were paying for a personnel program in their industry whether they had one or not. I was reminded of that story which no doubt most of you know of the traveling salesman who turned in his account after a trip, and on the good old swindle sheet he had charged a suit of clothes. When he handed the sheet in, his manager said to him: "Sam, ou haven't done anything wrong, but there's one thing y i've got to understand about your expense account. Yoi can't include any of your personal expenses in it. For i stance, if you buy a suit of clothes, that must come out of your own personal budget and must not be charged to your expense account with the company."

Well, after his next trip Sam came back with a pretty satisfactory expense account, and his manager, after looking it over, said to him this time: "Now you've got the idea, Sam.

Everything is accounted for properly, and there are no items here which are of a personal nature." It was just too much for Sam, and he smiled all over as he said, "Well, there's a suit of clothes in there anyhow."

However, I think that in an audience like this our speaker really has an easier job than the one I had. I would like to see you get back at him. Try to make him prove that his program does work and that it does accomplish what he says it accomplishes. Who has the first question? Maybe you are just starting a program of this kind? Maybe you are planning one? Maybe you don't have any at all? Or perhaps you have had one in existence in your company for nineteen years? Let's have your questions.

*   *   *

Edwin B. Moran, secretary of the National Association of Credit Men and author of The Credit Side of Selling, *introduces J. C. Aspley, president of The Dartnell Corporation, who is to serve as chairman for a luncheon program for the Rotary Club of Chicago. Mr. Moran and Mr. Aspley are close friends and Mr. Moran good-naturedly "kids" the chairman.*

And now! I present the chairman of the day.

Usually, this is a pleasure. Today it is only a duty.

I have personally known him for ten or twelve years, which is too long. For ten or twelve years before I met him, I read his publications and editorials, which proves that credit men are gluttons for punishment.

He claims Hamilton, Ontario, Canada, as his birthplace, although I have never heard that Hamilton has done any bragging about it.

I have heard that he is a naturalized citizen of the United States although I have never seen his papers.

He was educated at the University High School and Armour Institute of Technology, but is not known to have won any distinction or special honor at either.

He really got a good start in the advertising department of

Swift & Company, where he told them how to utilize the squeal in the pig, but he wandered away, to the editorial staff of *Printers' Ink*, and now is editor and publisher of *American Business* magazine, which is devoted to sales, advertising and public relations, and occasionally has a good article on credits. (Incidentally, the subscription is $3 annually, or two years for $5.)

He is president of The Dartnell Corporation, sales research counselors, whose monthly services can be obtained for a most moderate cost.

He is author of a number of books devoted to sales, sales management, advertising and competitive trade practices.

When he isn't busy telling folks how to spread the oil of successful selling, he may be telling you about his former forty-five-foot power cruiser, which holds the distinction of being the winner of the only Chicago to Mackinac endurance cruise.

He organized and was the first president of the Chicago Sales Executives Club, and later was president of the National Federation of Sales Executives.

He has served Chicago Rotary on the metropolitan area committee as chairman of our club publications committee, and as vice president in charge of the club service division.

I now present in this corner at 198 pounds, your chairman of the day, John Cameron Aspley.

*   *   *

Many times a chairman is called upon at the opening meeting of a convention to present the mayor of the convention city, who gives an address of welcome. Often this introduction is likely to be stereotyped. At a meeting of the National Foreign Trade Council, Philip D. Reed, chairman of the board of the General Electric Company and former chairman of the United States Associates, International Chamber of Commerce, Inc., introduced the mayor of St. Louis in the following interesting manner:

This great convention is not and cannot be legitimately

and appropriately launched without our having a word from
the mayor of this city. It would be inconceivable that we
should carry on these deliberations without knowing whether
or not he is glad to see us, whether or not he is pleased to
have us here, eating our gray matter away with consideration of these tremendous problems. So I give you, and I
hope he will say a word to us—the mayor of St. Louis.

❀   ❀   ❀

*Some clubs make special announcements at weekly
luncheon meetings relative to birthdays of members and
also make announcements at the time of the deaths of
members. Edwin B. Moran, some of whose introductions are included in this chapter, has used the following
statements on such special occasions.*

Birthdays

Birthdays are like stepping-stones
Along the path of years;
Here's hoping you will always find,
As each new one appears,
That it's a stepping-stone as well
To joys and pleasures new,
To still more happy hopes fulfilled,
And still more dreams come true.

❀   ❀   ❀

A happy birthday to each and every one of you.

❀   ❀   ❀

Count your garden by the flowers,
Never by the leaves that fall.
Count your days by golden hours,
Don't remember clouds at all.
Count your nights by stars—not shadows,
Count your life with smiles—not tears.
And with joy through all your lifetime,
Count your age by friends—not years.

A happy birthday and many more of them to each and every one of you.

* * *

Death

No one hears the door that opens
When they pass beyond our call;
Soft as loosened leaves of roses,
One by one, our loved ones fall.

Regretfully, and sorrowfully, I ask you to dwell for a moment upon the passing of two friends and fellow Rotarians, ———— and ————.

The shadows flit across the face of the earth, and are gone. So it appears sometimes with our lives.

But like the sunshine, and the shadows, and the rain, which have their eternal effect upon nature, so also is the influence of our lives eternal.

We take pride as Rotarians that the influence of Ernest and Henry was of the very finest, and will be remembered throughout our days.

Let us bow our heads in silent prayer in memory of these two, never to be forgotten fellow Rotarians, ———— and ————.

* * *

"His life was gentle, and the elements so mixed in him that Nature might stand up and say to all the world, 'This was a man!' "

So wrote Shakespeare, and so can we think and say of ————, for in every sense of the word, he was a man, a gentle, kindly man, whom we shall miss in fellowship, and in friendship.

"Brownie," as he was affectionately known to all Rotarians, had a devotion to his duties, as well as the principles and ethics of Rotary, which endeared him to all members.

O, for the touch of his vanished hands,
And the sound of his voice, that is still.

"Brownie" left us a week ago today. For him the play is done; the curtain drops.

We say "Farewell."

Let us bow our heads in silent remembrance and prayer for our friend and fellow Rotarian, —————.

*   *   *

An invocation by Rev. George M. Gibson before a national convention of the Office Management Association.

Oh, Almighty God, Eternal Lawgiver, Maker of all things, Judge of all men, Giver of every good and perfect gift! We invoke Thy presence upon this assembly today; and be with these Thy people in their deliberations, and grant that their vision will be widened and their hearts strengthened for new tasks. Be Thou with them all personally that they may serve an even wider field relative to the work of their hands and of their minds to the growing righteousness of the world. Grant to each one of them a new birth of freedom and righteousness and of justice.

Bless our land and all the lands of the earth today that men dwelling in them may find a new commonwealth of life; and eliminate conflicts everywhere, so that those who labor with hand and those who labor with mind may find that comradeship of spirit with spirit which is like unto that above. We pray Thy blessing upon this assembly and upon each one here. Be Thou with us in our undertakings, and grant that there may go from life to life and heart to heart throughout the whole world a new faith and devotion and confidence on which our institutions may rest. We ask this in Thy name. Amen.

*   *   *

*An invocation by the Rt. Rev. Daniel J. Gercke, D.D.,
bishop of the Tucson Diocese, before a convention of
the Arizona Bankers Association.*

Oh, God, our Father, all wise and loving, to know Whom
is to be truly wise; to serve Whom is to reign in this and in
the world to come—look down upon us, gathered here on
this memorable occasion, and bestow upon us Thy loving
benediction. Oh, God, from Whom are holy desires, right
counsels and just words, give to Thy servants that peace
which the world cannot give. Direct, we beseech Thee, Oh,
Lord, our actions by Thy holy inspirations, and carry them
on by Thy gracious assistance, that every prayer and word
of ours may begin always from Thee and through Thee be
happily ended. Amen.

*   *   *

*An invocation by Dr. Charles Ray Goff, pastor of Chi-
cago Temple, First Methodist Church, before the convention of the National Fraternal Congress of America.*

O Eternal God, our Father, we give Thee thanks for Thy
goodness and Thy mercy to us. We thank Thee for this wonderful land. We thank Thee for all the fine relationships of
life. We thank Thee for our friends and associates. Now, as
this convention gathers here, we pray Thy blessing upon every member, and upon all that is done. We ask Thee, O
God, that we might each seek in some way to build in this
world something of the spirit that moved in the heart of
Christ. We pray for the world, for our part in it, to ask
that soon the day may come when wars may cease to the
ends of the earth.

O God, we pray Thee that something new may be born
in the world, that we may find a new spirit moving in the
hearts of men. During the hours, we pray Thee, of this Congress, may that spirit be born in the hearts of those that are
here. God bless us all and forgive us for our failures in the

past. Give us, we pray Thee, Thy spirit. We ask it in Christ's name. Amen.

*   *   *

A mayor of Tucson, Arizona, welcomes the Arizona Bankers Association to Tucson.

I feel highly honored this morning to be asked, as mayor of this city, to greet you and extend to you the courtesies of Tucson. I feel that we are also very highly honored in having you select our city for your convention. There must be some attraction, or you would not come.

We hope that all your deliberations here will be entertaining and profitable to you and also to us, and we hope that it will not be long before our attractive city may attract you again, in the near future.

During your stay here, I again as mayor, and for the city, extend to you hearty greetings and all the privileges that the city can give you.

Chapter 12

ILLUSTRATIONS OF HOW SPEAKERS
RESPOND TO TOASTMASTERS

In this chapter there are presented many actual illustrations
of the opening remarks of speakers as they have responded
to the introductions of toastmasters. These examples should
be helpful both to speakers in preparing their responses, and
to toastmasters, who may find stories and interesting comments which they can adapt and use.

 ❁   ❁   ❁

*The introductory remarks of football coach Wally
Weber of the University of Michigan as he responds to
an introduction by Kenneth L. Wilson, athletic commissioner of the Intercollegiate Conference.*

Executives, vice presidents, office boys and assorted taxpayers: I'm not much of an after-dinner speaker, but I'm always after the dinner, as you can see by my rotund girth, so
round, so firm, so fully packed, so free and easy on the draw.

Not knowing the quantity of the fine victuals I might expect with your hospitality, I took it upon myself to participate in some sustenance in one of your more unhygienic
beaneries over on Wabash Avenue, to sustain my anemic
figure until I got to the banquet hall.

Incidentally, I haven't seen Tug Wilson in a good many
years. You know, he has reached the metallic age—gold in
his teeth, silver in his hair and lead in his feet. But he has a
very nice personality, a man of charming personality and
great force in the Western Conference.

He said something about Weber playing on the last Yost

team. It was really the highlight in my rather abbreviated career. It seems that in those days Mr. Yost was featuring a tremendous aerial game. It was featured by the throwing arm of the son of an impoverished tailor named Friedman, now a purveyor of jeeps in the city of Detroit, who threw passes into the receptive digits of a young man named Ooster-baan. My only function was to inflate the ball, which I did with consummate skill.

❋   ❋   ❋

Tom Collins, from Kansas City, Missouri, who is wide-ly known as one of the best humorous philosophers and speakers in the country, began an address as follows:

Thank you very much, sir. Ladies and gentlemen, good afternoon. I appreciate that gracious and very brief intro-duction, which leaves me little to live up to except to be a humorist and a philosopher. If I can get over those two hur-dles, I probably will get by this without falling flat on my puss.

I obviously feel very much at home here. After that elec-tion which I just witnessed, anybody from Kansas City would have a very homelike feeling. [The club before which he was speaking had just held its annual election with only one slate of candidates.] I do feel it my duty to tell you that about a third of my town went to the penitentiary for hold-ing elections in just such brisk manner as that. If you can get over that one, I'd think you could get by with pretty nearly anything.

Now, obviously, nobody would have asked a fellow with as silly a name and obvious lack of background as I have to come down here today had you wanted to be set right on anything. If you wanted a cultured message, you well know you wouldn't have gotten me, and I know it. And so I have but two promises to make to you—this will not be dignified; it will not take long. I have a watch and I know how to tell time. And I believe that speakers should be guided by an

old Biblical adage: "He who thinketh by the inch and speaketh by the yard ought to be kicketh by the foot."

I am here, frankly, ladies and gentlemen, to listen to my
own favorite speaker on your time.

*   *   *

*The opening paragraph of an address given by United
States Representative Dewey Short of Missouri offers an
interesting suggestion for beginning an address when a
speaker has been honored by being asked to speak several times before the same audience.*

When first I was invited to address this organization I felt
highly honored. The second time you had me here to speak
to you I really felt flattered, but now that I have been invited for the third time to appear before the same group I
am really beginning to wonder whether I am great or you
are just dumb. Anyway, I am overwhelmed by your capacity
for punishment.

*   *   *

*Roscoe Drummond, presently Chief of the Washington
News Bureau of the* New York Herald Tribune, *responds
to an introduction.*

The generous introduction which I received reminds me of
the press seminar which was held in Washington. It is cus-
tomary, as you may know, at the time of the President's annual budget for the budget director to attempt to explain the
budget to newspapermen. I recall that we were having an interesting session with the budget director and his colleagues
when there appeared to be a noticeable discrepancy of about
sixteen billion dollars in comparing two tables. It developed,
in the conversation, that there was a reasonable explanation.
It was a matter of using different comparisons, and one of
the speakers was able to explain the discrepancy of at least
fourteen billion dollars. However, a persevering newspaper-
man said, "What about the other two billion dollars?" "Well,"

the representative of the budget said, "what do you want me to do, explain it down to the last penny?"

Well, I am willing to say and grateful to say that the introduction was approximately accurate.

* * *

Dr. Deane W. Malott, chancellor, University of Kansas, responds to an introduction.

It is an honor to have this opportunity to be with you, and a pleasure to renew an old friendship with the chairman. I have not seen him for ten years. He has not quite as much hair as he once had, and I assume, from the introduction, that it is because so many ideas have gone over his head.

With such an introduction, one really ought to collapse, because it would have made such a wonderful obituary.

* * *

Admiral Richard E. Byrd, famous explorer, responds to an introduction.

I certainly appreciate all those fine things the chairman just said about me. I don't begin to deserve it, but I must admit I'm human enough to like it just the same.

A schoolgirl got on the train which brought me here, and she wanted an interview. She recognized me, and wanted an interview for the school paper, as she was one of the editors. We talked a while, and presently she said, "Admiral, where did you get that Southern accent—the South Pole?"

Sometimes, as I go around, I am introduced by ladies. The other day I was introduced by a lady as follows: "Ladies and gentlemen—Rear Richard Admirable Byrd."

This morning, on the train, a man asked me the difference between the top and the bottom of the world. He asked, "What do you miss down there from civilization? What do you miss the most?"

Well, of course we missed a lot of things. Some of them

we didn't mind missing, and others we did; some we were very glad to get away from.

I was discussing that very thing in the middle of the six months' night with one of the Irishmen in the camp, Jack O'Brien. It was right in the middle of the long Polar night. We were missing things, and we were also glad to get away from some things. I said, "Jack, what are you missing most from civilization?" He answered without any hesitation, "Temptation."

❖   ❖   ❖

Senator J. William Fulbright responds to an introduction.

It is very unusual for me to have an introduction like that. I think it's the first time I've been called a statesman since I have been outside my own state.

It reminds me a little of a story that they tell in Arkansas about the farmer who was taking a little white-faced calf down a country road, on the end of a rope, and he was having some difficulty in making headway. He came to a little bridge over a shallow creek, with a dry creek bed, and the calf wouldn't move forward. He was tugging on the rope when a man drove up behind him in a car. The car couldn't pass because of the calf in the road, so the driver thought he would urge him on, and he let out a loud blast on the horn. The calf responded by jumping sidewise, over the edge of the bridge, and fell down in the creek.

The man walked up to where the farmer stood looking at the calf. He saw that the calf had fallen and broken its neck, and was dead, and he didn't know what to say.

Finally the farmer looked up and said, "Well, stranger, I appreciate your intentions, but don't you think that was an awfully loud toot for such a little calf?"

❖   ❖   ❖

Samuel B. Pettengill, vice president of the Transportation Association of America and former congressman, began an address with the following interesting illustration:

During the height of the Supreme Court fight, my old friend John Garner was called to the White House for a conference. He said, "Chief, do you want it with the bark on or the bark off?" I am going to try to give it to you today with the bark on. I think you can take it.

*   *   *

Harold E. Stassen, former governor of Minnesota and distinguished statesman, responds to an introduction.

After hearing the introduction by your distinguished chairman, my pleasure at being invited to speak to you has changed to regret that I was not appearing before a court, because if I were at this moment before a court, I would say, "Your honor, I rest my case." Surely nothing that I can say from this point forward can do anything else than decrease your estimate of me.

*   *   *

Dr. Preston Bradley, pastor of the Peoples Church of Chicago, responds to an introduction by Paul Westberg.

I listened to the very magnanimous and gracious words spoken about me, and it reminded me of the time when I was invited to come up to St. Peters, Minnesota, to speak up there at a civic dinner at which all the luncheon clubs united. I was in Duluth, and we drove over to St. Peters. On the outskirts of the city, just as we were entering, is a very big billboard. That billboard says, "You are now entering St. Peters, Minnesota, home of five governors." And it is true that that little city has produced five governors for the state of Minnesota. But down below it, in small print was this sentence, "We have natural gas, too."

*   *   *

Tom Collins, publicity director of the City National Bank and Trust Company of Kansas City, Missouri, responds to an introduction which included only his name and his title.

Good afternoon, ladies and gentlemen. That was a very gracious and painless introduction. It reminds me of Mark Twain who said the best introduction he ever got was from the fellow that said, "I know two things about Clemens—he has never been in jail, and I don't know why." That seems to be the way I was pitched out here, with nothing to live up to, and I enjoyed it very much.

Obviously, I do not have the effrontery to come here to set you right on anything concerning the banking business. I am newly come to it, just a little over a year ago, and am very grateful for a chance to mingle with my betters. I would be stupid if I came here to tell you anything about the technical side of banking. You know I don't know and I know I don't know, and if I tried it I would run out of answers.

I would be like a gentleman who came to his local school and said, "Isn't it fine to come down here and get educated. To learn that two times two is four, and seven times eight is fifty-six—nine times twelve—(pause)—and then there is geography." I would be that way, too, I would run out of answers.

*   *   *

Dr. William H. Kiekhofer, for many years professor of economics at the University of Wisconsin, responds to an introduction.

After this altogether too generous introduction by Dr. Haake, who was one of our most brilliant students at the University of Wisconsin, and who later became one of my own delightful colleagues for some years, and always remained a devoted friend, my feelings are not unlike those of a certain bachelor-girl whose somewhat belated engagement was reported. When confronted with the story she blushed, but her eyes twinkled as she said, "Modesty and honesty compel me to deny the report, but thank heaven for the rumor."

I am quite willing to have Dr. Haake, at my time in life, go on and say nice things about me even if he has to stretch matters very considerably.

*   •   •

Alben W. Barkley, United States senator from Kentucky, responds to an introduction.

I am deeply grateful to the chairman for the very generous words with which he has presented me to this fine audience of men. I would not be entirely frank if I did not tell you that I do not deserve what he has said about me, and I would not be entirely frank or truthful if I didn't say that I am glad he said it.

I want to say at the outset that my remarks are entirely extemporaneous. I haven't had time to reduce these remarks to a manuscript, and I do not like to read a speech anyway. I read one once, and when I was the guest of the host who had invited me, I asked him what he thought of my speech. "Well," he said, "I have three criticisms to make. First," he said, "you read it; secondly, you read it poorly; and, thirdly, it was not worth reading."

*   •   •

Dr. Franklyn Bliss Snyder, who served for many years on the faculty and as president of Northwestern University, responds to an introduction by Harold O. McLain, president of the Railways Ice Company, Chicago.

I was just going to say most of that myself.

I appreciate the gracious technique of the toastmaster, Mr. McLain. It is not that which one usually experiences on such occasions. Not very long ago, looking into the faces of an audience a little larger than this gathered in my home town of Evanston, the chairman, looking at her watch, said: "Now we have come to the serious part of the evening: An address by Dr. Snyder. Some of us have heard him before and some have not. Those who have not are looking forward with great pleasure to hearing him now."

The bald literalism of that statement contrasts pleasantly with your very gracious exaggerations, and if I had to choose between the two, I would much prefer Mr. McLain's technique.

       ❀   ❀   ❀

Dr. Carroll Sibley, biographer, author and lecturer, responds to an introduction.

Thank you, Mr. McLain, for that unusually gracious introduction. I think there is nothing so rare on this earth as a superlatively good presiding chairman, but a presiding chairman like Mr. McLain presents one great difficulty. It keeps an audience wondering when the program is over why in the world they imported a speaker from two thousand miles away when they have an acre of diamonds in their own front yard. When I make that statement, gentlemen, I am polishing no apples, or, as we say in California, simonizing no citrus.

Mr. McLain referred to my published works, and while it is true I have written a number of books, I sometimes suspect that my literary following is so small that it might almost be said that my writings are confidential.

I understand that you have had the pleasure of several addresses from Lloyd Douglas, and it happens that Dr. Douglas lives very near our family in Southern California. Not long ago Mrs. Sibley and I had the privilege and pleasure of breaking bread with Dr. and Mrs. Douglas. As you recall, he is a man with a great sense of humor, and with a twinkle in his eye. After we had our fine meal, he said he suspected it was true in the case of each of us that the intellectual income of both of us was so much less than our oratorical output that we were both constantly in danger of mental bankruptcy.

Now I promise you several things about whatever I may say. In the first place, I shall give you no political oratory, which a friend of mine defines as: "The art of making deep sounds from the chest sound like messages from the brain."

And then I promise you another thing: I am going to be brief, because I have always felt that a speech in order to be immortal need not necessarily be eternal. I shall never forget the time that a certain well-known speaker came to Yale to address a class, and he took as his text the letters which are used in the word "Yale." And so he spoke for about thirty minutes on "Y"; how important "you" are to life, and how important life is to "you." Then he came to "A" which stands for "ambition," and how important that is, and without which no one ever got very far. And "L" stands for "loyalty," and he devoted about thirty minutes to loyalty to your friends, loyalty to your family, loyalty to your employer. Finally he came to "E," which he said stands for "energy" without which nobody can get very far in life. He talked about two hours, and one of the students upon leaving the lecture hall at the conclusion of his remarks was heard to say to a friend: "Thank heavens, we are not students at the Massachusetts Institute of Technology."

✱　　　✱　　　✱

Dr. Neil Carothers, for many years on the faculty of Lehigh University, responds to an introduction.

The kindly introduction of your chairman reminds me of two other occasions on which a chairman introduced me.

On one of them the chairman was most inexperienced, and he said that never having undertaken such a task before he had gone to a veteran toastmaster and asked him what the rule of introductions was, and this veteran told him that it was a very simple rule: "If the man is a big-shot and really amounts to something, simply state: 'We have with us today,' and say no more. But if he is small potatoes and does not amount to much in his home town, say just as much as you can about him." This young fellow then started with my birth and moved on down for the next fifteen minutes.

And on another occasion that I am reminded of, because

of the perfectly beautiful way in which your chairman in only five minutes has presented to you the economic problems that now face us, I was introduced by an ex-governor of the state of New Jersey who was, without doubt, the greatest orator that state had developed, but who had no terminal facilities whatever.

They warned me in advance that they had confined his introduction to ten minutes, which was far too long, but that I might expect the worst. The old gentleman did all right until he came to the subject of government policies at Washington, about which he appeared to feel very deeply. Instead of completing his introduction at that point, he talked about government policies at Washington for the next forty minutes.

When I got up to deliver my simple thirty-minute address, I told him that he reminded me of the Irishman who was trying to learn to ride a horse and who was mishandling the horse until the horse ended up by putting his back foot in the stirrup. The Irishman looked around at the horse and said: "Be gorrah, if you are going to get up, I am going to get down."

       *   *   *

Harold O. McLain, president of the Railways Ice Company, Chicago, responds to an introduction.

That is a very pleasant introduction and commentary your chairman has accorded me. You know someone has said that the three hardest things in the world to do are to climb a fence leaning toward you, to kiss a pretty girl leaning away from you and to acknowledge with proper humility a flattering introduction. In spite of many failures, I've had some success with the first two, but the last one has me licked.

I am glad what your chairman said really applied to me. Not this time, of course, but sometimes a chairman or toastmaster indulges in a little flattery about the speaker which doesn't carry conviction. That happened to the mayor of Des Moines a few years ago.

.That official, who was plagued, as are most of us, with embarrassingly forgetful moments, was to introduce at a large civic banquet the guest of the city, Mr. Wiley Post, who had just completed his remarkable solo flight around the world. In his introduction the mayor said something like this: "Fellow citizens, this is the proudest and most triumphant moment in my life. I am to present to you perhaps the greatest explorer, the most magnificent navigator, the most brilliant aviator in all history. He has just completed his astounding feat of circumnavigating the globe in solo flight. The feats of earlier explorers and navigators like Columbus and Balboa and Ponce de Leon and Coronado pale in insignificance beside the accomplishment of our guest, the great pilot at whose feet the world bows in homage and whose name is on everyone's lips. It is the high privilege of my career to present to you our guest, the world renowned . . ." and then a horrible blank look came over the mayor's face as he experienced a lapse of memory. He stooped down and said in an audible whisper to Wiley, "What did you say your name is?" and receiving the reply he straightened up and declared dramatically, "the great Wiley Post."

Wiley arose in acknowledgment of the introduction and said: "Friends, as your honorable mayor has intimated, I have been a great traveler. I have felt the charm of Oriental Tokyo and Shanghai, the mystery of St. Petersburg, the courtly brilliance of Vienna, the fascinating lure of Berlin, Paris and Rome and the sturdy enormity of London. I have had the privilege of being entertained by the crowned heads and ruling potentates of most of the countries of the world, but I want to say to you that never have I visited such a delightful and charming city with such magnificent parks and boulevards, such splendid public buildings, and peopled by such beautiful women and hospitable and capable men as this your own world renowned city of . . ." and then Wiley allowed a blank look to come over his face as he leaned over and said in a loud and hoarse whisper to the mayor, "What did you say is the name of this burg?"

*   *   *

Jans J. Vander Graff, formerly Protestant chaplain at Vaughn General Hospital, Hines, Illinois, responds to an introduction.

The introduction sounded somewhat like an obituary, and I hope I can live up to all the things the chairman has just told you. I feel just a little bit like the man who had recently been married and didn't know just how he was going to stack up with his wife when he came home late one night, so when he put the key in the door, he said, "I wonder what I am letting myself in for." I don't know whether you know what you are letting yourself in for today.

*   *   *

Clyde R. Hoey, the late senator of the state of North Carolina, responds to an introduction in a speech before the American Bankers Association.

I count it a high privilege to come this morning to say just a few words to this great assembly. Of course I am highly indebted to my friend of the years, your distinguished president, for his most gracious presentation of me. He was so much kinder than a friend of the late Senator James of Kentucky was in presenting him that I am doubly contented. This friend of Senator James was a very plain, blunt man, and in introducing the senator he said: "Ladies and gentlemen, I am not going to bore you with a speech today, but I will present to you a man who will."

*   *   *

General James H. Doolittle responds to an introduction.

I am delighted to be with you today.

I am very pleased with the introduction; but that sort of introduction can't give you the "big head" if you deal with children.

I am reminded of an experience I had here while I was still in uniform, immediately after returning from Okinawa after the war was over. I was walking along Michigan Avenue when a little boy came along, recognized me and said, "May I have your autograph?" I said, "Certainly." Presently I was surrounded by boys who wanted my autograph. I was in a hurry, but continued signing autographs until one little mucous-nosed fellow came through the crowd, elbowing his way in, put a scrap of paper in my hand and said, "Sign your name here," and then turned to the kid next to him and said, "Who is the old buzzard anyway?"

Chapter 13

INTERESTING STORIES FROM
INTRODUCTIONS AND SPEECHES

Often a toastmaster or speaker will find it helpful if he can refer to a humorous or otherwise interesting story which someone else has told. He may say, for example, in illustrating a point, "United States Senator Leverett Saltonstall of Massachusetts said that he once received a letter from a gentleman which read, 'I have two children. One of them has been sick, unfortunately. Now my wife is about to have twins, and what are you going to do about it?'" The speaker may then state, "Now I should like to ask a similar question: What are we going to do about this matter?" The speaker is thus able to tell a story with credit to someone else and use it to bring out a point he himself is seeking to emphasize. Any story takes on additional interest if it can be credited to someone who is well-known.

This chapter contains a great many stories actually used in introductions and speeches, as well as interesting comments on various subjects.

The name of the person who told the story is given in each case at the end of the story.

Never Satisfied

I guess football coaches are a lot like the actor Frank Mc-Glenn, who himself attempted always to be a perfectionist. The actor spent his life doing Lincoln, both on the legitimate stage and in the movies. In his living room he assumed Lincoln postures, he walked like Lincoln, dressed like Lincoln. On this particular day he was coming out of his apartment in the habiliment of Lincoln—top hat, frock coat, striped trousers—and when he reached the sidewalk he surveyed one end of the block, and then the other, very deliberately, and then with long strides, very similar to Lincoln's, he walked up the street. A fellow standing across the street watching him said, "Look; that guy will never be satisfied until he's assassinated."—*James Conzelman, well-known football coach.*

Married Life

A long time ago, when Mrs. Chandler and I were courting, she made me a proposition which seemed entirely all right, but, in the state that I found myself, I think I would have taken it anyway. The married men will know what I mean, and the single ones will know what to expect. She said that, during the time we lived together, if important subjects came up, I could have the say. She said if they were not very important, she wouldn't bother me with them; she would just decide them and let it go. Well, we have been married quite a while; we got two baby girls and two baby boys and a grandbaby, but no major problems have come up.

She said she was going to try to teach the children good manners—and she thought she was doing very well, until one day during her temporary absence from the house, an elderly lady came suddenly into the room. Our six-year-old put his hands on his hips and said, "Well, who are you?" "Why," she said, "honey, I am your grandmother on your father's side." He said, "Huh, you'll not be here very long until you find out you're on the wrong side."—*Albert B. Chandler, former United States senator from Kentucky and former baseball commissioner.*

Courage of His Convictions

Down in Mississippi we have a squirrel law, and half of the people are for it and half of them are against it. Well, during a certain campaign down there, one of the campaign fellows came in one day and was making a big speech, and after he had finished, he said, "Now, does anybody have any questions?"

One of the people in the crowd said, "Yeah, how do you stand on the squirrel law?"

Well, when we heard that, we were scared to death, because we knew he'd say the wrong thing, but he said, "Glad you asked me that question. I understand that half of my friends are for it and half are against it. I want it definitely understood that I'm for my friends!"

Beggar's Choice

Freud says that in a great deal of joking we set up a situation in which there is a joker, a hidden change of values. Something looks like something and turns out to be something else.

Freud gives a number of amusing illustrations of that. In one, two beggars meet at the door of a rich man. This rich man has taken a vow never to turn a beggar away—always to give a beggar something. Of course the beggars found this out, and it was a regular business among the beggars to go there every day.

Well, one beggar is coming out of the door when he encounters another going in. The one going in says—referring to the rich patron—"How is he today?" The one coming out says, "He's in a very bad humor today; he only gave me a dollar." The one going in stops for a moment and then says, "Oh, well, I'll go in, anyway. Why should I give him a dollar?"

Satire

The great composer Liszt is said to have called upon Rossini with a letter of introduction. Rossini asked him to play, listened politely, and when he was done asked him what the piece was. Liszt said, "It is a march which I have written on the death of Meyerbeer. How do you like it?"

Rossini replied, "I like it very much, but don't you think it would have been better if you had died and Meyerbeer had written the music?"—*From speeches by Professor Bergen Evans of Northwestern University, author of* The Natural History of Nonsense.

Failure

I am one of these foolish fellows who believe that I can train kids to be inventors, and somebody made a study—I think it was the Brookings Institution—one time that proved that a man who had an education was less likely to make an invention than a fellow who had no education. Well, that should be just exactly the other way. So I tried to find out why that was, and I think the reason is quite elementary. That kid, from the time he was six or eight years old, was examined three or four times a year in school, and, if he flunked once, he was out and it was a pretty disgraceful thing; while a research fellow fails 999 times, and if he succeeds once, he is in.

Research

The word "research" has been so glamorized that it really doesn't hold the factors at all that I think it should have. We have tried to get definitions. We tried to get a definition for research that makes it something that takes it out of the academic and very intangible phase. Most people think of research men as being either highbrows or nuts. Well, we don't like either one of them, because we think that all the research there is, is trying to find out something that we don't know. So we devised this definition: "Research is a process of finding out what you are going to do when you can't keep on doing what you are doing now, or what are you going to do when you quit doing what you are doing now." One fellow said, "I don't know!" He needs research.

Imagination

Some fellows in my office one time said, "What are some of the problems that are worrying you?" "Well," I said, "one is why I can see through a pane of glass." "Well," they said, "that is simple. It is transparent." If you look into a Webster dictionary, it says that something transparent is something you can see through. What he said was, "You can see through a pane of glass because you can see through a pane of glass," but it sounded much better when he said "transparent." There is an awful lot we don't know. In fact, most everything we don't know very well. Therefore, the opportunities that are in the world are just as great as we have the imagination to create.—*Charles F. Kettering, formerly vice president and director, General Motors Corporation.*

Better Keep Quiet

When the microphone was being tested, I was reminded of a speaker who didn't have very good attention, which is usually true of very poor speakers, and the fellow was talking away and talking away, and he noticed that he wasn't getting attention. He stopped and said, "Can you hear me back there? I can't hear myself talk." A little fellow out in front said, "Go right ahead, brother, you're not missing a thing."—*Emil Schram, former president of the New York Stock Exchange.*

Weapon of War

Someone asked Mr. Einstein one day what kind of weapons would be used in the third world war. "Well," he answered, "I don't know. I don't know what they are developing, because things are progressing so rapidly, but I can tell you what they'll use in the fourth world war," he said. "They'll use rocks."—*J. William Fulbright, United States senator from Arkansas.*

They Were Right

Everyone that goes to Mexico, or wants to go to Mexico, always asks me one question and I shall answer it so that it won't bother you. What about travel conditions in Mexico?

What about the problem of food and water? The first time I went to Mexico I rode a donkey from Mexico City down south over the mountains to Guatemala, and when I told them I planned such a trip, they said, "They will bring you back in a pine box."

"Well," I said, "I am going anyway." They said to take all precautions and "you might conceivably come back to us alive. You have to get inoculated for typhoid, vaccinated for smallpox, sleep under mosquito netting every night, peel all your vegetables and boil all your drinking water." The first time I went down to Mexico, I didn't get inoculated or vaccinated for anything, and I slept in the swamps and up in the mountains with never a mosquito net. I ate enchiladas and drank water running in streams, backyard ditches and any place in Mexico—and, boy, was—I—sick!—*Robert Friars, travel lecturer.*

No Taxes—No Debts

A boy came home from school and asked his father, "Father, was the white man superior to the Indian?" The father thought for a minute and said, "Well, when the Indians were running things, they had no taxes, they had no debts, and the women did all the work. How can you improve on that?"

Foolish Question

A small boy was practicing his piano lessons because he had to, and a traveling salesman stuck his head in the door, and said, "Son, is your mother home?" The boy said, "What do you think?"

Don't Touch It

I heard of two moonshiners down in Kentucky who were fifty-five years of age on the same day and wanted to celebrate. They didn't know what to do. Someone who knew them well suggested that they take a train ride. Well, they thought that was a good idea so they walked ten miles across country to the little railroad station.

Someone showed them how to buy tickets so they purchased tickets and got on the train. After getting on the train someone said, "Why don't you sit down?" They didn't know they were allowed to sit down, but finally they sat down.

The moment they sat down a big, burly fellow with a blue uniform and brass buttons came along for their tickets. They had never seen a conductor or heard of a conductor. This man took the tickets away from them and that made them mad because they hadn't even read them.

Another fellow they didn't know went to the platform at the end of the car and yelled the name of the next town—something that people couldn't possibly understand—and people got up and left the train and more people got on. They didn't know where they were—they didn't know anybody lived on the other side of the mountains.

Well, a boy came by selling peanuts, popcorn, chocolate bars and soda pop. They had heard of the first three things but had never seen soda pop before. One of the other passengers said, "Boy, give me a bottle of soda pop." Well, the minute he said "bottle," these moonshiners were all attention. They watched the fellow take the bottle of pop, knock off the top and slowly drink the contents. The moonshiners winked at each other and one of them said, "Give us a bottle of that stuff, boy." They decided to "go halvers" on the first bottle to see how they liked it.

One of them started to drink his half of the contents just as the train went into a big, black tunnel. "How is it, Lem?" asked the other. "Don't touch the stuff," said the first man. "I've been struck blind!"

Knew What to Do

A friend of mine and I went to Coney Island, and we had a wonderful time. He knew what to see and what to avoid that wasn't worthwhile. The last attraction we visited was a shooting gallery, and there they had celluloid balls propelled by jets of water. The balls rose and fell and when they fell, they fell out of sight. The idea was to hit them as you saw them. I shot all the cartridges in my rifle and didn't hit one of the balls. My friend picked up a gun, took careful aim, shot once and all the balls fell.

I said, "Bill, that's the most wonderful shooting I ever saw in my life. How on earth did you do it?" Bill replied, "I shot the fellow working the pump!" It was just a matter of knowing what to do.—*James E. Gheen, humorous lecturer.*

Honest

The warm ocean current near Alaska has some disadvantages. It produces a lot of rain. Alaskans are not Californians. They confess freely that they have a lot of rain. Sometimes I think they overstress it. In fact, it has often occurred to me that if an Alaskan and a Californian could meet and marry, the offspring would probably be an honest person.—*Ernest T. Gruening, former governor of Alaska.*

Poor Hearing

A man was very hard of hearing, and went to the doctor. The doctor examined him and said, "I think you are drinking too much." He said, cupping his ear, "How is that, Doc?" And the doctor repeated, "You are drinking too much." The man said, "Maybe I am." "Well," the doctor said, "cut it out and see if you can't hear better." Six weeks later he came to see the doctor, and he was hearing perfectly. Six weeks more and he came back and he couldn't hear a thing, and the doctor said, "I thought, when you stopped drinking, you were hearing all right." He said, "I was, Doc, but I liked what I was drinking so much better than what I was hearing that I went back to drinking again."—*Mark Brown, retired president of the Harris Trust & Savings Bank of Chicago.*

Useless Words

Pat and Mary were in some difficulty in court. They had been fighting, and the judge said: "Pat, I understand you and Mary had some words." "Yes, I had some," said Pat, "but I didn't get to use mine."—*United States Senator John W. Bricker of Ohio.*

No Handicap Desired

[Mr. Halleck had no prepared manuscript for his speech.]
When it comes to a manuscript, I am kind of like the boy
who wanted to join the Army. They asked him if he wanted
to be in the cavalry, and he said, no, when they started shooting at him, he didn't want to be bothered with any horse!

Chaplain and Congress

The young fellow said to his dad: "Dad, why do they have
a chaplain in Congress?" He said, "They have a chaplain
there to pray." "Well, who does he pray for? Does he pray
for the Congress?" He said, "Oh, no, he stands up and takes
a look at the Congress, and then prays for the country!"—
*Hon. Charles A. Halleck, member of the House of Represent-
atives from Indiana.*

Accurate

The great baseball manager Connie Mack has a son who
married a North Carolinian, and Connie used to go up there
for his vacations after the season. He liked to hunt some. Not
a particularly good shot, he went out one day with a fine
rifle and excellent equipment, and came back without a squirrel. He met a native mountain North Carolina boy with a
bag full of squirrels, and he said, "Son, where did you get
all those squirrels?" "Well," he said, "mister, I killed them
chunking rocks at them." Connie said, "I don't believe that
can be done, young man." "Well, sir," he said, "come on with
me and if we find one I'll show you."

So they walked on through the woods of that beautiful
mountain section, and soon the leaves shook and the boy
reached down with his left hand and sailed a rock into the
trees and down came the squirrel. Connie then had a new
interest. He said, "Son, I need you for the Athletics. You
will be the greatest left-handed pitcher the world has ever
known." The boy said, "Thank you, Mister, but I ain't left-
handed." Connie said, "Pray tell me then, if you are not left-

handed, why didn't you use your right hand when you threw
that rock at that squirrel?" "Well, sir, when I uses my right
hand, I mangles them too bad."

Correction, Please

It is sometimes hazardous to speak without a manuscript,
because you might get misquoted, but my experience has
been with the press that, whenever I have been misquoted,
it constitutes an improvement in what I otherwise would
have said. Sometimes you get into difficulty. My distinguished
predecessor in office, who is quite a courtly, handsome, magnificent gentleman, had a little incident occur in the mansion
there one day. He was lifting one of those heavy windows in
that old building and sustained a slight hernia while lifting
this window, and the morning papers the next morning said
the "Governor had sustained a slight hernia while lifting a
widow in the Governor's Mansion."—*Joseph Melville Brough-
ton, former governor of North Carolina.*

Can't Know Everything

I like to tell the story about a little Protestant boy who
came home with a big black eye, and his mother said, "Where
on earth did you get that black eye?" He said, "The O'Reilly
kids hung it on me." She said, "How did they come to do
that?" "Well," he said, "I was over at their house, making
some cracks about the Pope." His mother said, "Didn't you
know the O'Reilly's were Catholics?" "Yes," he said, "but I
didn't know the Pope was."

The Boy and the Drum

I live next door to a little boy, and some misguided guy
gave him a drum for his birthday. I hope none of you have
ever had to endure that reprehensible combination. It almost drove me out of my wits. I didn't know the answer to
it. Finally I got a fellow I know and who likes me a little
bit. I said, "Joe, what are we going to do with this, before I

lose what passes for my wits?" He said, "I've got a notion. We'll go and see the kid." And we called on that little guy and my neighbor pulled out his pocket knife, and he said, "Son, I am making you a present of this knife. Wouldn't you love to know what is in the middle of that drum?"

Fear

A worry, a fear of failure, has often held you and me back and you know it. I've got a friend who has done very well calling on tough customers, the kind that usually say no, and I said to him, "How do you get in a frame of mind to call on a tough guy?" He said, "I say to myself: Where am I? I am out here. Where is he? He is in there in his office. Where do I have to go? I have to go in where he is. What if he says no and throws me out—where am I? Out here—that's where I am now. I've got nothing to lose."

He Knew

I have a friend who plays the 'cello—in a kind of queer fashion. He clamps his finger on the neck and saws away, and he never moves that finger. He holds the 'cello in one spot, tight. One tone is all he ever produces, and his wife said to him, "Other people don't play the 'cello the way you play it. They fiddle up and down on the neck. They don't just leave their finger in one spot the way you are doing." "Oh," he said, "they are just hunting the place to play, but me, I've found it."—*Tom Collins, humorist and philosopher.*

He Had to Stay

A speaker talked and talked and talked on endlessly like the proverbial brook. Finally there came an end to the patience of the audience, and gradually the crowd began to leave. On and on the speaker went until finally there remained but one man who sat right out in front of him.

The speaker leaned over and said: "I would like to say in conclusion, sir: You are a gentleman." And the fellow looked up and said: "You are still wrong, mister. I am the next speaker."—*Charles Francis Coe, executive vice president and general counsel of the Motion Picture Producers & Distributors of America, Inc.*

Modernization

The story is told of an *Uncle Tom's Cabin* company that was touring in Russia. They came to the place in the play where Little Eva dies and goes to heaven, but since the Russians didn't believe in heaven, they had her get well and go to work in a cement factory.—*Charles Milton Newcomb, humorist and philosopher.*

Missed Him

Back in '32, in the depths of the depression, they invited President Hoover down to Charleston, West Virginia, to dedicate some sort of a public institution. He got there at eight o'clock in the morning, and was greeted by an appropriate committee, taken to a hotel for breakfast and out to the scene of the ceremony about eleven o'clock.

There were about twenty thousand people assembled. They had erected a platform, and they escorted the President up on the platform. Immediately they gave him the presidential salute of twenty-one guns. They boomed out from cannons close by. Everything was deathly still while the cannons were booming and for a moment afterward. Back in the middle of the audience an old man shaded his eyes with his hand, and peered up on the platform and saw Hoover still standing there, and he said to himself, "By Gosh! They missed him."—*Alben W. Barkley, United States senator from Kentucky.*

Not Particular

A gentleman who was slightly under the weather decided to leave the party he was attending at a hotel and go home. He went out to the front door and there, on the sidewalk, was a man dressed in a blue uniform with gold braid and brass buttons, so he said, "Call me a cab." The uniformed man said, "I'm not a doorman; I'm a United States naval officer." The drunk said, "Well, call me a boat; I've got to get home."—*James E. Gheen, humorist.*

Better Work

A little girl was pirouetting in front of a mirror one day, wearing her first long gown. She said, "Mamma, did God make Papa?"

Mamma said, "Yes." She said it with a kind of a gulp, but she admitted that God made him.

The little girl asked, "Mamma, did God make you?"

"Well, yes," replied the mother.

After a pause, the little girl took another pirouette and looked at herself very keenly from top to bottom, then she said, "Mamma, God's doing better work lately, isn't he?"—*Upton Close, radio commentator and lecturer.*

Cash

One time a man was introducing me to a meeting, and he said, "I've just heard this man, LeTourneau, talking about giving the Lord credit. I know a lot of folks who will give the Lord the credit, but they won't give him the cash."—*Robert G. LeTourneau, president of R. G. LeTourneau, Inc., who has given substantially of his time and funds to further Christian activities.*

Proper Address

Soon after being elected a bishop, I happened to be out in Wichita, Kansas. In the lobby of a hotel, I noticed my friend Channing Pollock, the playwright, sitting there. It was the first time I had seen him since my election to this office. I called out—he didn't see me, but I called out so he could hear me—"There's old Channing Pollock!" He rushed over.

He was a spontaneous, effervescent type of personality. He said this—I didn't say it, for a bishop wouldn't say this. He grabbed my hand and said, "My God, Bishop, I'm glad to see you!" Then I looked at him for a moment and I said, "Mr. Pollock, you may know all about the theater, sir, but the proper way to address a bishop is Me Lord—not My God!"—*Bishop G. Bromley Oxnam, noted Methodist churchman, educator and leader in public affairs.*

Sizzle

When I was just a little fellow, back in Penfield, every Sunday I put a box out in front of Grandpa's farm; an old apple box. Grandpa had built me the prettiest handpainted sign, in three colors, Eggs—30¢, with a beautiful white Leghorn up in the corner, and I did a fair business.

But, one time, the wind came along and destroyed my sign and I made myself a homemade one, and just being a young fellow, I couldn't spell very well and I had the *s* marked backwards and the cent mark in the wrong place. That is the day success came to me, because all the city folks driving down the highway would see the crude, homemade sign, and figured, he is just a dumb country boy and his prices will be cheap. So, they pulled up in front of my sign and the wife would always nudge her husband and say, "Charlie, go on out and get me a dozen eggs."

He would come out in front of the car and then she would stick her head out the door and say, "Ask the boy if they are fresh." Now, I could have been ordinary. I could have been trite. I could have said to the lady, "Of course, they are fresh, lady; one-day-old eggs." But, I knew all the city fellows could say the same thing.

When she asked me if they were fresh, I looked the woman smack in the eye and said, "Madam, do you mind waiting a moment while I get them fresh from the henhouse?"

She would say, "No, go right ahead."

So, I went to the henhouse. Of course, just inside the henhouse door, I had a big bushel basket of eggs that I had been saving up all week for Sunday's business. So, I would put twelve eggs in my little bag, but here was my big selling sizzle. Every Sunday, I had a hen in the henhouse. I always knew she would be there because I had her roped in. And, just before I came out of the henhouse, I used to kick the hen just enough to make her cackle. Just when she cackled the loudest, that is when I walked out of the henhouse with the eggs in my right hand.

After hearing all that cackling, did I have to tell the woman how old my eggs were? Why, some of the customers thought I went in, swept the hens off the nests that had one-second-old eggs.—*Elmer Wheeler, author of* How to Sell Yourself to Others, *and president of the Tested Selling Institute of New York.*

Cooperation

Dr. Leverett S. Lyon, former chief executive officer, The Chicago Association of Commerce and Industry, was acting as moderator of a discussion in which one of the participants defined marriage as a status of antagonistic cooperation. Dr. Lyon said, "This interesting and intriguing definition of marriage, in which it turns out to be a 'status of antagonistic cooperation' reminds me of the definition of 'cooperation' which one man used when he said that every time he had been asked to cooperate, he was expected to *coo* while the other fellow *operated*."

If It Doesn't Rain

A young man had just returned from an enjoyable date with his girl friend. He immediately sat down and wrote her a letter, asserting his undying devotion.

"There is nothing I would not do to reach your side," he wrote. "I would climb the highest mountains, I would cross the trackless desert, I would swim the widest ocean to be near you, my beloved!" Then he added: "P.S. I'll see you Saturday night, if it doesn't rain."

That is the danger of public speeches! We may be so entertained, or so enthusiastic about a problem, or so enamoured of great, shining generalities that we never do get around to taking appropriate action!—*Edward G. Olson, director of school and community relations, Washington State Office of Public Instruction.*

Skinned

Some time ago one of my countrymen, who was engaged in the prosperous business of tailoring in Singapore, had a rather exciting idea. He was getting along very well with his men's tailoring and he thought he would extend and expand his business by entering the ladies' clothing field, and he wanted to start with fur coats. He then devoted the second story of his premises to the new enterprise, putting up a sign in big letters, LADIES' FUR COATS MADE TO ORDER—YOUR SKIN OR MINE.—*Dr. V. K. Wellington Koo, ambassador of China to the United States.*

Exercise

A man was celebrating his eightieth birthday and his fiftieth wedding anniversary. The reporters gathered around and congratulated him, and asked, "Can you tell us how you account for this?"

He said, "I never thought about it. I do know that when I got married my wife and I had an agreement that any time we saw an argument coming on, I would grab my hat and walk three times around the block, and you'd be surprised what fifty years of outdoor exercise will do for your health."—*Dr. W. Ballentine Henley, president of The College of Osteopathic Physicians and Surgeons of Los Angeles.*

There Are Too Many Like This Church Member

A Negro parson, who was trying to arouse his membership to action and get people personally to participate in whatever matter he had at hand, told his "brethren and sistern" that "dis yere church should do things . . . dey should walk forward." And the brother in the back row called out, "Amen, let her walk, brother, let her walk."

The preacher continued, "Not only should she walk but she should run." The brother in the back said, "Amen, let her run, brother, let her run."

"But," said the preacher, "not only should she walk and run, but she should fly." And the brother in the back said, "Amen, brother, let her fly, let her fly."

"But," said the parson, "to fly, dat means dat every membah of dis church has got to sacrifice, he has got to give more, every Sunday to de work ob de Lawd. Dey has got to gib ob dere time and ob dere money." The same voice in the back of the room said, "Let her walk, brother, let her walk."—*E. P. Hamilton, president of the Hamilton Manufacturing Company of Two Rivers, Wisconsin.*

Opposed

A New York newspaper reporter who went up to Maine to interview a centenarian quite politely approached the old gentleman, who was sitting in his chair with his cane in his hand, and said, "Sir, you must have seen a great many changes during your hundred years." The old man replied, "Yes, and I've been agin' all of 'em."—*George V. Denny, Jr., founder and moderator of "America's Town Meeting of the Air."*

Living

I enjoy living so much I want everyone else to feel as I do. There is never a day when I drive out to my home in California that I don't look up and see the beautiful sky and see the sun—and see what God put here for us to enjoy. Instead of thinking what is wrong with the other guy, or the other fellow that is driving alongside of you, the best thing for us to do is see what is good in the other person, and bring that out instead of criticizing and finding what is wrong.—*Joe E. Brown, star of stage, screen and radio.*

Long-winded

One time, Irvin Cobb was listening to some speeches in which a group of government people had talked. After listening for two or three hours, he turned to the man next to him and said, "Now I know why they wrote 'The Stars and

Stripes Forever.' "—*Tom C. Clark, Associate Justice of the Supreme Court of the United States.*

Foresight

A boy was taking Latin, and he was not exactly the best student in the class. I observed that he had written something in the front of his Latin book. I thought it must be very important if he had written it down, so I read it. This was what it said: "In case of fire, throw this book in."

Knowledge

A man said to his friend, "You know, when I was a boy, I used to think Sodom and Gomorrah were man and wife." His friend answered, "You've got nothing on me. I thought Epistles were the wives of the Apostles."—*Charles Milton Newcomb, humorist and philosopher.*

No Mud-Slinging

Chauncey Depew was a very ardent Republican, a great entertainer, a great after-dinner speaker. In the course of one political campaign, he was approached by a stalwart Democrat, who said to him, "Chauncey, can't we conduct this campaign now without any mud-slinging?" Chauncey said, "Why, of course we can. If you will promise not to tell any lies about the Republican party, then I will promise you that I will not tell the truth about the Democratic party."—*Dwight H. Green, former governor of Illinois.*

Hadn't Seen Anything

One of the leading citizens of a small Ohio city, the first in the community to make such a trip, went around the world. He could hardly wait to get home to go to the club and tell all the fellow about the wonders he had seen and the interesting experiences he had had in India, China, Egypt and all around the globe. He got up to the club one evening, and had orated for two or three hours in front of the bar and, finally, a chap down at the end, about half asleep and sort of leaning over, roused himself sufficiently to address this fellow, and said to him, "As one gentleman to another, may I ask you a question?" Our friend said, "Why, certainly. What is it?" He said, "Have you ever had delirium tremens?" My friend said, "No." "Well," he said, "brother, you hain't seen nothing and you hain't been nowhere!"—*James S. Kemper, chairman of the board, Lumbermen's Mutual Casualty Company of Chicago.*

God

This universe of ours hasn't any meaning, it can't have any meaning, unless somewhere there is a power or a ruler that holds it all together. You cannot explain the very world in which you live unless you begin with the thing that you call God. I am not thinking of God as he might be described in a book, as he might be given to you by a Mohammedan or a Confucian or Brahman, or any other human being. I am thinking of God as a Power, as Someone who reveals His Will in the manifestations of nature.

You can't escape that. We know there is such a thing as the law of gravity, and we know if there were no law of gravity, this universe would fly apart; it couldn't hold together. Explain the law of gravity, if you will. Explain how all these spheres hold their proper relationships to each other.

Explain, if you will, so common a phenomenon—all of us know it and very few of us appreciate its significance—that the world turns on its axis once every twenty-four hours, traveling at the rate of one thousand miles an hour. What difference does it make? Suppose it traveled only one hundred miles an hour? Why not? Who made it travel a thousand miles an hour? Why didn't He make it travel a hundred miles an hour? If that thing were sheer accident, if there were no Will, no God who determined that, why one thousand miles an hour? Why not five hundred? Why not two thousand? Why not one hundred? And what a difference it would make! If this world traveled at the rate of one hundred miles an hour, your days and nights would be ten times as long as they now are. For what amounts to five full days now, ten times as long, you would be in night, without the warmth of the sun, and the world would freeze up, freeze up so solidly that everything would be dead before dawn came. And that which was still alive would roast during the day that was ten times as long as it is now. Suppose your noon hour, which is already threatening in some places in the world to burn things up sometimes—suppose it lasted ten times as long.

The world couldn't exist if it didn't turn at that rate of one thousand miles an hour.

Or take so simple a thing as the freezing of water. When water freezes, it gets lighter. Why should it get lighter? Why should water, as it turns into ice, weigh less than it weighed before? Who did that? Who ordered that, and made it that way? What are the conveniences of it? As it becomes lighter, as it freezes, the ice floats on top of the water, and the water that is underneath can never freeze but remains above the freezing point, and the life that is in the water lives. But if the water as it froze became heavier, or remained just as heavy as it was, it would go down to the bottom—this ice— and the lake and the ocean and the river would freeze solid. There wouldn't be any life there when the spring came, and when the summer came the solid ice at the bottom would never be reached by the rays of the sun. You could not have life on the earth if it weren't for the simple fact that ice is lighter than water.

Who ordered it that way? All through the manifestations of nature you will find a will, a sense of orderliness, a sense of relationship. What some of us call accepting or following God, the things that the Communist shrinks from in horror, in the last analysis mean nothing more difficult than accepting the laws of nature as they are manifested all about us every day.—*Dr. Alfred P. Haake, economist and consultant for the General Motors Corporation.*

Is the Young Man, Absalom, Safe?

Revolt was in the air. Anybody could feel it, though it was not easy to find the source of it. David was growing old and it seemed obvious to some of the enlightened members of the younger generation that the nation needed a change. The king still believed in the old-fashioned virtues of the "good old days," and the older he grew, the more cautious he became. Absalom did the best he could to enlighten his aged father, but it seemed to him that David simply had lived too long. It was time for a younger hand to take over the leadership of the nation, Absalom thought, but he was depressed by the realization that old though his father was, he was disgustingly healthy and vigorous.

Absalom covered his trail well and few suspected his intrigues. He knew how to use his attractive personality for all it was worth and his ingratiating ways made him popular everywhere. The fact that he was David's son gave him access to the "right people" and enabled him to sidetrack the suspicion that might have fallen upon him. All in all, Absalom cut no mean figure in his father's kingdom.

When Absalom finally showed his hand, much to his father's amazement, it was almost too late to save the kingdom. David and his servants fled from Jerusalem while his captains rallied the loyal remnants of the army. Perhaps it was overconfidence or an excessive estimate of his military genius that led to Absalom's disaster, but in any event, his armies were defeated and he lost his life.

Then there follows one of the most dramatic incidents in the Old Testament. Joab, the king's captain, sent Ahimaaz, a runner, from the battlefield to the king to inform him that Absalom was dead. David was watching for the messenger, who, when he arrived, was startled by the king's first question: "Is the young man, Absalom, safe?" The question was so eager, so anguished, that Ahimaaz had not the courage to tell the truth. He retreated behind a halfhearted evasion. A second runner, however, broke the old man's heart with the callous and exultant announcement that Absalom was dead. Weeping, David cried out: "O Absalom, my son, my son, would I had died for thee."

"Is the young man, Absalom, safe?" The question should have occurred to David long before it did. Absalom had been playing with fire for years and anybody should have been able to see that he was riding for a fall. Pride, self-will, ruthless ambition, lack of integrity—these were forerunners of disaster and David should have known it. The valiant faith and the striking idealism that had made David great had made no claim upon his son. The stirring traditions of Israel and the spiritual heritage of the nation meant nothing to Absalom; he could sweep away the glory of the past without a qualm.—*From a sermon by Dr. Harold Blake Walker of The First Presbyterian Church of Evanston.*

Three Stories

In an ancient literature, which I happen to teach at the University of Chicago, is to be found this little story: Three men were in a boat, none of whom could swim. When they got out to midstream, one man took out an augur and started to bore a hole in the bottom of the boat. The other two shouted, "What are you doing?"

"Tend to your own business," said he. "I am boring a hole beneath my seat only, and not beneath yours."

"But," shouted the other two, "we are *all* in the same boat."

That story is two thousand years old. It is as true, if not truer, than when it was written. We are all in the same boat.

*   *   *

Whittier tells how two rabbis, on the Day of Atonement, prayed the whole day long, each for his sins to be forgiven. Just before nightfall each still felt the burden of sin on his conscience. Finally, one rabbi prayed, "Oh, Lord God, if it be Thy will not to forgive my sins, do Thou forgive the sins of my brother who writhes in the agony of his soul."

And just then he felt that he, himself, had been forgiven. The great climax of that poem reads:

"Heaven's gate is not opened to him who comes alone;
Save another's soul, and thus thou'lt save thine own."

We are all in the same boat! Are we not?

In the sixteenth century, John Donne wrote a little poem that Hemingway has resurrected in his novel *For Whom the Bell Tolls*. Listen to these lines:

"No man is an island in himself; he is part of the main land.
If a clod be washed away, Europe is less.
Any man's death diminishes me.
Never send to know for whom the bell tolls;
    It tolls for thee."

What did John Donne mean? *We live in and through every man's life. We die in and through every man's death.* Evidently, even our souls are in the same boat.—*Dr. Louis L. Mann, rabbi, Sinai Temple, Chicago.*

Insomnia

I was talking to a friend who was complaining of his inability to sleep. He finally went to a doctor about it. The doctor suggested that he try counting sheep. He did so that night, and returned to the doctor the next day more exhausted than before, stating that he didn't sleep at all.

He said: "For four, maybe five, hours, I count sheep. I count up to 20,000. Then I begin thinking—20,000 sheep would produce 80,000 pounds of wool—that would be 30,000 yards of cloth—that would make 12,000 overcoats! And, man, who can sleep with an inventory like that?"—*Edwin B. Moran, secretary of the National Association of Credit Men.*

Form Letters

A man found bedbugs in his bed and complained to the hotel. He got a very nice letter back explaining that those things would happen once in a while. They were very careful and so forth, and they thanked him for writing the letter. But somebody had forgotten to detach a little slip that said, "Send this customer the bedbug letter."

I think our form letters need overhauling every once in a while. I know after I have read mine for a while I say to myself, "How could anybody think this is anything but a form letter?" It isn't personal any more, after several months. You might look over your own, however, and see how they sound.—*Paul A. Mertz, director of company training of Sears, Roebuck & Company and past president of the Industrial Relations Association of Chicago.*

Horse Sense

Somebody once said that horse sense is the quality you never find in a jackass. American people have a lot of that horse sense.

Another definition of horse sense is "stable" thinking.

The one I like best of all—and this is very typical of the American people—horse sense is what keeps a horse from betting on a man.

Yes or No

A gentleman in Texas some years back wrote in and inquired if we would take a survey on what the public thinks about the whole subject of gold and the gold standard for our dollar. He also took the trouble to write out the question which he wanted us to put on the ballot. I want to read you the question as he suggested it because it illustrates the problem we are up against in the matter of wording the inquiries that we put on our ballots.

This man said, "Kindly poll the American people on this question: Do you believe that instead of allowing a free open market with bidding for gold unavoidably determining its value and production in keeping with the law of supply and demand, automatically maintaining the gold supply properly apace growing industry's needs for financing unrestricted production of desired goods, employment, wages, profits, and consumption of goods—answer yes or no."—*William A. Lydgate, editor of the Gallup Poll.*

Modern Medicine

My little daughter was sent to the store supposedly to get a thermometer because her daddy was quite ill. She forgot what she went after and got the thing mixed up. When she got home, my wife supposedly put the thing in my mouth, and when she took it out after waiting the proper period for the reading, she discovered it was a barometer instead of a thermometer and the reading was Dry and Windy.—*Jans J. Vander Graff, formerly Protestant chaplain of Vaughn General Hospital, Hines, Illinois, tells this story which others are said to have originated about him.*

Conditions Change

Things are going to keep on changing and we have got to be flexible in our thinking. A man called up the doctor in the middle of the night and said, "Doctor, come over here right away! My wife is awfully sick. I think she is going to need an operation for appendicitis."

The doctor said, "Man! You're crazy! Your wife couldn't have appendicitis. I took her appendix out myself six or seven years ago." He said, "Did you ever hear of a woman having a second appendix?"

The fellow said, "No, Doc, but didn't you ever hear of a man with a second wife?"

So, things do change.—*Arthur H. Brayton of Des Moines, Iowa.*

Little Journeys into Famous Lives

Very few persons know the name of George Matheson, but millions have sung the hymn he wrote. Mr. Matheson decided to study for the ministry. He was a brilliant scholar with a promising career but suddenly lost his sight. All the bright prospects of life seemed closed to him. His career appeared ended, but he would not have it so. He became a great preacher and wrote many books. In that period of terrible disaster, when the darkness first fell on him, he wrote that immortal hymn, a part of which follows:

"O Light that followest all my way
   I yield my flickering torch to Thee;
My heart restores its borrowed ray,
That in Thy sunshine's blaze its day
   May brighter, fairer be.

"O Joy that seekest me through pain,
   I cannot close my heart to Thee;
I trace the rainbow through the rain,
And feel the promise is not vain
   That morn shall tearless be."

This hymn takes rank with Cardinal Newman's "Lead, Kindly Light," as one of the greatest hymns of the Christian church. It is notable for its beauty, its freshness, its devotional appeal; it is even more conspicuous as a hymn of courage. But its beauty is infinitely magnified when one understands that suffering out of which it came. Trials and hardships frequently unlock men's greatest virtue.

•   •   •

Two of the three greatest epic poets of the world were blind—Homer and Milton. Dante was in his later years almost blind. Beethoven was almost deaf when he produced his greatest works.

•   •   •

When Sir George Stephenson was working on the invention of the railroad engine, people said he was crazy. They said, "Smoke will pollute the air," and, "Carriage makers and coachmen will starve for want of work." A House of Commons committee asked many `questions. This was one of them: "If a cow gets on the track of the engine traveling ten miles an hour, will it not be an awkward situation?" "Yes, very awkward, indeed, for the cow," replied Stephenson. A government inspector said that if an engine ever went ten miles an hour, he would attempt to eat a stewed locomotive for breakfast. "What can be more palpably absurd than the prospect held out of locomotives traveling twice as fast as horses?" asked a writer in the English *Quarterly Review* for March, 1825.

＊   ＊   ＊

One of the greatest writers and novelists in American history, Nathaniel Hawthorne, owed his success as a writer and the composition of his masterpiece to the loss of his job and the inspiration of his wife. One day he came home broken-hearted because of the loss of his job. He told his wife he was a failure. She replied, to his surprise, that the loss of his job had given him a wonderful opportunity to write a book. When he remarked that they had nothing on which to live in the meantime, she showed him that she had saved, out of her allowance and without his knowledge, enough so they could live for a year. She had implicit confidence in the fact that Hawthorne was a man of great ability. Hawthorne began work and wrote an exceptionally good book, *The Scarlet Letter.*

＊   ＊   ＊

Alexander Hamilton said, "Men give me credit for genius. All the genius I have lies just in this: when I have a subject in hand I study it profoundly. Day and night it is before me. I explore it in all its bearings. My mind becomes pervaded with it. Then the effort which I make the people are pleased to call the fruit of genius; it is the fruit of labor and thought." The law of labor is equally binding on genius and mediocrity.

Achieving Greatness

Great achievement demands giving life itself. See Webster working thirty-six years on his dictionary; Bancroft writing twenty-six years on his *History of the United States.* Gibbon devoted twenty years to his *Decline and Fall of the Roman Empire* and rewrote his autobiography nine times. Vergil spent twelve years writing the *Aeneid.*

＊   ＊   ＊

The publishers of the *Atlantic Monthly* returned Louisa

Alcott's writing with the suggestion that she had better stick to schoolteaching. A leading magazine ridiculed young Tennyson's first poems. Only one of Emerson's books had a profitable sale. Thackeray's *Vanity Fair* was turned down by a dozen publishers. Milton worked on *Paradise Lost* when he could not see.

*   *   *

When young Disraeli was ridiculed and hissed from the House of Commons, he said, "The time will come when you will hear me." And the time did come when this boy, with no opportunity, furnished England with her leadership for a quarter of a century.

*   *   *

Morse, the inventor of the telegraph, wrote: "So straitened were my circumstances that, in order to save time to carry out my invention and to economize my scanty means, I had for some months lodged and eaten in my studio, procuring my food in small quantities from some grocery, and preparing it myself. To conceal from my friends the stinted manner in which I lived, I was in the habit of bringing my food to my room in the evenings, and this was my mode of life for many years."

*   *   *

Daniel Webster, the youngest of ten children, as a child was so feeble in health he could not work. He developed physically and helped to earn his way through college, later becoming the leading lawyer in New England. He served in Congress, both as a representative and a senator, later becoming secretary of state under President Harrison.—*The foregoing are excerpts from speeches by Herbert V. Prochnow, vice president of The First National Bank of Chicago.*

Redemption or Conversion

Bill Michaels, vice president of the First National Bank of Tulsa, told the story about the woman who telephoned the bank to arrange for the disposal of a thousand-dollar bond. "Is the bond for redemption or conversion?" she was asked. There was a long pause, then the woman demanded: "Am I talking to the First National Bank or the First Baptist Church?"—*Finance.*

Medicine and Law

I well remember a young legal friend of mine who went to a great gathering of the medical profession, trying to curry favor with them, which is a fault of some members of the legal profession. He tried to draw an analogy between the medical profession and the legal profession, and said: "I know not why I was invited here unless it be there is some affinity between your great profession and mine, because I know that whenever I finish a case I say to myself, 'Now, have I left anything out?' whereas the medical profession, at the end of a case, say, 'Have I left anything in?' "—*Sir Norman Birkett, judge of King's Bench, England.*

Difficult Question

In a class on Americanism the teacher of the class, just before turning his students over to the official who was there to give them the oath of allegiance to complete their papers on Americanism, wanted to impress the official with what the men had learned. The teacher said to them: "What is it, gentlemen, that flies over the City Hall on the Fourth of July?" Well, that stumped the boys. They could not get the answer.

As the teacher looked upon the class in despair, one fellow held up a hand rather reluctantly. The teacher said: "All right, Ole, what is it that flies over the City Hall on the Fourth of July?" What do you suppose Ole's answer was? "Pigeons."—*George McCarty, head of the speech department, South Dakota State College.*

Legal Ethics

After I was graduated from Harvard, I went out to Wyoming to practice law. The attorney-general of Wyoming at that time was an old cowpuncher. He was a salty old character and loved to give advice. I went around to see him. He asked me: "Did you ever have a course in legal ethics?"

I said: "No, they don't consider it necessary to teach that at Harvard."

He said: "I am very happy to hear that, because I can in one sentence tell you all the legal ethics that any lawyer needs to know."

I said: "Go ahead, General."

He replied: "Remember this. Whenever you are involved in any litigation and it becomes apparent that someone has got to go to jail, be sure it is your client."—*Thurman W. Arnold, former assistant attorney-general of the United States.*

Do Your Best

Some years ago a Negro defendant was convicted before the late Judge David on a charge of arson on ten separate counts of 99 years each, a total of 990 years. "Judge, yo honor," said the defendant, "that's gonna be moughty hard for me to do!"

"Well," replied Judge David, "just do the best you can!"—*Thomas R. Mulroy, Chicago attorney.*

Quoting the Bible

Justice Chase was a very famous justice of the supreme court of Ohio. He was a Republican.

Before assuming the bench he was governor, and in his position as governor issued a Thanksgiving proclamation. To make it very realistic he decided that he could do no better than go to the source of Thanksgiving, the Bible. So he studded the entire proclamation with Biblical phrases, thinking that surely the people of Ohio, who read it, would know where it came from and would not accuse him of plagiarism. He never put the quotation marks in it.

The next day a Democratic newspaper came forth with a statement as follows: "The Editor wishes to state that these statements made by Governor Chase sound suspiciously familiar; he has read them somewhere but he cannot recall where, and he is inclined to believe that they are rank plagiarism."

Now, that would have been enough but the following day the Republican newspaper came out in defense of their governor and said:

"The statement of the Democratic editor is a lie. These are original statements and I challenge anybody to show where they were ever used before."—*Rabbi Charles E. Shulman.*

A Few Kind Words

There was a Britisher visiting the United States for the first time, and he was going up and down the country. He arrived in a little junction-town out West in the morning and wanted some breakfast. So he went into one of these greasy-spoon affairs that you find about those places and sat down. The waitress came to him and he said: "If you don't mind, you know, I should like some three-minute eggs, please, and some buttered toast, a little bacon, a pot of coffee, and a few kind words." In a moment the coffee was back and the eggs were back and the bacon was back, and they were all placed in front of this Britisher, all very lovely and fine. He looked up and said: "It *is* very nice, you know, and now for the few kind words." She leaned over to him and said: "If I were you, I wouldn't eat the eggs."—*Dr. Preston Bradley, pastor, People's Church of Chicago.*

Active

A Negro gentleman had been a preacher for some little time.

Someone said: "Uncle Amos, how many members have you got in your church?"

And he replied: "I got sixteen."

"Are they all active?"

And the old preacher answered: "Yes, eight of them fur me and eight of them agin' me."

Difficult Question

A little fellow asked his mother: "Do you know what makes the Tower of Pisa lean?" And she said: "No, if I did, I would take some."

Greatness

I think I am a great man. I will tell you why. In claiming greatness for myself I am claiming greatness for every one of you. I can think; I can love; I can purpose; I can dream; I can hope; I can aspire; I can grow. I can peer through the telescope and see the skies and understand the stars. I am bigger than the stars themselves. I am great. You are.

California

I come from Los Angeles. I always like to make that plain. A little schoolboy was asked by his teacher to define California, and he said: "It is Los Angeles and outlying territory." The teacher said: "That cannot be; there is no territory that can outlie Los Angeles."—*Dr. Roy L. Smith, editor, author and well-known preacher.*

Chapter 14

EPIGRAMS AND WITTICISMS

This chapter contains several hundred epigrams and concise humorous comments which frequently may be more effective than anecdotes in introductions. Brevity may be imperative in an introduction, and the epigram meets this requirement perfectly. A humorous story followed later in an introduction by an epigram provides a "change of pace" that is not made possible by telling two or three humorous stories. A chairman who plans his introductions carefully will find many occasions to use epigrams. Epigrams are also exceptionally helpful in speeches.

* * *

If a man has more personality than brains, he soon gets to the point where he is overpaid.

When the census taker asked how old she was, she couldn't remember whether she was thirty-eight or thirty-nine, so she said twenty-five.

A doctor will order you to stop working and rest. Then he will give you a bill that will keep your nose to the grindstone for six months.

All a good executive needs for an office is a room that's big enough for his brains.

Most of us are broadminded; in an argument we see both points of view, the one that is wrong and our own.

When in doubt (also when not), do the friendliest thing.

He wasn't exactly a sculptor, just a chiseler.

Advice—The cheapest commodity in all the world. "What

older men offer to younger men when they no longer can set them a bad example."—*Irvin S. Cobb.*

A small town businessman is one who conducts a business so small he doesn't have to bribe a government official to let him alone.

Short Book Review—Little girl describing a book: "This book tells more about birds than I am interested in knowing."

If a person has no education he just has to use his brains.

Grapefruit—A California lemon.

A mother may hope that her daughter will get a better husband than she did, but she knows her son will never get as good a wife as his father did.

April showers bring May doubleheaders.

Rotarian—A person who is sober when he sings at luncheon.

The world is divided into people who do things and people who get the credit. Try, if you can, to belong to the first class. There's far less competition.—*Dwight Morrow.*

James McNeill Whistler was invariably tart of tongue. To a man who remarked, "I passed your house last night," Whistler retorted, "Thanks!"

Every executive knows there is nothing common about common sense.

Professor—"If the young man in the back row will remove his hat, I shall continue and point out a concrete example."

Seven Ages of Woman—Baby, infant, miss, young woman, young woman, young woman, young woman.

Bubble gum has certainly made this a country of the wide open faces.

Death and taxes may always be with us, but death at least doesn't get any worse.

No man enjoys life like the man who doesn't think, but thinks he does.

Socialism becomes popular whenever hard-working, thrifty people build something worth owning which other people want.

If the world is too much with you, put a coin in a telephone booth slot and you will be cut off from everything.

What the world needs is a diplomat who can satisfy the Communists without giving them what they want.

Economics Simplified—Prosperity is the period when it is easy to borrow money to buy things which you should be able to pay for out of your own income.

In a budget of billions it ought to be possible to set aside enough money to teach the Internal Revenue Department the basic English necessary to write a readable income tax form.

Statistics show great increases in marriages. Life seems to be just a marry chase.

The five B's of middle age—Baldness, bridgework, bifocals, bay-windows and bunions.

Something ought to be done to improve sandwiches sold in depots. A coat of clear shellac would make them more attractive and easier to dust.

A conference is a gathering of important people who singly can do nothing, but together can decide that nothing can be done.—*Fred Allen.*

A man said he was glad he didn't like olives, because he knew if he did, he'd eat a lot of them, and he hated the things.—*Charles Milton Newcomb, humorist and philosopher.*

Nobody ever listened himself out of a job.—*Calvin Coolidge.*

The mystery to a married man is what a bachelor does with his money.

The worst telegram we ever saw was the one the father received reading: "Twins arrived tonight. More by mail."

Love starts when she sinks in your arms and ends with her arms in the sink.

Life—A span of time, of which the first half is ruined by our parents and the second half by our children.—*The Phoenix Flame.*

A man is as old as he feels; a woman as old as she feels— like admitting.

An army rifle weighs 8.69 pounds. After it has been carried a few miles, the decimal point drops out.—*Banking.*

A cynic defined professional courtesy as a lawyer swimming through shark-infested waters.

Do the best you can. The forests would be very quiet if all the birds were quiet except the best singers.

Boids is on the wing—I hoid; but that's absoid, 'cause wings is on the boid—I hoid.

Sign on a store which went bankrupt after two weeks' business: OPENED BY MISTAKE.

"As the earth is round," remarked a lecturer the other day, "it is obvious that we could go east by going far enough west." That's the sort of thing that puts ideas into taxi-drivers' heads.

Advice is what a person asks for when he wants you to agree with him.

No person who has to ask the price of a mink coat should think of buying one.

Marriage is somewhat like a cafeteria. You look the possibilities over carefully, select what you like best and pay later.

When the average man says he loves greens, he is speaking of a golf course.

A modest pat on the back develops character—if given young enough, often enough and low enough.

It's an ill wind that blows a saxophone.

We have often wondered what it is about windshield glass that makes a pedestrian look like a fly and a forty-ton locomotive like a toy train.

If you win at either love or war, it doesn't mean the expense has ended.

Progress is slow. Four thousand years of civilization and not more than ten good shortstops in the country.

Truth is not only stranger than modern fiction but more decent.

It might be a good idea to put some of our crossword puzzle experts at work on our unsolved crimes.

There is never any traffic congestion on the straight and narrow path.

Nothing helps a person's complexion like putting it to bed before 1:00 A.M.

It pays to be honest even though you may be a long time collecting.

Prizefighting rules now prevail in many European nations. When one side leads with the Right, the other counters with the Left.

If the number of automobiles shows a big increase in the next two or three years, we may have to adopt the lily as our national flower.

Some author is going to make a fortune not in writing a book on building your vocabulary but on giving it a rest.

The income tax payment in June keeps many a bride from getting the thirty gravy bowls or compotes.

Hope springs eternal in the suburban gardener.

Apparently the same persons write the seed catalogs and the resort folders.

The most wonderful thing about a popular song is that it can't last.

Many persons seem to think that when the Declaration of Independence says they are entitled to the pursuit of happiness it means at sixty miles per hour.

A parking place is where you leave your car to have the wheelbase shortened and the trunk caved in.

No matter how many new translations of the Bible come out, the people still sin the same way.

A man is happily married if his wife is boss but doesn't know it.

It's a comfort to know that the wars the world fought in the eleventh and twelfth centuries are paid for.

We often wonder what became of the old eighth-grade copy books with their maxims on economy.

Out in the country, life is what you make it, but in the city it too often is what you make.

Despite what the cartoonists make him look like, Uncle Sam is a gentleman with a very large waste.

Almost all businesses have strikes but not the Internal Revenue Department.

Just because a man passes you with his car is no sign that he isn't behind with his payments.

Famous last words—"Go right ahead, don't let that big truck crowd you off the road."

One improvement we would like to see on automobiles is a device to make the brakes get tight when the driver does.

If you lend a friend ten dollars, you lose either a friend or ten dollars.

We never knew who wrote the descriptions in the seed catalogs until we read *Jack and the Beanstalk*.

Green seems to be the color that gives the eyes the most rest—especially the long green.

What we like about spring is that you can call plain laziness spring fever.

When a politician says that the nation is due for a re-awakening, it means he is running for office.

It's a good thing that Moses didn't have to submit the Ten Commandments to a council of foreign ministers for approval.

We suggest to some enterprising young American who is looking for a business opportunity that he establish a junk shop near an important railroad crossing.

Publishers ought to take the description of promissory notes out of the banking books and put it in the books on international relations.

With 40,000,000 automobiles this is going to be a tough world for a horsefly.

We have sometimes wondered whether those automobile-type trolley cars that can go from one side of the road to the other were meant to catch dodging pedestrians.

Let him who doesn't wish to die yet diet.

The average man knows as much about an atomic bomb as he does about his income tax form.

If a man can remember what he worried about last week, he has a very good memory.

Of the sounds the human ear cannot hear it is a sad fact that none are made by the human tongue.

The poor house is always the last house on Easy Street.

What this country needs is a pair of shoestrings that will last as long as a pair of shoes.

Even chaos has almost become normal now.

What Latin-Americans need is a way to satisfy their longing to be generals without starting revolutions.

If one marries in haste, there is sometimes no leisure for repentance.

For most of us ice skating is a sedentary sport.

The trouble with opportunity is that it generally comes disguised as hard work.

Whenever you get disgusted with a movie, think how utterly idiotic the rejected movie scenarios must be.

The lost chord in the harmony of nations is accord.

The only person we know who beats time is a drum player.

There is a vast difference between realism and reelism in the movies.

A lame duck is never so lame he can't waddle as far as a new government job.

American Indians used to eat pine bark. We still do, only we call it breakfast food.

They say every worm finally turns, but if he does he probably meets either a chicken or a fisherman.

Newspaper advertisement: "Farmhouse, barn and garden for rent. Room to keep animals; suitable for summer boarders." We think we stayed there.

When they award the Pulitzer book prizes for the best definitive biography, we should like to submit our last income tax report.

The millennium will be here when the pedestrians keep inside the traffic safety zones and the automobiles stay outside of them.

A newspaper reported a certain well-known man had no friends except his wife. In Hollywood that wouldn't be a bad showing.

When a man opposes change, he probably has his.

When you try to define a living wage, it depends on whether you are giving or getting it.

The chances are that the American who criticizes India for judging a man by his caste judges his own neighbor by his cash.

There is just a faint possibility that a kangaroo is nature's evolutionary process of developing a safe pedestrian.

An attorney said, "Moses was a great lawgiver. But the way

he was satisfied to keep the Ten Commandments short an' to the point shows he wasn't a regular lawyer."

It's almost reached the point where if a person takes a day off he falls behind in his income tax payments.

What a banker calls unsecured paper, a politician calls an election pledge and a diplomat calls a treaty.

We have often wondered why men lie about each other. The plain truth would be bad enough.

Many a driver runs a dead heat trying to beat a streamliner to a railroad crossing.

An intelligent businessman not only knows how to take advice but also how to reject it.

A street lamp never hits an automobile except in self-defense.

No government ever cuts off an expense that is capable of voting.

If you want to teach history realistically, print a picture of a tax receipt on the front of each book.

The doctors are trying to find out what makes men tall or short. We'll gladly explain why we're short.

Technical progress has been great. But we'll bet on the locomotive against an automobile at a railroad crossing.

There is some relationship between stable government and horse sense.

After you watch the crowd at a hockey game when the referee makes a close decision against the home team, you have some idea of the problem of world peace.

To a young boy there is no such period as "between meals."

For most businessmen success not only brings poise but avoirdupois.

Let's not be unreasonable. People went crazy before there were any double feature movies or singing radio commercials.

Any time you think a college freshman is a dumbbell, we suggest you try a college entrance examination.

Convention speaker: "These are not my own figures I'm quoting. They're the figures of someone who knows what he's talking about."

There's no secret about "Button, button, who's got the button?" The laundries have.

An economist says women are lovely. When economists eliminate theory and get down to fact, they are easier to understand.

We suggest to the ladies of Hollywood that less interest in permanent waves and more interest in permanent wives would be a stimulating example for the rest of the country.

We think the fellow ought to go to the foot of the class who said, "A dog's lungs are the seat of his pants."

A diplomat is a man who knows what it isn't safe to laugh at.

The fellow who saves knows there is nothing like cash down to feather a nest.

The dove of peace after a war brings not only an olive branch in her bill, but an olive branch and the bill.

Washington made the cherry tree popular, but the plum is more common in politics now.

Oil may be a lubricant, but it never is in international affairs.

The greatest general to emerge from any war is General Taxation.

From the size of the tips you have to leave to get any service in a restaurant, you realize the truth of the old saying that all things come to him who waits.

A penny saved is a penny taxed.

Unlike a tree, a salesman who stays rooted to a spot never branches out.

Women wear funny things, but a hard collar isn't one of them.

Sometimes we think the world is growing worse, but it may be that the news and radio coverage is better.

The records of the history of nations are merely scrap books.

Being a senator isn't so difficult. All you have to do is satisfy the farmers, labor unions, businessmen and a few other groups.

The one thing we have never been able to save for a rainy day is an umbrella.

Governments trim their expenditures when there is nothing else left to trim.

The ambitious folks who are always trying to introduce simplified spelling might read some of the papers written by our recent high school graduates.

Most men never get so pessimistic they can't see the bright side of the other fellow's misfortune.

Advertisement: "After 30 washings, how do your undies look?" How do you get undies back from the laundry 30 times?

As a reward in life, popularity is small change.

The trouble with modern civilization is that we so often mistake respectability for character.

The one advantage of a dictatorship over a republic is that you have one particular individual to criticize when things go wrong—that is, if you have the right to criticize.

A successful marriage is one in which two persons learn to get along happily without the things they have no right to expect anyway.

When you are completely satisfied, remember what happens to a fat turkey.

The lines and wrinkles in a person's face are generally trade-marks.

Want ad in a Kansas newspaper: "For sale—a full-blooded cow, giving milk, three tons of hay, a dozen chickens, and four turkeys." What a cow!

The public has the idea that no banker is a yes-man.

Capital and labor should pull together. We don't mean on the public's leg.

At election time political candidates are more candied than candid.

A man doesn't have to live as long as Methuselah to learn there is nothing common about common sense.

When a person has no more illusions, he is suffering from old age.

An ignorant person is one who doesn't know anything

about what you know, and knows things you don't know anything about.

A diplomat leads a terrible life. When he isn't straddling an issue, he is dodging one.

We're inclined to think American wild life isn't disappearing. It's just merging with domestic life.

You can't say much for the average father's skin, but he certainly has a pocketbook they love to touch.

What Lord Macaulay apparently tried to say years ago was that a democracy may be ushered in by a liberty bell and ushered out by the dumbbells.

We wonder whether the University of Chicago includes a passbook in its list of 100 great books.

Judging from our experience we would say that a summer resort is a place where the mosquitoes start work when the flies quit.

The difference between a man and a woman buying a hat is about four hours.

The politician who keeps his ear to the ground may limit his vision.

A magazine featured a story about a Colorado rooster living without his head. What's so unusual about that? All kinds of human beings seem to get along without using their heads.

We have always envied the fellow who can tell whether the violinist in the symphony orchestra is tuning up or playing.

A banker recently caught a sixty-pound fish off the coast of Florida and in describing the feat dislocated both shoulders.

A friend is a person who dislikes the same people you do.

With these modern beauty shops many a young girl is as old as her mother looks.

This generation can fly, talk by wireless radio and harness atomic power. It can do about everything but bring up children.

Millions of Americans may have only the mentality of children. But if you have tried to work your child's arithmetic you may think that's not so bad.

What our engineers should concentrate on is an automobile that will get over a railroad crossing after the gates are down.

Being bald on the outside of one's head is not so bad. What is serious is when the baldness is on the inside.

About the only difference between history and hysteria is the spelling.

It is almost getting so a respectable person is ashamed to carry a modern book.

You can say one thing at least for the United States. It's about the only country where the people don't want to move to another country.

If all the pedestrians were laid end to end, it would greatly simplify the task for some automobile drivers.

We have often wondered what would happen with the numbers if telephone operators worked in shoe stores.

One thing we learn each summer is that what this country needs is a lawn grass that will grow an inch high and quit.

The fellow who puts up the billboards on country roads must have some sense of beauty because he always picks out the best views to obstruct.

A farmer is a fellow who gets up at 5:00 A.M. and hurries through his work by 9:30 P.M. so he can read a farm paper about how to make money by farming more intensively.

Why not arrange loans to European nations so payments would be made to us after each tourist season?

In the old days spirited chargers carried noble knights on their backs. Nowadays spirited chargers run the winter and summer vacation resorts.

The easiest thing for anyone to run into is debt.

When a diplomat comes to the parting of the ways, he goes both ways.

They now say that we will live fifteen years longer than our grandfathers, but they don't say why.

The great trouble in government is that the men who have wisdom enough to run it have wisdom enough to stay away from the job.

After our experience at picnics each summer we still think Noah had more than two ants in the Ark.

American highways are filled with tourists and detourists.

Classical music is music that threatens every other bar to develop a tune and then disappoints you.

The Life of Man—School tablet, aspirin tablet, stone tablet.

The greatest undeveloped resources of any nation are its people.

An egotist is a person of quéstionable taste more interested in himself than in me.

Nothing recedes like success.

If it's a sin to die rich, few businessmen will have to bear that reproach in the future.

A conservative statesman is one who wishes to continue existing evils whereas a liberal wishes to replace them with others.

When some women shop, it looks like they were taking an inventory of the stock.

It is easy to be in favor of government ownership of something that belongs to somebody else.

It has been said that if you take an average group of 100 men, 1 will later become rich, 4 well-to-do, 30 independent, and 65 will be supported by relatives. Apparently, they all will have it easy.

We wonder whether it ever occurred to the archaeologists that some of the deserted cities they have discovered over the world may represent communities where people paid the taxes as long as they could and then moved.

Satisfaction is a state of mind produced when you witness another person's discomfort.

A statesman thinks he belongs to the nation, but a politician thinks the nation belongs to him.

Hunger is an instinct placed in man to make certain that he will work.

Only three things are found in sand—petroleum, gold and spinach.

A prudent man today is one who never asks the waitress what a Salisbury steak is.

If we had had today's taxes a generation ago, the world

would never have heard of a guy named Horatio Alger. His books would now read *From Riches to Rags*.

The best thing you can do for spring fever is absolutely nothing.

A conviction is that commendable quality in ourselves that we call bullheadedness in others.

We understand some savage tribes in Africa pay no taxes. Then what makes them savage?

The fellow who traces his ancestors way back admits he has been descending for centuries.

There may be, as a professor has said, over 10,000 useless words in the dictionary, but a great many come in handy in framing the political platforms.

The difficulty of a cocktail "hour" is that it generally stretches into four or five.

A traffic safety committee has announced most automobile accidents are avoidable. We wish pedestrians were also.

The modern American is a fellow who can answer the $64 question on a radio program but can't tell you the name of his congressman.

Tolerance is the patience shown by a wise man when he listens to an ignoramus.

Political leaders seldom look for the biggest man for the job. Experience has shown them you can win without that kind.

A dentist says it takes over fifty pounds' pressure to chew a steak. What we want to know is where he buys those tender cuts.

It takes the old family album to convince some people that the truth is a terrible thing.

The average American woman is not old at forty. In fact, she isn't even forty.

Newspaper headline: "Farmers to Hear Pest Talk." We believe we have heard the same fellow.

The country is really in bad shape when you think that 160,000,000 people wake up every morning with halitosis, B.O. and athlete's foot.

When a diplomat puts his cards on the table, he still has a deck up each sleeve.

About the only class of downtrodden people America has ever had are those in the aisle seats at the movies.

Mr. Kettering of the Research Department of General Motors wants to know why grass is green and glass is transparent. We would like to know why a fly invariably picks out a bald head on which to land.

The way to avert another war is to have peace long enough now to learn the lessons of the last war.

The test of whether any government can survive is its ability to ring the dinner bell.

What the average woman wants is a great big strong he-man who can be wrapped around her finger.

There is no one so narrow-minded as the fellow who disagrees with you.

Summer is the time when the weather gets too hot to cook and the relatives come to visit you.

The only place a woman's intuition doesn't work is when she is trying to decide which way to turn the car at a corner.

The elephant and the donkey were probably chosen as political party emblems because they are beasts of burden. If a new party is started, a taxpayer might suitably be used as the emblem.

Any earthquake shocks the world may feel in the years ahead will probably not be due to the fact that the nations are settling.

There are some scientists who believe the height of intelligence is reached at sixteen. Well, at that age one generally feels sure of it.

Egotism is a drug that enables some people to live with themselves.

It isn't the $100,000 a mile that a good road costs which is so expensive; it's the wrecked cars and funeral expenses that follow.

Federal aid is simply a system of taking money from the people and making it look like a gift when you hand it back.

Foreign missionaries will be more successful when they

can show civilization to the heathens and not merely tell them about it.

We never could quite understand why children are too young to work under eighteen, but are old enough to drive an $1,800 car seventy miles an hour.

Some of the big guns are silenced when a war ends; others begin work on their memoirs.

There is an old story about an ass being disguised with a lion's skin. Every now and then some college does it with a sheepskin.

Economics Lesson—Even when a debt is canceled, somebody pays it.

An army travels on its stomach, but some individuals travel on their gall.

No politician is ever as bad as he is painted by his enemies or as good as he is whitewashed by his friends.

We wonder if nations experience declining birth rates because the stork is a bird with a big bill.

Americans will have to learn that for every export there must be an import, or we shall continually be sending out relief ships to the world to keep peace.

When a woman demands equal rights, she is simply indulging in flattery.

You can get a government bulletin on almost every subject except curbing government expenditures.

When God made man he didn't arrange the joints of his bones so he could pat himself on the back.

It is reported by scientists that man's jaw has dropped half an inch in several thousand years. That's not so bad when you consider the government budgets he has faced.

The pessimist says, when a diplomat lays his cards on the table it's a good idea to count 'em.

A government bureau often turns out to be a group of people organized to keep the taxpayers worried.

Several million people in this country cannot read or write They devote themselves to writing our popular songs.

The market reports often say, "Hogs are little changed." Well, what is new about that?

A good politician is a fellow who has prejudices enough to suit the needs of all his constituents.

It won't be long now until American tourists will see Europe's poverty and will bring it back with them.

If a man wants to borrow trouble, he never needs collateral.

A wise husband remembers his wife's birthday but forgets which one it is.

Ulcers are said to be the occupational disease of radio announcers. We wonder what affliction is reserved for the news commentators.

The modern city consists of a large number of persons striving to avoid being hit by an automobile.

America may spend more money on chewing gum than on books, but judging from some best sellers that doesn't necessarily mean we have bad judgment.

Sometimes when we look at the headlines, we're not sure the fellow who can't read is missing so much.

A cynic has defined a politician as a man who keeps his ear to the ground and his hand in the taxpayer's pocket.

A false alarm may cost a city fire department $100. In business one costs even more.

Convictions are what an employee has after he knows what the boss thinks.

How far a little scandal throws its beams.

Mud thrown is ground lost.

" 'Too many husbands being shot,' says worried judge" (*Chicago Daily News*). Judge, would you mind telling us just how many would be the right number?

A man who owns a summer cottage on a lake may not have a good time during the summer season, but the chances are dozens of his friends who visit him do.

The bone of contention in most quarrels is generally just a little above the ears of those doing the arguing.

It's not a bad idea for a politician to remember that no newspaper can misquote silence.

In the concert of nations too many nations want to beat the drum and too few want to play second fiddle.

He was the kind of fellow who would rather blow his own horn than listen to the marine band.

The fellow who laughs last may laugh best, but he gets the reputation of being a dumbbell.

Some oldtimer spoke of the political pot boiling. That never happens. The old applesauce is just warmed over.

You can't fool all the people all the time, but that doesn't keep some persons from trying.

We didn't think it would go this far, but our laundry has just sent back some buttons with no shirt on them.

There, little luxury, don't you cry—you'll be a necessity by and by.

The big problem on the average home reading table is to keep those old next month's magazines from cluttering up the place.

You may fear that much of the world is going to destruction. But after you read the tabloids and the confession magazines you don't much care.

If a woman can be a sweetheart, valet, audience, cook and nurse, she is qualified for marriage.

If you want to know how much a man can't remember, call him as a witness to an automobile accident.

Some day a progressive newspaper is going to develop a comic feature for grownups.

Every once in a while you find a police department that seems to work on the theory that if you leave the burglars alone they will soon become rich enough to quit.

The modern teacher believes that spanking misses its aim. If so, the method must be different than it was in the days when we were on the receiving end.

Did you ever meet anyone who said he couldn't sleep last night because of his conscience?

Life is often a battle of the wits, but some folks are unarmed.

This is the day of youth and they can have it. They'll age rapidly when the taxpaying starts.

It often takes a speaker twice as long to tell what he thinks as to tell what he knows.

An Illustration of Financial Illiteracy—The young woman who said the bank had sent back all the checks she used to pay bills with last month and so she hadn't spent a cent.

Wars may come and wars may go, but a politician never forgets the new sources of revenue that are discovered.

First you have to teach a child to talk; then you have to teach it to keep quiet.

An excavating archaeologist at least proves that you can't keep a good man down.

A landlord is a fellow who pays for a house once and then quits. Write your own definition of a renter.

No one thinks faster on his feet than a pedestrian—if he wants to live.

It looks like eventually we will all make our living by collecting taxes from each other.

A radical is a person who feels he might get a little more if he howled a little louder.

The disgusted professor: "Class is dismissed. Please don't flop your ears as you pass out."

The world's worst: Are airmail stamps fly paper?

It's remarkable when you think that under the American system a man can have a savings account and an automobile at the same time.

Intelligence tests may be a means of grading intelligence, but there is nothing that equals a grade crossing for effectiveness.

With the increasing output of new automobiles now, some enterprising manufacturer ought to start making spare parts for pedestrians.

Secret diplomacy is never secret long and seldom diplomatic.

Someone says love is a solvent; but whoever saw a solvent lover?

We can't think of anything so urgent to any man that he can't wait until the train gets past the crossing.

The genius of another world war will be the fellow who figures out how to run it on a cash instead of an accounts-payable basis.

When the average man looks at what he has left after paying his taxes, he realizes social security may have some real meaning for him.

A man who is not in need certainly is a friend.

The higher taxes go, the sharper the voter grinds his ax.

Question for Experts: Is the zebra a white animal with black stripes or a black animal with white stripes?

Why is it that a man will always marry the woman who sweeps him off his feet rather than the one who keeps him on them.

When we look at the price tags on some articles, we don't know whether they represent value or nerve.

He was in his salad days—very particular about his dressing.

Author: "She dropped her eyes and her face fell." Total collapse we'd call it.

The kind of reference book that ought to sell in Hollywood is a "Who's Whose."

We don't wish the folks who have some $100 bills hoarded any bad luck, but we remember once upon a time there were some counterfeits out of this denomination.

Communists seem to labor under the impression that everybody wants to die poor.

In September most of the folks return from the summer resorts for a greatly needed rest.

Many a member of a union has an eight-hour day for himself but sixteen for his wife.

The easiest way to remain poor is to pretend to be rich.

If they ever start making paper suits, we're going to need a little better service from the weather man.

Solomon said, "There is no new thing under the sun," but he didn't say it over a coast-to-coast television network.

A public speaking instructor says, "Not one person in ten thinks on his feet." Why add "on his feet"?

The fellow who says he would go through anything for his girl friend doesn't necessarily mean his bank account.

A politician is a person who keeps the people loyal to him by keeping them angry at someone else.

Someone has said nothing is done as well as it might be done. Well, what about the American taxpayer?

The modern girl has accepted the advertising motto, "Save the surface and you save all."

Never cling to a liberal idea too long unless you want to be called a reactionary five years from now.

Some people are bent with work; others get crooked trying to avoid it.

A conservative is a fellow who thinks a rich man should have a square deal.

When the folks who have something to sell are courteous, it's a buyer's market.

Sometimes a nation abolishes God, but fortunately God is more tolerant.

After listening to some commencement speeches, we gather that the world is in such terrible shape that nothing can save it except the graduating class.

Many caddies become good golfers. Unlike businessmen they never read one of those books on how to play golf.

"Chickens," said the Negro philosopher, "is de usefulest animal dere is. You kin eat 'em fo' dey is born an' after dey is dead."

Some animals can understand but can't talk, whereas it's just the other way with some human beings.

Perhaps we should say that freedom of speech is for those who know the speech of freedom.

From a newspaper: "Henry Jones has bought a cow and will now supply his neighbors with milk and fresh eggs." Apparently an advance model.

Civilization is a slow process of adopting the ideas of minorities.

We think the juvenile problem is not so much one of ruling youngsters with a firm hand as using a firm hand with a ruler.

When the people aren't sure of what they want in democracy, they vote for something different from what they have.

In the future the world will need guns of smaller, and men of larger, caliber.

Supreme Example of Conceit—The father who tries for twenty years to make his child just what he is.

Someone wants to know where the population is most dense. Well, one answer might be—from the neck up.

It's remarkable how large a part ignorance plays in making a man satisfied with himself.

Our idea of Utopia would be a nation in which principles would win the battles with expediency in politics.

There is no assurance that wealthy parents will not make poor parents.

Money may talk, but it doesn't talk as loud as it used to when we pay the bills.

It is never the initial outlay that floors you; it's the running expenses that keep you out of breath.

When a man thinks he is important, he should ask what the world would miss if he were gone.

The inventive genius who first makes a good combination small car and cigarette lighter will make a fortune.

Every time I see a bald-headed man sporting a mustache, I keep wondering whether it is a case of overproduction or just poor distribution.

The only thing wrong with the world is the people.

What we would like is an alarm clock that goes off when we are ready to get up.

A joint checking account is one in which the wife writes the checks and the husband makes the deposits.

Chapter 15

QUOTATIONS FOR MANY OCCASIONS

The toastmaster will frequently find it necessary to refer to the speeches or speechmaking ability of those whom he is called upon to introduce. Consequently, any quotation, epigram or proverb that deals with such subjects as speeches, speechmaking, eloquence, discussions or oratory may on some occasion be helpful to him in preparing an introduction for a speaker. There are included in this chapter a number of short items of this character which the toastmaster may adapt for various uses and various situations. They will help to make introductions more colorful and sparkling.

In addition, the toastmaster may find it very helpful to have quotations, epigrams and proverbs on different occupations and professions. For example, if he is called upon to introduce a businessman, lawyer, teacher or musician, some pertinent quotation may assist him greatly in preparing an introduction that will be interesting and directly to the point. Many quotations of this type are also included in the following pages.

Sometimes a toastmaster will be called upon to introduce young people; at other times some reference may be necessary to those who have reached old age. Quotations have therefore been included on both youth and age. All of the quotations in this chapter are arranged alphabetically by groups such as actors, age, authors, doctors, lawyers, musicians, speeches and speechmaking, teachers, wedding anniversaries and youth. These quotations will also be equally helpful to anyone who is to make a speech.

Actors

An actor is a sculptor who carves in snow.—*Lawrence Barrett.*

The profession of the player, like that of the painter, is one of the imitative arts, whose means are pleasure, and whose end should be virtue.—*Shenstone.*

> Let him who plays the monarch be a king;
> Who plays the rogue, be perfect in his part.
> —*Erskine.*

Actors are the only honest hypocrites. Their life is a voluntary dream; and the height of their ambition is to be beside themselves. They wear the livery of other men's fortunes: their very thoughts are not their own.—*Hazlitt.*

The actor who took the role of King Lear played the king as though he expected someone to play the ace.—*Eugene Field.*

All the world's a stage, and all the men and women in it merely players. They have their exits and their entrances; and one man in his time plays many parts.—*Shakespeare.*

> Our Garrick's a salad; for in him we see
> Oil, vinegar, sugar and saltiness agree.
> —*Goldsmith.*

It is with some violence to the imagination that we conceive of an actor belonging to the relations of private life, so closely do we identify these persons in our mind with the characters they assume upon the stage.—*Lamb.*

> On the stage he was natural, simple, affecting,
> 'Twas only when he was off, he was acting.
> —*Goldsmith.*

At the Academy Award dinners all the actors and actresses in Hollywood gather around to see what someone else thinks about their acting besides their press agents.—*Bob Hope.*

Aside from the moral contamination incident to the average theater, the influence intellectually is degrading. Its lessons are morbid, distorted, and superficial; they do not mirror life.—*T. T. Munger.*

Advertisers

There is too much culture in the advertising business.—*C. F. Kettering.*

The advertising man is a liaison between the products of business and the mind of the nation. He must know both before he can serve either.—*Glenn Frank.*

Advertising is the mouthpiece of business.—*James R. Adams.*

You can tell the ideals of a nation by its advertisements.—*Norman Douglas.*

One-third of the people in the United States promote, while the other two-thirds provide.—*Will Rogers.*

Age

It is not by the gray of the hair that one knows the age of the heart.—*Bulwer.*

A graceful and honorable old age is the childhood of immortality.—*Pindar.*

How beautiful can time with goodness make an old man look.—*Jerrold.*

A person is always startled when he hears himself seriously called old for the first time.—*O. W. Holmes.*

We do not count a man's years until he has nothing else to count.—*Emerson.*

One of the many things nobody ever tells you about middle age is that it's such a nice change from being young.—*Dorothy Canfield Fisher.*

Some fall into their "anecdotage."—*Disraeli.*

Let us respect gray hairs, especially our own.—*J. P. Senn.*

When we are young, we are slavishly employed in producing something whereby we may live comfortably when we grow old; and when we grow old, we perceive it is too late to live as we proposed.—*Pope.*

They say music and women should never be dated.—*Goldsmith.*

To be seventy years young is sometimes far more cheerful and hopeful than to be forty years old.—*O. W. Holmes.*

> The best of friends fall out, and so
> His teeth had done some years ago.
> —*Thomas Hood.*

No wise man ever wished to be younger.—*Swift.*

Years do not make sages; they only make old men.—*Mme. Swetchine.*

Forty is the old age of youth; fifty is the youth of old age.—*Victor Hugo.*

Every one desires to live long, but no one would be old.—*Swift.*

How many fancy they have experience simply because they have grown old.—*Stanislaus.*

Whenever a man's friends begin to compliment him about looking young, he may be sure that they think he is growing old.—*Washington Irving.*

Men of age object too much, consult too long, adventure too little, repent too soon, and seldom drive business home to the full period, but content themselves with a mediocrity of success.—*Bacon.*

As we grow old we become both more foolish and more wise.—*La Rochefoucauld.*

Childhood itself is scarcely more lovely than a cheerful, kindly, sunshiny old age.—*L. M. Child.*

Age is the most terrible misfortune that can happen to any man; other evils will mend, this is every day getting worse.—*George James.*

Old age is a tyrant, which forbids the pleasures of youth on pain of death.—*La Rochefoucauld.*

Architects

Architecture is the printing press of all ages, and gives a history of the state of society in which the structure was erected, from the cromlechs of the Druids to the toyshops of bad taste. The Tower and Westminster Abbey are glorious pages in the history of time, and tell the story of an iron despotism, and of the cowardice of an unlimited power.—*Lady Morgan.*

> Old houses mended,
> Cost little less than new before they're ended.
> —*Colley Cibber.*

The architecture of a nation is great only when it is as universal and established as its language, and when provincial differences are nothing more than so many dialects.—*Ruskin.*

Architecture is frozen music.—*Mme. de Staël.*

Greek architecture is the flowering of geometry.—*Emerson.*

Architecture is a handmaid of devotion. A beautiful church is a sermon in stone, and its spire a finger pointing to heaven. —*Schaff.*

A Gothic church is a petrified religion.—*Coleridge.*

Architecture is the art which so disposes and adorns the edifices raised by man that the sight of them may contribute to his mental health, power, and pleasure.—*Ruskin.*

Artists

True art is reverent imitation of God.—*Tryon Edwards.*

All great art is the expression of man's delight in God's work, not his own.—*Ruskin.*

The highest art is always the most religious, and the greatest artist is always a devout man.—A scoffing Raphael, or an irreverent Michael Angelo, is not conceivable.—*Blaikie.*

Artists are nearest God. Into their souls He breathes His life, and from their hands it comes in fair, articulate forms to bless the world.—*J. G. Holland.*

The little dissatisfaction which every artist feels at the completion of a work forms the germ of a new work.—*Auerbach.*

When a work of art appears to be in advance of its period, it is really the period that has lagged behind the work of art.—*Jean Cocteau.*

A photograph is a portrait painted by the sun.—*Dupins.*

> In the vaunted works of Art,
> The master-stroke is Nature's part.
> —*Emerson.*

Art is the surest and safest civilizer.—*Charles B. Fairbanks.*

A highbrow is the kind of person who looks at a sausage and thinks of Picasso.—*A. P. Herbert.*

Only God Almighty makes painters.—*Sir Godfrey Kneller.*

A room hung with pictures is a room hung with thoughts.—*Joshua Reynolds.*

When love and skill work together, expect a masterpiece.—*Ruskin.*

What garlic is to salad, insanity is to art.—*Homer Saint-Gaudens.*

Every time I paint a portrait I lose a friend.—*John Sargent.*

Painting is silent poetry, and poetry is painting with the gift of speech.—*Simonides.*

To sit for one's portrait is like being present at one's own creation.—*Alexander Smith.*

Every artist writes his own autobiography.—*H. Ellis.*

Nothing can come out of the artist that is not in the man.—*Proverb.*

Astronomers

An undevout astronomer is mad.—*Young.*

The contemplation of celestial things will make a man both speak and think more sublimely and magnificently when he comes down to human affairs.—*Cicero.*

He that looks for a star puts out his candle.—*Proverb.*

> He that strives to touch the stars
> Oft stumbles at a straw.
> —*Spenser.*

Hitch your wagon to a star.—*Emerson.*

Too low they build, who build beneath the stars.—*Young.*

Authors

Clear writers, like clear fountains, do not seem so deep as they are; the turbid seem the most profound.—*Landor.*

No fathers or mothers think their own children ugly; and this self-deceit is yet stronger with respect to the offspring of the mind.—*Cervantes.*

The most original authors are not so because they advance what is new, but because they put what they have to say as if it had never been said before.—*Goethe.*

For people who like that kind of a book—that is the kind of book they will like.—*Lincoln (on being asked for an opinion).*

The chief glory of a country, says Johnson, arises from its authors. But this is only when they are oracles of wisdom. Unless they teach virtue they are more worthy of a halter than of the laurel.—*Jane Porter.*

Next to doing things that deserve to be written, nothing gets a man more credit, or gives him more pleasure than to write things that deserve to be read.—*Chesterfield.*

There are three difficulties in authorship: to write anything worth publishing, to find honest men to publish it, and to get sensible men to read it.—*Colton.*

Talent alone cannot make a writer; there must be a man behind the book.—*Emerson.*

Books are men of higher stature; the only men that speak aloud for future times to hear.—*Barrett.*

Bankers

Neither a borrower nor a lender be; for loan oft loses both itself and friend.—*Shakespeare.*

Put not your trust in money, but put your money in trust.—*O. W. Holmes.*

The use of money is all the advantage there is in having it.—*Franklin.*

If money be not thy servant, it will be thy master.—*Italian Proverb.*

Money and time are the heaviest burdens of life, and the unhappiest of all mortals are those who have more of either than they know how to use.—*Johnson.*

He that wants money, means, and content, is without three good friends.—*Shakespeare.*

He who has no money in his purse, should have honey on his tongue.—*French Proverb.*

Men are seldom more innocently employed than when they are honestly making money.—*Johnson.*

Who steals my purse steals trash.—*Shakespeare.*

No man will take counsel, but every man will take money. Therefore, money is better than counsel.—*Swift.*

A person who can't pay gets another person who can't pay to guarantee that he can pay.—*Dickens.*

However gradual may be the growth of confidence, that of credit requires still more time to arrive at maturity.—*Disraeli.*

The covetous man never has money; the prodigal will have none shortly.—*Ben Jonson.*

Ready money is Aladdin's lamp.—*Byron.*

Money is the life blood of the nation.—*Swift.*

Creditors have better memories than debtors; they are a superstitious sect, great observers of set days and times.—*Franklin.*

Breakfasts, Luncheons and Dinners

For the sake of health, medicines are taken by weight and measure; so ought food to be, or by some similar rule.—*Skelton.*

To eat is human; to digest, divine.—*C. T. Copeland.*

One should eat to live, not live to eat.—*Franklin.*

They are as sick that surfeit with too much, as they that starve with nothing.—*Shakespeare.*

A full belly makes a dull brain.—*Franklin.*

It isn't so much what's on the table that matters, as what's on the chairs.—*W. S. Gilbert.*

At table it becomes no one to be bashful.—*Latin Proverb.*

By suppers more have been killed than Galen ever cured. —*George Herbert.*

When the crowd of your admirers is shouting, "Bravo! Hear, hear!" it is not you, Pomponius, but your dinner that is eloquent.—*Martial.*

Business and Businessmen

In business, three things are necessary, knowledge, temper, and time.—*Feltham.*

The playthings of our elders are called business.—*St. Augustine.*

Business will be either better or worse.—*Calvin Coolidge.*

A man who cannot mind his own business, is not to be trusted with that of the King.—*Saville.*

It is a wise man who knows his own business; and it is a wiser man who thoroughly attends to it.—*H. L. Wayland.*

A business, like an automobile, has to be driven, in order to get results.—*B. C. Forbes.*

Rare almost as great poets, rarer perhaps than veritable saints and martyrs are consummate men of business.—*Helps.*

To business that we love, we rise betime, and go to it with delight.—*Shakespeare.*

No nation was ever ruined by trade.—*Franklin.*

Big business makes its money out of by-products.—*Elbert Hubbard.*

The merchant has no country.—*Jefferson.*

When two men in a business always agree, one of them is unnecessary.—*William Wrigley, Jr.*

The Christian must not only mind heaven, but attend diligently to his daily calling, like the pilot, who, while his eye is fixed on the star, keeps his hand upon the helm.—*T. Watson.*

It is not the crook in modern business that we fear, but the honest man who doesn't know what he is doing.—*Owen D. Young.*

The secret of success in life is for a man to be ready for his opportunity when it comes.—*Disraeli.*

> Seek not for fresher founts afar,
> Just drop your bucket where you are.
> —*S. W. Foss.*

Everyone lives by selling something.—*Proverb.*

Clergymen

The Christian ministry is the worst of all trades, but the best of all professions.—*John Newton.*

"Three things," says Luther, "make a Divine—prayer, meditation, and trials." These make a Christian; but a Christian minister needs three more—talent, application, and acquirements.—*C. Simmons.*

If a minister takes one step into the world, his hearers will take two.—*Cecil.*

The preaching that comes from the soul, most works on the soul.—*Fuller.*

"I have heard many great orators," said Louis XIV to Massillon, "and have been highly pleased with them; but whenever I hear you, I go away displeased with myself." This is the highest encomium that could be bestowed on a preacher.—*C. Simmons.*

It is bad preaching to deaf ears.—*German Proverb.*

The life of a pious minister is visible rhetoric.—*Hooker.*

Men of God have always, from time to time, walked among men, and made their commission felt in the heart and soul of the commonest hearer.—*Emerson.*

Actors speak of things imaginary as if they were real, while you preachers too often speak of things real as if they were imaginary.—*Thomas Betterton.*

Certain thoughts are prayers. There are moments when, whatever be the attitude of the body, the soul is on its knees. —*Victor Hugo.*

Let not him who prays, suffer his tongue to outstrip his heart; nor presume to carry a message to the throne of grace, while that stays behind.—*South.*

I have been driven many times to my knees by the overwhelming conviction that I had nowhere else to go. My own wisdom, and that of all about me, seemed insufficient for the day.—*Abraham Lincoln.*

A prayer in its simplest definition is merely a wish turned Godward.—*Phillips Brooks.*

God's way of answering the Christian's prayer for more patience, experience, hope, and love, often is to put him into the furnace of affliction.—*Cecil.*

It is no use walking anywhere to preach unless we preach as we walk.—*St. Francis of Assisi.*

Our prayers should be for blessings in general, for God knows best what is good for us.—*Socrates.*

Whatsoever we beg of God, let us also work for it.—*Jeremy Taylor.*

He who runs from God in the morning will scarcely find Him the rest of the day.—*Bunyan.*

Trouble and perplexity drive me to prayer, and prayer drives away perplexity and trouble.—*Melanchthon.*

Practice in life whatever you pray for, and God will give it to you more abundantly.—*Pusey.*

Improve your style, monsieur! You have disgusted me with the joys of heaven!—*François de Malherbe.*

The simple heart that freely asks in love, obtains.—*Whittier.*

Death

It is impossible that anything so natural, so necessary, and so universal as death, should ever have been designed by Providence as an evil to mankind.—*Swift.*

We understand death for the first time when he puts his hand upon one whom we love.—*Mme. de Staël.*

Death to a good man is but passing through a dark entry, out of one little dusky room of his father's house, into another that is fair and large, lightsome and glorious, and divinely entertaining.—*Clarke.*

The sole equality on earth is death.—*Philip J. Bailey.*

The gods conceal from men the happiness of death, that they may endure life.—*Lucan.*

Death is the golden key that opens the palace of eternity.—*Milton.*

> Much talking man, in earth thou soon wilt lie;
> Be still, and living think what 'tis to die.
> —*Palladas.*

Be absolute for death. Either death or life shall thereby be the sweeter.—*Shakespeare.*

To neglect, at any time, preparation for death, is to sleep on our post at a siege; to omit it in old age, is to sleep at an attack.—*Johnson.*

Is death the last sleep? No, it is the last and final awakening.—*Walter Scott.*

> ... death,
> The undiscover'd country, from whose bourn
> No traveller returns.
>
> —*Shakespeare.*

Cullen, in his last moments, whispered, "I wish I had the power of writing or speaking, for then I would describe to you how pleasant a thing it is to die."—*Derby.*

The darkness of death is like the evening twilight; it makes all objects appear more lovely to the dying.—*Richter.*

Death is the liberator of him whom freedom cannot release; the physician of him whom medicine cannot cure; the comforter of him whom time cannot console.—*Colton.*

Diplomats

An ambassador is an honest man sent to lie and intrigue abroad for the benefit of his country.—*Sir H. Wotton.*

A court is an assemblage of noble and distinguished beggars.—*Talleyrand.*

Falsehood and dissimulation are certainly to be found at courts; but where are they not to be found? Cottages have them, as well as courts, only with worse manners.—*Chesterfield.*

The court is a golden but fatal circle, upon whose magic skirts a thousand devils sit tempting innocence, and beckon early virtue from its center.—*N. Lee.*

The two maxims of any great man at court are, always to keep his countenance and never to keep his word.—*Swift.*

The court is like a palace built of marble—made up of very hard, and very polished materials.—*La Bruyère.*

The chief requisites for a courtier are a flexible conscience and an inflexible politeness.—*Lady Blessington.*

See how he sets his countenance for deceit, and promises a lie before he speaks.—*Dryden.*

International arbitration may be defined as the substitution of many burning questions for a smouldering one.—*Ambrose Bierce.*

> Diplomacy is to do and say
> The nastiest thing in the nicest way.
> —*Isaac Goldberg*

Men, like bullets, go farthest when they are smoothest.—*J. P. Richter.*

Ambassadors are the eye and ear of the state.—*Italian Proverb.*

Doctors

The building of a perfect body crowned by a perfect brain, is at once the greatest earthly problem and grandest hope of the race.—*Dio Lewis.*

Half the spiritual difficulties that men and women suffer arise from a morbid state of health.—*H. W. Beecher.*

> . . . physicians mend or end us,
> *Secundum artem:* but although we sneer
> In health—when ill, we call them to attend us,
> Without the least propensity to jeer.
> —*Byron*

Dyspepsia is the remorse of a guilty stomach.—*A. Kerr.*

Happy the doctor who is called in at the end of the disease.—*French Proverb.*

A good surgeon operates with his hand, not with his heart. —*Dumas.*

Every doctor thinks his pills the best.—*German Proverb.*

The only way for a rich man to be healthy is by exercise and abstinence, to live as if he were poor.—*Sir W. Temple.*

With stupidity and sound digestion man may fret much; but what in these dull unimaginative days are the terrors of conscience to the diseases of the liver.—*Carlyle.*

It's no trifle at her time of life to part with a doctor who knows her constitution.—*George Eliot.*

From the physician and lawyer keep not the truth hidden. —*Italian Proverb.*

People who are always taking care of their health are like misers, who are hoarding up a treasure which they have never spirit enough to enjoy.—*Sterne.*

Farmers

Let the farmer forevermore be honored in his calling, for they who labor in the earth are the chosen people of God.— *Jefferson.*

Agriculture, for an honorable and high-minded man, is the best of all occupations or arts by which men procure the means of living.—*Xenophon.*

Trade increases the wealth and glory of a country; but its real strength and stamina are to be looked for among the cultivators of the land.—*Lord Chatham.*

The farmers are the founders of civilization and prosperity. —*Daniel Webster.*

He that would look with contempt on the pursuits of the farmer, is not worthy the name of a man.—*H. W. Beecher.*

Tools were made, and born were hands,
Every farmer understands.

—*Blake.*

Whoever makes two ears of corn, or two blades of grass,
to grow where only one grew before, deserves better of mankind, and does more essential service to his country, than the
whole race of politicians put together.—*Swift.*

We may talk as we please of lilies, and lions rampant, and
spread eagles in fields of *d'or* or *d'argent,* but if heraldry were
guided by reason, a plough in the field arable would be the
most noble and ancient arms.—*Cowley.*

Farmers fatten most when famine reigns.—*Proverb.*

To plow is to pray—to plant is to prophesy.—*Proverb.*

Florists

What a desolate place would be a world without flowers!
It would be a face without a smile; a feast without a welcome. Are not flowers the stars of the earth? And are not our
stars the flowers of heaven?—*Mrs. Balfour.*

To me the meanest flower that blows can give thoughts
that do often lie too deep for tears.—*Wordsworth.*

What a pity flowers can utter no sound! A singing rose, a
whispering violet, a murmuring honeysuckle—oh, what a rare
and exquisite miracle would these be!—*H. W. Beecher.*

The flowers are nature's jewels, with whose wealth she
decks her summer beauty.—*Croly.*

The instinctive and universal taste of mankind selects flowers for the expression of its finest sympathies, their beauty
and fleetingness serving to make them the most fitting sym-
bols of those delicate sentiments for which language seems
almost too gross a medium.—*Hillard.*

Flowers are love's truest language.—*P. Benjamin.*

To analyze the charms of flowers is like dissecting music; it is one of those things which it is far better to enjoy, than to attempt fully to understand.—*Tuckerman.*

Fourth of July

We hold these truths to be self-evident, that all men are created equal, that they are endowed by their Creator with certain inalienable Rights, that among these are Life, Liberty, and the pursuit of Happiness.—*Jefferson.*

Is life so dear, or peace so sweet, as to be purchased at the price of chains and slavery? Forbid it, Almighty God! I know not what course others may take, but as for me, give me liberty, or give me death!—*Patrick Henry.*

There is no liberty worth anything which is not a liberty under law.—*N. J. Burton.*

Freedom is not worth having if it does not connote freedom to err.—*Mahatma Gandhi.*

Liberty has restraints but no frontiers.—*Lloyd George.*

Personal liberty is the paramount essential to human dignity and human happiness.—*Bulwer.*

Give me the liberty to know, to think, to believe, and to utter freely, according to conscience, above all other liberties. —*Milton.*

Easier were it to hurl the rooted mountain from its base, than force the yoke of slavery upon men determined to be free.—*Southey.*

No free government, or the blessings of liberty can be preserved to any people but by a firm adherence to justice, moderation, temperance, frugality, and virtue, and by a frequent recurrence to fundamental principles.—*Patrick Henry.*

Personal liberty is the right to act without interference within the limits of the law.—*J. Oerter.*

Safe popular freedom consists of four things, the diffusion of liberty, of intelligence, of property, and of conscientiousness, and cannot be compounded of any three out of the four. —*Joseph Cook.*

Christianity is the companion of liberty in all its conflicts, the cradle of its infancy, and the divine source of its claims.—*Tocqueville.*

Where the press is free, and every man able to read, all is safe.—*Jefferson.*

Liberty is the right to do what the laws allow; and if a citizen could do what they forbid, it would no longer be liberty, because others would have the same powers?

A nation may lose its liberties in a day, and not miss them in a century.—*Montesquieu.*

Liberty will not descend to a people; a people must raise themselves to liberty; it is a blessing that must be earned before it can be enjoyed.—*Colton.*

Liberty may make mistakes but tyranny is the death of a nation.—*Matteotti.*

Where liberty dwells, there is my country.—*Milton.*

A country cannot subsist well without liberty, nor liberty without virtue.—*Rousseau.*

The human race is in the best condition when it has the greatest degree of liberty.—*Dante.*

Liberty and union, one and inseparable, now and forever. —*Daniel Webster.*

A Bible and a newspaper in every house, a good school in every district—all studied and appreciated as they merit— are the principal support of virtue, morality, and civil liberty. —*Franklin.*

Historians

History is philosophy teaching by example, and also by warning; its two eyes are geography and chronology.—*Dionysius*.

History is but the unrolled scroll of prophecy.—*Garfield*.

History is a voice forever sounding across the centuries the laws of right and wrong. Opinions alter, manners change, creeds rise and fall, but the moral law is written on the tablets of eternity.—*Froude*.

Sin writes histories, goodness is silent.—*Goethe*.

History is little more than the register of the crimes, follies, and misfortunes of mankind.—*Gibbon*.

History is but a kind of Newgate calendar, a register of the crimes and miseries that man has inflicted on his fellow man.—*Washington Irving*.

All the historical books which contain no lies are extremely tedious.—*Anatole France*.

We read history through our prejudices.—*Wendell Phillips*.

What is history but a fable agreed upon?—*Napoleon*.

What are all histories but God manifesting himself, shaking down and trampling under foot whatsoever he hath not planted.—*Cromwell*.

History is neither more nor less than biography on a large scale.—*Lamartine*.

It is not deeds or acts that last: it is the written record of those deeds and acts.—*Elbert Hubbard*.

The best thing which we derive from history is the enthusiasm that it raises in us.—*Goethe*.

If men could learn from history, what lessons it might teach us! But passion and party blind our eyes, and the light which experience gives is a lantern on the stern which shines only on the waves behind us.—*Coleridge.*

History is merely gossip.—*Oscar Wilde.*

The men who make history have not time to write it.—*Metternich.*

History makes us some amends for the shortness of life.—*Skelton.*

The impartiality of history is not that of the mirror, which merely reflects objects, but of the judge who sees, listens, and decides.—*Lamartine.*

Out of monuments, names, words, proverbs, traditions, private records and evidences, fragments of stories, passages of books, and the like, we do save and recover somewhat from the deluge of time.—*Bacon.*

Housewives—Wives

Nothing lovelier can be found in woman than to study household good, and good works in her husband to promote. —*Milton.*

She was a woman of a stirring life, whose heart was in her house; two wheels she had . . . this large, for spinning wool, that small, for flax; and if one wheel had rest, it was because the other was at work.—*Wordsworth.*

A house is no house unless it contain food and fire for the mind as well as for the body.—*Margaret Fuller.*

A hundred men may make an encampment, but it takes a woman to make a home.—*Chinese Proverb.*

The strength of a nation, especially of a republican nation, is in the intelligent and well-ordered homes of the people.—*Mrs. Sigourney.*

Try praising your wife, even if it does frighten her at first. —*Billy Sunday.*

The fingers of the housewife do more than a yoke of oxen. —*German Proverb.*

The homes of a nation are the bulwarks of personal and national safety and thrift.—*J. G. Holland.*

Her pleasures are in the happiness of her family.—*Rousseau.*

A wife is essential to great longevity; she is the receptacle of half a man's cares, and two-thirds of his ill-humor.— *Charles Reade.*

An ideal wife is any woman who has an ideal husband.— *Booth Tarkington.*

The sum of all that makes a just man happy consists in the well choosing of his wife.—*Massinger.*

The way to fight a woman is with your hat. Grab it and run.—*John Barrymore.*

The three virtues of a woman: Obey the father, obey the husband, obey the son.—*Chinese Proverb.*

Kind words and few are a woman's ornament.—*Danish Proverb.*

No man can live piously or die righteously without a wife. —*Richter.*

Woman would be more charming if one could fall into her arms without falling into her hands.—*Ambrose Bierce.*

A woman who looks much in the glass spins but little.— *French Proverb.*

Women have more strength in their looks, than we have in our laws; and more power by their tears, than we have by our arguments.—*Saville.*

A handsome woman is always right.—*German Proverb.*

Silence gives grace to a woman.—*Sophocles.*

I'm not denying the women are foolish: God Almighty made 'em to match the men.—*George Eliot.*

Journalists

Great is journalism. Is not every able editor a ruler of the world, being the persuader of it?—*Carlyle.*

Get your facts first, and then you can distort 'em as you please.—*Mark Twain.*

Burke said there were Three Estates in Parliament; but, in the Reporters' Gallery yonder, there sat a fourth estate more important far than they all.—*Carlyle.*

We live under a government of men and morning newspapers.—*Wendell Phillips.*

I fear three newspapers more than a hundred thousand bayonets.—*Napoleon.*

A newspaper is the history for one day of the world in which we live, and with which we are consequently more concerned than with those which have passed away, and exist only in remembrance.—*Bishop Horne.*

A newspaper should be the maximum of information, and the minimum of comment.—*Cobden.*

Newspapers are the schoolmasters of the common people— a greater treasure to them than uncounted millions of gold.— *H. W. Beecher.*

Journalism is organized gossip.—*Edward Eggleston.*

In these times we fight for ideas, and newspapers are our fortresses.—*Heine.*

The newspaper press is the people's university. Half the readers of Christendom read little else.—*J. Parton.*

Do not read newspapers column by column; remember they are made for everybody, and don't try to get what isn't meant for you.—*Emerson.*

Let it be impressed upon your minds, let it be instilled into your children, that the liberty of the press is the palladium of all the civil, political, and religious rights.—*Junius.*

The most truthful part of a newspaper is the advertisements.—*Jefferson.*

Judges

To be perfectly just is an attribute of the divine nature; to be so to the utmost of our abilities is the glory of man.—*Addison.*

Judges ought to be more learned than witty, more reverent than plausible, and more advised than confident. Above all things, integrity is their portion and proper virtue.—*Bacon.*

> Justice while she winks at crimes,
> Stumbles on innocence sometimes.
> —*Samuel Butler.*

If judges would make their decisions just, they should behold neither plaintiff, defendant, nor pleader, but only the cause itself.—*B. Livingston.*

Justice is truth in action.—*Disraeli.*

Justice discards party, friendship, and kindred, and is therefore represented as blind.—*Addison.*

One man's word is no man's word; we should quietly hear both sides.—*Goethe.*

Justice is the constant desire and effort to render to every man his due.—*Justinian.*

Justice is itself the great standing policy of civil society; and any departure from it, under any circumstance, lies under the suspicion of being no policy at all.—*Burke.*

A just man is not one who does no ill,
But he who, with the power, has not the will.
—*Philemon.*

Justice without wisdom is impossible.—*Froude.*

How can a people be free that has not learned to be just?
—*Sieyès.*

Justice is the great and simple principle which is the secret of success in all government, as essential to the training of an infant, as to the control of a mighty nation.—*Simms.*

Labor

Next to faith in God, is faith in labor.—*Bovee.*

Labor is the divine law of our existence; repose is desertion and suicide.—*Mazzini.*

Industry cannot flourish if labor languish.—*Calvin Coolidge.*

There is a perennial nobleness and even sacredness in work. Were he ever so benighted and forgetful of his high calling, there is always hope in a man who actually and earnestly works.—*Carlyle.*

Labor disgraces no man; unfortunately you occasionally find men disgrace labor.—*Ulysses S. Grant.*

Blessed is he who has found his work; let him ask no other blessedness.—*Carlyle.*

Labor is life; from the inmost heart of the worker rises his God-given force, the sacred celestial life-essence breathed into him by Almighty God!—*Carlyle.*

Toil, says the proverb, is the sire of fame.—*Euripides.*

Work is the meat of life, pleasure the dessert.—*B. C. Forbes.*

The workman still is greater than his work.—*Menander.*

It is to labor, and to labor only, that man owes everything of exchangeable value. Labor is the talisman that has raised him from the condition of the savage; that has changed the desert and the forest into cultivated fields; that has covered the earth with cities, and the ocean with ships; that has given us plenty, comfort, and elegance, instead of want, misery, and barbarism.—*J. Macculloch.*

Lawyers

No man can be a sound lawyer who is not well read in the laws of Moses.—*Fisher Ames.*

The law is the last result of human wisdom acting upon human experience for the benefit of the public.—*Johnson.*

Accuracy and diligence are much more necessary to a lawyer than great comprehension of mind, or brilliancy of talent. His business is to refine, define, split hairs, look into authorities, and compare cases. A man can never gallop over the fields of law on Pegasus, nor fly across them on the wing of oratory. If he would stand on *terra firma,* he must descend. If he would be a great lawyer, he must first consent to become a great drudge.—*Daniel Webster.*

As well open an oyster without a knife, as a lawyer's mouth without a fee.—*Proverb.*

He that is his own lawyer has a fool for his client.—*Proverb.*

If there were no bad people there would be no good lawyers.—*Proverb.*

Agree, for the law is costly.—*Proverb.*

Librarians

Libraries are as the shrines where all the relics of saints, full of true virtue, and that without delusion or imposture, are preserved and reposed.—*Bacon.*

> Through and through the inspired leaves,
> Ye maggots make your windings;
> But, oh, respect his lordship's taste,
> And spare the golden bindings!
> 　　　　　　　　　*—Burns.*

Libraries are the wardrobes of literature, whence men, properly informed, may bring forth something for ornament, much for curiosity, and more for use.—*Dyer.*

There are books of which the backs and covers are by far the best parts.—*Dickens.*

My library was dukedom large enough.—*Shakespeare.*

I would define a book as a work of magic whence escape all kinds of images to trouble the souls and change the hearts of men.—*Anatole France.*

> Camerado, this is no book,
> Who touches this touches a man.
> 　　　　　　　　　*—Whitman.*

Consider what you have in the smallest chosen library. A company of the wisest and wittiest men that could be picked out of all civil countries, in a thousand years, have set in best order the results of their learning and wisdom. The men themselves were hid and inaccessible, solitary, impatient of interruption, fenced by etiquette; but the thought which they did not uncover to their bosom friend is here written out in transparent words to us, the strangers of another age.—*Emerson.*

A great library contains the diary of the human race. The great consulting room of a wise man is a library.—*G. Dawson.*

Men—Husbands

Men are but children, too, though they have gray hairs; they are only of a larger size.—*Seneca.*

But, oh! ye lords of ladies intellectual,
Inform us truly—have they not henpeck'd you all?
—*Byron.*

The real difference between men is energy. A strong will, a settled purpose, an invincible determination, can accomplish almost anything; and in this lies the distinction between great men and little men.—*Fuller.*

A husband is always a sensible man; he never thinks of marrying.—*Dumas.*

All great men are in some degree inspired.—*Cicero.*

A master of a house, as I have read,
Must be the first man up, and the last in bed.
—*Robert Herrick.*

A man's ledger does not tell what he is, or what he is worth. Count what is *in* man, not what is *on* him, if you would know what he *is* worth—whether rich or poor.—*H. W. Beecher.*

The only time that most women give their orating husbands undivided attention is when the old boys mumble in their sleep.—*Wilson Mizner.*

Men, in general, are but great children.—*Napoleon.*

Man is an animal that cooks his victuals.—*Burke.*

Man is to man all kinds of beasts; a fawning dog, a roaring lion, a thieving fox, a robbing wolf, a dissembling crocodile, a treacherous decoy, and a rapacious vulture.—*Cowley.*

An institution is the lengthened shadow of one man.—*Emerson.*

It is not what he has, or even what he does which expresses the worth of a man, but what he is.—*Amiel.*

Man is an animal that makes bargains; no other animal does this—one dog does not change a bone with another.—*Adam Smith.*

Man is a reasoning rather than a reasonable animal.—
Alexander Hamilton.

The record of life runs thus: Man creeps into childhood,
bounds into youth, sobers into manhood, softens into age,
totters into second childhood, and slumbers into the cradle
prepared for him—thence to be watched and cared for.—
Henry Giles.

There is no fact more observable in literature than how
many beautiful things have been said about man in the ab-
stract, and how few about men in particular.—*Mme. l'Estrange.*

In my youth I thought of writing a satire on mankind; but
now in my age I think I should write an apology for them.—
Walpole.

Man is but a reed, the weakest in nature, but he is a thinking reed.—*Pascal.*

Man at his birth is content with a little milk and a piece of
flannel: so we begin, that presently find kingdoms not enough
for us.—*Seneca.*

Show me the man you honor, and I will show you what
kind of a man you are, for it shows me what your ideal of
manhood is, and what kind of a man you long to be.—*Carlyle.*

Musicians

There is something marvelous in music. I might almost say
it is, in itself, a marvel. Its position is somewhere between
the region of thought and that of phenomena; a glimmering
medium between mind and matter, related to both and yet
differing from either. Spiritual, and yet requiring rhythm;
material, and yet independent of space.—*H. Heine.*

> Swans sing before they die; 'twere no bad thing
> Should certain persons die before they sing.
> —*Coleridge.*

All musical people seem to be happy; it is to them the engrossing pursuit; almost the only innocent and unpunished passion.—*Sydney Smith.*

Music can noble hints impart, engender fury, kindle love, with unsuspected eloquence can move and manage all the man with secret art.—*Addison.*

The man that hath no music in himself, nor is not moved with concord of sweet sounds, is fit for treasons, stratagems, and spoils; . . . let no such man be trusted.—*Shakespeare.*

Music is the fourth great material want of our nature—first food, then raiment, then shelter, then music.—*Bovee.*

> And music pours on mortals
> Her magnificent disdain.
> —*Emerson.*

Music is the art of the prophets, the only art that can calm the agitations of the soul; it is one of the most magnificent and delightful presents God has given us.—*Luther.*

Music is the only language in which you cannot say a mean or sarcastic thing.—*John Erskine.*

Music, of all the liberal arts, has the greatest influence over the passions, and is that to which the legislator ought to give the greatest encouragement.—*Napoleon.*

Next to theology I give to music the highest place and honor. And we see how David and all the saints have wrought their godly thoughts into verse, rhyme, and song.—*Luther.*

> A squeak's heard in the orchestra,
> The leader draws across
> The intestines of the agile cat
> The tail of the noble hoss.
> —*Lanigan.*

We love music for the buried hopes, the garnered memories, the tender feelings it can summon at a touch.—*L. E. Landon.*

Music washes away from the soul the dust of every-day life.—*Auerbach.*

Naturalists

This is the forest primeval. The murmuring pines and the hemlocks, bearded with moss and in garments green, indistinct in the twilight, stand like Druids of eld, with voices sad and prophetic, stand like harpers hoar, with beards that rest on their bosoms.—*Longfellow.*

> I think that I shall never see
> A poem lovely as a tree.
>
> . . . .
>
> Poems are made by fools like me,
> But only God can make a tree.
> —*Joyce Kilmer.*

Nature is the art of God.—*Sir Thomas Browne.*

The groves were God's first temples. Ere man learned to hew the shaft, and lay the architrave, and spread the roof above them—ere he framed the lofty vault, to gather and roll back the sound of anthems; in the darkling wood, amidst the cool and silence, he knelt down and offered to the Mightiest solemn thanks and supplication.—*Bryant.*

Drive away nature, it comes back apace.—*French Proverb.*

We talk of our mastery of Nature, which sounds very grand; but the fact is we respectfully adapt ourselves, first, to her ways.—*Clarence Day.*

Study Nature as the countenance of God.—*Charles Kingsley.*

Nature does not proceed by leaps.—*Latin Proverb*.

Nature is the time-vesture of God that reveals him to the wise, and hides him from the foolish.—*Carlyle*.

Nature does nothing in vain.—*Latin Proverb*.

Philosophers

To be a philosopher is not merely to have subtle thoughts; but so to love wisdom as to live according to its dictates.—*Thoreau*.

To be a husbandman, is but a retreat from the city; to be a philosopher, from the world; or rather a retreat from the world as it is man's, into the world as it is God's.—*Cowley*.

True philosophy invents nothing; it merely establishes and describes what is.—*Cousin*.

There are more things in heaven and earth, Horatio,
Than are dreamt of in your philosophy.
                                        —*Shakespeare*.

Philosophy did not find Plato already a nobleman, it made him one.—*Seneca*.

The discovery of what is true, and the practice of that which is good, are the two most important objects of philosophy.—*Voltaire*.

To philosophize in a just sense, is but to carry good breeding a step higher. For the accomplishment of breeding is, to learn what is decent in company or beautiful in arts; and the sum of philosophy is to learn what is just in society, and beautiful in nature and the order of the world.—*Shaftesbury*.

Philosophy is the art of living.—*Plutarch*.

Philosophy consists not in airy schemes or idle speculations; the rule and conduct of all social life is her great province.—*Thomson*.

Adversity's sweet milk, philosophy.—*Shakespeare.*

Philosophy is the science which considers truth.—*Aristotle.*

A man gazing on the stars is proverbially at the mercy of the puddles on the road.—*Alexander Smith.*

The idea of philosophy is truth; the idea of religion is life. —*Peter Bayne.*

To study philosophy is nothing but to prepare oneself to die.—*Cicero.*

Philosophy does the going, and wisdom is the goal.—*Latin Proverb.*

The first business of a philosopher is, to part with self-conceit.—*Epictetus.*

Philosophy, when superficially studied, excites doubt; when thoroughly explored, it dispels it.—*Bacon.*

Poets

Poetry is the art of substantiating shadows, and of lending existence to nothing.—*Burke.*

Poetry is music in words: and music is poetry in sound: both excellent sauce, but those have lived and died poor who made them their meat.—*Fuller.*

Words become luminous when the poet's finger has passed over them its phosphorescence.—*Joubert.*

A poet must needs be before his own age, to be even with posterity.—*J. R. Lowell.*

Sad is his lot who, once at least in his life, has not been a poet.—*Lamàrtine.*

By poetry we mean the art of employing words in such a manner as to produce an illusion on the imagination; the art of doing by means of words, what the painter does by means of colors.—*Macauley.*

Poetry is truth in its Sunday clothes.—*French Proverb*.

> Sir, I admit your general rule,
> That every poet is a fool;
> But you yourself may serve to show it,
> That every fool is not a poet.
>
> —*Pope.*

> Would you have your songs endure?
> Build on the human heart.
>
> —*Browning.*

Politicians and Statesmen

If ever this free people—if this government itself is ever utterly demoralized, it will come from this incessant human wriggle and struggle for office, which is but a way to live without work.—*Abraham Lincoln.*

When connected with morality and the character and interest of a country, politics is a subject second only to religion in importance—*Charles Hodge.*

Nothing is politically right which is morally wrong.—*Daniel O'Connell.*

How little do politics affect the life, the moral life of a nation. One single good book influences the people a vast deal more.—*Gladstone.*

An honest politician is one who, when he is bought, will stay bought.—*Simon Cameron.*

Responsibility educates, and politics is but another name for God's way of teaching the masses ethics, under the responsibility of great present interests.—*Wendell Phillips.*

There is an infinity of political errors which, being once adopted, become principles.—*Abbé Raynal.*

All political parties die at last by swallowing their own lies.—*Arbuthnot.*

To be a chemist you must study chemistry; to be a lawyer or a physician you must study law or medicine; but to be a politician you need only to study your own interests.—*Max O'Rell.*

Any party which takes credit for the rain must not be surprised if its opponents blame it for the drought.—*Morrow.*

People vote their resentment, not their appreciation. The average man does not vote for anything, but against something.—*Munro.*

I hate all bungling as I do sin, but particularly bungling in politics, which leads to the misery and ruin of many thousands and millions of people.—*Goethe.*

All politics is apple sauce.—*Will Rogers.*

Politics is the science of exigencies.—*Theodore Parker.*

Politics—a rotten egg; if broken open, it stinks.—*Russian Proverb.*

Every political question is becoming a social question, and every social question is becoming a religious question.—*R. T. Ely.*

A politician thinks of the next election; a statesman of the next generation. A politician looks for the success of his party; a statesman for that of his country. The statesman wishes to steer, while the politician is satisfied to drift.—*J. F. Clarke.*

In politics, merit is rewarded by the possessor being raised, like a target, to a position to be fired at.—*Bovee.*

Republics end through luxury; monarchies through poverty. —*Montesquieu.*

True statesmanship is the art of changing a nation from what it is into what it ought to be.—*W. R. Alger.*

> How a minority,
> Reaching majority,
> Seizing authority,
> Hates a minority.
> —*L. H. Robbins.*

The three great ends for a statesman are: security to possessors, facility to acquirers, and liberty and hope to the people.—*Coleridge.*

Scholars

The criterion of a scholar's utility is the number and value of the truths he has circulated, and the minds he has awakened.—*Coleridge.*

One wise man's verdict outweighs all the fools'.—*Browning.*

A man doesn't begin to attain wisdom until he recognizes that he is no longer indispensable.—*Admiral Byrd.*

The scholar who cherishes the love of comfort is not fit to be deemed a scholar.—*Confucius.*

If common sense has not the brilliancy of the sun, it has the fixity of the stars.—*Caballero.*

The more we study, the more we discover our ignorance. —*Shelley.*

> Defer not till tomorrow to be wise,
> Tomorrow's sun to thee may never rise.
> —*Congreve.*

Impatience of study is the mental disease of the present generation.—*Johnson.*

> Knowledge is proud that he has learn'd so much;
> Wisdom is humble that he knows no more.
> —*Cowper.*

When God lets loose a great thinker on this planet, then all things are at risk. There is not a piece of science, but its flank may be turned tomorrow; nor any literary reputation, nor the so-called eternal names of fame, that may not be revised and condemned.—*Emerson.*

Scientists

The highest reach of human science is the recognition of human ignorance.—*Sir W. Hamilton.*

Science is nothing but perception.—*Plato.*

Science ever has been, and ever must be, the safeguard of religion.—*Sir David Brewster.*

Don't hesitate to be as revolutionary as science. Don't hesitate to be as reactionary as the multiplication table.—*Calvin Coolidge.*

> Nature and Nature's Laws lay hid in Night:
> God said, Let Newton be! and all was Light.
> —*Pope on Newton.*

The person who thinks there can be any real conflict between science and religion must be either very young in science or very ignorant in religion.—*Professor Henry.*

The study of science teaches young men to think, while study of the classics teaches them to express thought.—*J. S. Mill.*

Speeches and Speechmaking

Speech is a faculty given to man to conceal his thoughts. —*Talleyrand.*

Take care of the sense and the sounds will take care of themselves.—*Lewis Carroll.*

Speeches cannot be made long enough for the speakers, nor short enough for the hearers.—*Perry.*

There is no eloquence without a man behind it.—*Emerson.*

One may think what he dare not speak.—*Proverb.*

Rhetoric is nothing but reason well dressed, and argument put in order.—*Jeremy Collier.*

Speak and speed: the close mouth catches no flies.—*Proverb.*

Sheridan once said of some speech, in his acute, sarcastic way, that "it contained a great deal both of what was new and what was true; but that what was new was not true, and what was true was not new."—*Hazlitt.*

A good talker or writer is only a pitcher. Unless his audience catches him with heart and mind he's defeated.—*Wilson Mizner.*

There are three things that ought to be considered before some things are spoken—the manner, the place, and the time. —*Southey.*

Speaking without thinking is shooting without aiming. —*Proverb.*

A printed speech is like a dried flower: the substance, indeed, is there, but the color is faded and the perfume gone. —*Lorain.*

Young man, thy words are like the cypress, tall and large, but they bear no fruit.—*Phocion.*

A man's character is revealed by his speech.—*Proverb.*

Never rise to speak till you have something to say; and when you have said it, cease.—*Witherspoon.*

Gentlemen, you have just been listening to that Chinese sage, On Too Long.—*Will Rogers.*

Many a man's tongue shakes out his master's undoing.
—*Proverb.*

What a spendthrift he is of his tongue.
                                —*Shakespeare.*

What is an epigram? a dwarfish whole,
Its body brevity, and wit its soul.
                                —*Coleridge.*

We often say things because we can say them well, rather than because they are sound and reasonable.—*Landor.*

He is a good orator who convinces himself.—*Proverb.*

An epigram is but a feeble thing
With straw in tail, stuck there by way of sting.
                                —*Cowper.*

. . . out of the abundance of the heart the mouth speaketh. —*Matthew 12:34.*

Men are never so likely to settle a question rightly, as when they discuss it freely.—*Macaulay.*

He misses what is meant by epigram
Who thinks it only frivolous flim-flam.
                                —*Martial.*

An epigram is a half-truth so stated as to irritate the person who believes the other half.—*Matthews.*

Where judgment has wit to express it, there is the best orator.—*Penn.*

Everyone is eloquent in his own cause.—*Proverb.*

He that hath ears to hear, let him hear.—*Mark 4:9.*

He is the eloquent man who can treat subjects of an humble nature with delicacy, lofty things impressively, and moderate things temperately.—*Cicero.*

It is the first rule in oratory that a man must appear such as he would persuade others to be; and that can be accomplished only by the force of his life.—*Swift.*

He is eloquent enough for whom truth speaks.—*Proverb*.

What too many orators want in depth, they give you in length.—*Montesquieu*.

There is no power like that of true oratory. Caesar controlled men by exciting their fears; Cicero, by captivating their affections and swaying their passions. The influence of the one perished with its author; that of the other continues to this day.—*Henry Clay*.

In oratory, the greatest art is to conceal art.—*Swift*.

An epigram often flashes light into regions where reason shines but dimly.—*E. P. Whipple*.

An orator without judgment is a horse without a bridle. —*Theophrastus*.

Orators are most vehement when they have the weakest cause, as men get on horseback when they cannot walk. —*Cicero*.

The effective public speaker receives from his audience in vapor, what he pours back on them in a flood.—*Gladstone*.

Eloquence is vehement simplicity.—*Cecil*.

It is the heart which makes men eloquent.—*Proverb*.

An orator or author is never successful till he has learned to make his words smaller than his ideas.—*Emerson*.

Success—Fame—Reputation

Success is full of promise till men get it, and then it is as a last year's nest, from which the bird has flown.—*H. W. Beecher*.

Every man who is high up loves to think that he has done it all himself; and the wife smiles, and lets it go at that.—*J. M. Barrie*.

Success soon palls. The joyous time is when the breeze first strikes your sails, and the waters rustle under your bows. —*Charles Buxton.*

The gent who wakes up and finds himself a success hasn't been asleep.—*Wilson Mizner.*

Herein the only royal road to fame and fortune lies:
Put not your trust in vinegar—molasses catches flies!
                                        —*Eugene Field.*

After a feller gits famous it don't take long fer some one t' bob up that used t' set by him at school.—*Kin Hubbard.*

If fame is to come only after death, I am in no hurry for it. —*Martial.*

Nothing succeeds so well as success.—*Talleyrand.*

Glory arrives too late when it comes only to one's ashes. —*Martial.*

Let them call it mischief; when it is past and prospered, it will be virtue.—*Ben Jonson.*

How prudently we proud men compete for nameless graves, while now and then some starveling of Fate forgets himself into immortality.—*Wendell Phillips.*

The way to fame is like the way to heaven, through much tribulation.—*Sterne.*

A contemplation of God's works, a generous concern for the good of mankind, and the unfeigned exercise of humility— these only denominate men great and glorious.—*Addison.*

Difficulty is a nurse of greatness—a harsh nurse, who rocks her foster children roughly, but rocks them into strength and athletic proportions. The mind, grappling with great aims and wrestling with mighty impediments, grows by a certain necessity to the stature of greatness.—*Bryant.*

Great men are meteors designed to burn so that the earth may be lighted.—*Napoleon.*

The superiority of some men is merely local. They are great because their associates are little.—*Johnson*.

No man has come to true greatness who has not felt in some degree that his life belongs to his race, and that what God gives him he gives him for mankind.—*Phillips Brooks*.

> Not that the heavens the little can make great,
> But many a man has lived an age too late.
> —*R .H. Stoddard*.

What millions died that Caesar might be great.—*Campbell*.

High stations, tumult, but not bliss, create; none think the great unhappy, but the great.—*Young*.

Some men are born great; some achieve greatness; and some have greatness thrust upon them.—*Shakespeare*.

He who comes up to his own idea of greatness, must always have had a very low standard of it in his mind.—*Ruskin*.

The man who does his work, any work, conscientiously, must always be in one sense a great man.—*Mulock*.

Reputation is what men and women think of us; character is what God and angels know of us.—*Paine*.

The solar system has no anxiety about its reputation.—*Emerson*.

The way to gain a good reputation is to endeavor to be what you desire to appear.—*Socrates*.

It is a sign that your reputation is small and sinking, if your own tongue must praise you.—*Matthew Hale*.

Reputation, reputation, reputation! Oh, I have lost my reputation! I have lost the immortal part of myself; and what remains is bestial.—*Shakespeare*.

Good will, like a good name, is got by many actions, and lost by one.—*Jeffrey*.

One may be better than his reputation, but never better than his principles.—*Latena.*

I would to God thou and I knew where a commodity of good names were to be bought.—*Shakespeare.*

In all the affairs of this world, so much reputation is, in reality, so much power.—*Tillotson.*

Reputation is sometimes as wide as the horizon, when character is but the point of a needle. Character is what one really is; reputation what others believe him to be.—*H. W. Beecher.*

A man's reputation is not in his own keeping, but lies at the mercy of the profligacy of others. Calumny requires no proof.—*Hazlitt.*

Reputation is an idle and most false imposition, oft got without merit, and lost without deserving.—*Shakespeare.*

Associate with men of good quality, if you esteem your own reputation; it is better to be alone than in bad company. —*Washington.*

Teachers

The true aim of every one who aspires to be a teacher should be, not to impart his own opinions, but to kindle minds. —*F. W. Robertson.*

In the education of children there is nothing like alluring the interest and affection; otherwise you only make so many asses laden with books.—*Montaigne.*

Whatever you would have your children become, strive to exhibit in your own lives and conversation.—*Mrs. Sigourney.*

> Charming women can true converts make,
> We love the precepts for the teacher's sake.
> —*George Farquhar.*

The one exclusive sign of a thorough knowledge is the power of teaching.—*Aristotle.*

The teacher who is attempting to teach without inspiring the pupil with a desire to learn is hammering on cold iron. —*H. Mann.*

Those who educate children well are more to be honored than even their parents, for these only give them life, those the art of living well.—*Aristotle.*

The best teacher is the one who suggests rather than dogmatizes, and inspires his listener with the wish to teach himself.—*Bulwer.*

If ever I am a teacher, it will be to learn more than to teach.—*Mme. Deluzy.*

He that governs well, leads the blind; but he that teaches, gives him eyes; and it is glorious to be a sub-worker to grace, in freeing it from some of the inconveniences of original sin. —*South.*

The object of teaching a child is to enable him to get along without his teacher.—*Elbert Hubbard.*

He is to be educated not because he is to make shoes, nails, and pins, but because he is a man.—*Channing.*

Education is only like good culture; it changes the size, but not the sort.—*H. W. Beecher.*

Educate men without religion, and you make them but clever devils.—*Wellington.*

Next in importance to freedom and justice is popular education, without which neither justice nor freedom can be permanently maintained.—*Garfield.*

The teacher is one who makes two ideas grow where only one grew before.—*Elbert Hubbard.*

The true object of education should be to train one to think clearly and act rightly.—*H. J. van Dyke.*

An industrious and virtuous education of children is a better inheritance for them than a great estate.—*Addison.*

It is on the sound education of the people that the security and destiny of every nation chiefly rest.—*Kossuth.*

'Tis education forms the common mind, just as the twig is bent, the tree's inclined.—*Pope.*

He that teaches himself has a fool for his master.—*Proverb.*

He who can, does. He who cannot, teaches.—*G. B. Shaw.*

We loved the doctrine for the teacher's sake.—*Proverb.*

Travelers—Explorers

Usually speaking, the worst bred person in company is a young traveller just returned from abroad.—*Swift.*

> How much a dunce that has been sent to roam
> Excels a dunce that has been kept at home!
> —*Cowper.*

The bee, though it finds every rose has a thorn, comes back loaded with honey from his rambles, and why should not other tourists do the same.—*Halliburton.*

It is not worth while to go round the world to count the cats in Zanzibar.—*Thoreau.*

The travelled mind is the catholic mind, educated out of exclusiveness and egotism.—*A. B. Alcott.*

The vagabond, when rich, is called a tourist.—*Paul Richard.*

If a goose flies across the sea, there comes back a quack-quack.—*German Proverb.*

He who never leaves his own country is full of prejudices. —*Goldoni.*

The world is a great book, of which they who never stir from home read only a page.—*Augustine.*

See one mountain, one sea, one river—and see all.—*Greek Proverb.*

Wedding Anniversaries

To be man's tender mate was woman born, and in obeying Nature she best serves the purposes of heaven.—*Schiller.*

Take the daughter of a good mother.—*Fuller.*

I . . . chose my wife, as she did her wedding gown, [for] such qualities as would wear well.—*Goldsmith.*

If it were not for the Presents, an Elopement would be Preferable.—*George Ade.*

[Take not] a time too short to make a world-without-end bargain in.—*Shakespeare.*

Married in haste, we may repent at leisure.—*Congreve.*

It is always incomprehensible to a man that a woman should refuse an offer of marriage.—*Austen.*

Marriage has many pains, but celibacy has few pleasures. —*Johnson.*

O, friendly to the best pursuits of man, friendly to thought, to virtue, and to peace, domestic life in rural leisure passed! Few know thy value, and few taste thy sweets.—*Cowper.*

In the opinion of the world marriage ends all, as it does in a comedy. The truth is precisely the reverse, it begins all. —*Mme. Swetchine.*

God has set the type of marriage everywhere throughout the creation. Every creature seeks its perfection in another. The very heavens and earth picture it to us.—*Luther.*

One should believe in marriage as in the immortality of the soul.—*Balzac.*

O marriage! marriage! what a curse is thine, where hands alone consent, and hearts abhor!—*A. Hill.*

A good wife is like the ivy which beautifies the building to which it clings, twining its tendrils more lovingly as time converts the ancient edifice into a ruin.—*Johnson.*

When a man and woman are married their romance ceases and their history commences.—*Rochebrune.*

There is more of good nature than of good sense at the bottom of most marriages.—*Thoreau.*

The honeymoon is not actually over until we cease to stifle our sighs and begin to stifle our yawns.—*Rowland.*

Men should keep their eyes wide open before marriage, and half shut afterward.—*Mme. Scuderi.*

The sanctity of marriage and the family relation makes the cornerstone of our American society and civilization.—*Garfield.*

The surest way to hit a woman's heart is to take aim kneeling.—*Douglas Jerrold.*

> That man that hath a tongue, I say, is no man,
> If with his tongue he cannot win a woman.
> —*Shakespeare.*

Courtship consists in a number of quiet attentions, not so pointed as to alarm, nor so vague as not to be understood.—*Sterne.*

Respect is what we owe; love, what we give.—*Philip J. Bailey.*

We are shaped and fashioned by what we love.—*Goethe.*

The supreme happiness of life is the conviction of being loved for yourself, or, more correctly, being loved in spite of yourself.—*Victor Hugo.*

Youth

Young men have a passion for regarding their elders as senile.—*Henry Adams.*

Youth is the gay and pleasant spring of life, when joy is stirring in the dancing blood, and nature calls us with a thousand songs to share her general feast.—*Ridgeway.*

Youth is the opportunity to do something and to become somebody.—*T. T. Munger.*

> In sorrow he learned this truth—
> One may return to the place of his birth,
> He cannot go back to his youth.
> —*John Burroughs.*

Youth is the season of hope, enterprise, and energy, to a nation as well as an individual.—*W. R. Williams.*

Youth, with swift feet, walks onward in the way; the land of joy lies all before his eyes.—*Bulwer.*

The excesses of our youth are drafts upon our old age, payable with interest, about thirty years after date.—*Colton.*

> Life is but thought; so think I will,
> That youth and I are house-mates still.
> —*Coleridge.*

The majority of men employ the first portion of their life in making the other portion miserable.—*La Bruyère.*

Youth holds no society with grief.—*Aristotle.*

Youth is a wonderful thing. What a crime to waste it on children.—*G. B. Shaw.*

Whilst the morning shines, gather the flowers.—*Latin Proverb.*

Unless a tree has borne blossoms in spring, you will vainly look for fruit on it in autumn.—*Hare.*

My salad days, when I was green in judgment.—*Shakespeare.*

The fairest flower in the garden of creation is a young mind, offering and unfolding itself to the influence of divine wisdom, as the heliotrope turns its sweet blossoms to the sun. —*J. E. Smith.*

The self-conceit of the young is the great source of those dangers to which they are exposed.—*Blair.*

No young man believes he shall ever die.—*Hazlitt.*

Girls we love for what they are; young men for what they promise to be.—*Goethe.*

I have often thought what a melancholy world this would be without children, and what an inhuman world without the aged.—*Coleridge.*

I love little children, and it is not a slight thing when they, who are fresh from God, love us.—*Dickens.*

It is good to be children sometimes, and never better than at Christmas, when its mighty Founder was a child himself. —*Dickens.*

Childhood has no forebodings; but then, it is soothed by no memories of outlived sorrow.—*George Eliot.*

Infancy is the perpetual Messiah, which comes into the arms of fallen men, and pleads with them to return to paradise.—*Emerson.*

The proper time to influence the character of a child is about a hundred years before he is born.—*Dean Inge.*

Children have more need of models than of critics.—*Joubert.*

> The childhood shows the man,
> As morning shows the day.
> —*Milton*

Children begin by loving their parents; as they grow older they judge them; sometimes they forgive them.—*Oscar Wilde.*

The child is father of the man.—*Wordsworth.*

Chapter 16

HUMOROUS STORIES FOR ALL
OCCASIONS

"Hello, Joe"

"Perkins, Parkins, Peckham, and Potts—good morning."

"I want to speak with Mr. Perkins."

"Who's calling, please?"

"Mr. Pincham, of Pincham, Pettam, Poppum, and Potter."

"Just one moment, please. I'll connect you with Mr. Perkins' office."

"Hello, Mr. Perkins' office."

"I want to speak to Mr. Perkins."

"Mr. Perkins? I'll see if he's in. Who's calling, please?"

"Mr. Pincham."

"Just one moment. Here's Mr. Perkins. Put Mr. Pincham on, please."

"Just one moment, please. I have Mr. Pincham right here. O.K. with Perkins, Parkins, Peckham, and Potts, Mr. Pincham. Go ahead."

" 'Lo, Joe? How's about lunch?"

"O.K."

A Problem

"Now, what we gwine do 'bout dat billy goat in de crate, boss?" asked the Negro employee at the express office. "He's done et whar he's gwine!"

243

No More Bragging

"Is your son's college education of any real value?"

"Yes, indeed. It has cured his mother of bragging about him."

Competition

A young doctor and a young dentist shared the services of a receptionist and both fell in love with her.

The dentist was called away on business, so he sent for the receptionist and said: "I am going to be away for ten days. You will find a little present in your room."

She went in and found ten apples.

Salesmanship

The life-insurance agent called upon a big businessman at the close of a busy day. When the agent had been admitted, the big fellow said: "You ought to feel honored, highly honored, young man. Do you know that today I refused to see several insurance agents?"

"I know," said the agent. "I'm them."

Plenty Big Enough

Friend: "That wasn't a very big account of your daughter's wedding in the paper this morning."

Father (sadly): "No, the big account was sent to me."

Paid in Full

A man received a big check for services rendered, and discovered that it was one penny short. A stickler for detail, he insisted that the difference be paid—and in due course received another check for the single penny. He presented it for payment at his bank.

The teller examined it closely and then asked, "How would you like this, sir? Heads or tails?"

Good Pay

Johnny, ten years old, applied for a job as grocery boy for the summer. The grocer wanted a serious-minded youth, so he put Johnny to a little test.

"Well, my boy, what would you do with a million dollars?" he asked.

"Oh, gee, I don't know—I wasn't expecting so much at the start."

Satisfied

Personnel Director: "Have you any reference?"

Applicant: "Sure, here's the letter: 'To whom it may concern. John Jones worked for us one week and we're satisfied.'"

Opened by Mistake

Wife: "Let me see that letter you've just opened. I can see from the handwriting it's from a woman and you turned pale when you read it."

Husband: "You can have it. It's from your milliner."

Ordeal

Two Irishmen met. Said the first, "How are you, Mike?"

"Terrible, terrible!" replied the other. "It is shtarvation that is staring me in the face."

"Is that so," said the other. "It couldn't be very pleasant for aither of ye, I'm shure!"

Hold It, Please

Photographer: "Please smile and watch for the little birdie."

Modern Youngster: "Oh, drop that 'little birdie' stuff! Get out your light meter and make some tests, adjust your lighting properly, and set your lens correctly so you won't ruin a sensitized plate."

Good Precedent

Mrs. (*belligerently*): "Do you think I'm going to wear this old squirrel coat all my life?"

Mr. (*brightly*): "Why not, dear? The squirrels do."

Next Case

Judge: "Have you ever been up before me?"

Accused: "I don't know, Judge. What time do you get up?"

Opportunist

"As soon as I realized it was a crooked business, I got out of it."

"How much?"

Not His Territory

Diner (*beckoning waiter*): "Is it raining outside?"

Waiter: "Sorry, sir, but this is not my table."

He Was Eligible

"I told the club they were a set of blind, stupid, obstinate, unmitigated asses."

"And what did they do?"

"They made me an honorary member."

That Reminds Me

A traveler just home from abroad was describing an earthquake. "Most amazing thing I ever saw," he said dramatically. "The hotel rocked. Cups and saucers were flying all over the room, and—"

His meek-looking companion turned suddenly white. "Great Scott!" he cried. "That reminds me. I forgot to post a letter my wife gave me two days ago."

Inflation

Lady: "How much are those tomatoes?"
Grocer: "Thirty-five a pound, ma'am."
Lady: "Did you raise them yourself?"
Grocer: "Yes, they were thirty cents a pound yesterday."

Could Use Them!

"The new baby has its father's nose and its mother's eyes."
"Yes, and if Grandpop doesn't stop leaning over the crib, it's going to have his teeth."

You're Telling Me!

On Christmas Eve, Jones was discovered by Brown trying to shove a horse onto his doorstep.

"Give a hand, old man," he pleaded. Brown, wondering, did so. They pushed the horse into the hall.

"Now just let's get him up the stairs." So they pushed and shoved.

"Now into the bathroom," said Jones.

When they had got the horse safely in, Jones closed the door softly.

"Why? Why? Why?" asked Brown.

"I'll tell you," said Jones. "I've got a brother-in-law who lives with us and knows everything. But when he goes up to bathe tomorrow, he'll shout down: 'Hey, there's a horse in the bathroom'; and for the first time I'll be able to shout back: 'You're tellin' me.'"

To the Head of the Class

Teacher: "Bobby, what is an oyster?"
Bobby: "It's a fish built like a nut."

Pipe Down

Professor Albert Einstein, in the course of a newspaper interview, offered his idea of success in life in the following formula: "If a is success in life, I should say that the formula is a equals x plus y plus z, x being work and y being play."

"And what is z?" asked the reporter.

"That," replied the great scientist, with a laugh, "is keeping your mouth shut."

Truth

Foreman: "How long have you been working here?"
Apprentice: "Ever since you came in the door."

A Large Group

A man was looking for a good church to attend and happened into a small one in which the congregation was reading with the minister. They were saying: "We have left undone those things we ought to have done, and we have done those things which we ought not to have done."

The man dropped into a seat and sighed with relief as he said to himself: "Thank goodness, I've found my crowd at last."

Fore and Four

Jones is devoted to golf and his wife is equally fond of auction sales. They both talk in their sleep. The other night the people in the next apartment heard him shout, "Fore!" and immediately his wife yelled, "Four and a quarter!"

A Shocking Story

A certain village paper had not been able to print any sensational news for weeks, when during an electrical storm a live wire fell across Main Street. Everyone feared to go near it. The city editor sent out two reporters. One to touch the wire and the other to write the story.

His Equal

Husband: "I passed Joe on the street yesterday and he refused to recognize me. Thinks I'm not his equal, I guess."

Wife: "You certainly are his equal! He's nothing but a bluffing, conceited idiot!"

You Know the Answer

A man said he feared he would be of no use in the world because he had only one talent.

"Oh, don't let that discourage you," said his pastor. "What is your talent?"

"The talent of criticism," was the answer.

"Well," replied the pastor, "I advise you to do with it what the man of one talent in the parable did with his."

Bingo

In his announcement one Sunday morning the minister regretted that money was not coming in quickly enough—but he was no pessimist.

"We have tried," he said, "to raise the necessary money in the usual manner. We have tried honestly. Now we are going to see what a bazaar can do."

Slight Understatement

Said the Florida man, picking up a watermelon: "Is this the largest grapefruit you can grow in these parts?"

"Stop!" said the Californian. "You're crushing that raisin."

Courtesy

The Quaker had heard a strange noise in the night and, waking, found that a burglar was busy ransacking the living room.

Eliphalet took up his fowling piece, or, as it is called nowadays, shotgun, and addressed the startled intruder: "Friend,

I would do thee no harm for this vile world, and all that is in it—but thee stands where I am about to shoot!"

The burglar decamped.

Perfect Understanding

"Who's calling?" was the answer to the telephone.

"Watt."

"What is your name, please?"

"Watt's my name."

"That's what I asked you. What's your name?"

"That's what I told you. Watt's my name."

A long pause, and then, from Watt, "Is this James Brown?"

"No, this is Knott."

"Please tell me your name."

"Will Knott."

Whereupon they both hung up.

Good Memory

"So you really think your memory is improving under treatment. You remember things now?"

"Well, not exactly, but I have progressed so far that I can frequently remember I have forgotten something, if I could only remember what it is."

Foreign Missions

Gothamite: "I'm from New York. I suppose you do not know where New York is?"

Salt Lake Citizen: "Oh, yes, I do. Our Sunday school has a missionary there."

Be Calm

A passenger in an airplane was far up in the sky when the pilot began to laugh hysterically.

Passenger: "What's the joke?"

Pilot: "I'm thinking of what they'll say at the asylum when they find out I have escaped."

Self-Indicted

Missus (*at height of quarrel*): "They say marriage makes people look alike and now I even talk like you."
Mister: "Oh, for goodness' sake don't talk like a fool."

Did She See Them!

He had never been outside the United States, and neither had she, but both were recounting their experiences abroad.
"And Asia. Ah, wonderful Asia. Never shall I forget Turkey, India—all of them. And most of all China, the celestial kingdom. How I loved it!"
"And the pagodas—did you see them?"
She held her ground.
"Did I see them?" She powdered her nose. "My dear, I had dinner with them."

Station Announcement

Uncle (*to six-year-old after church service*): "And how did you like it, dear?"
Six-Year-Old: "I liked the music, but the commercial was too long."

That Explains Everything

An ardent golfer was visiting a friend and playing golf at his friend's club. On the first tee, he took his stance, gave a wild swing, and missed completely. "Gosh," he said to his opponent, "it's a good thing I found out early in the game that this course is at least two inches lower than the one I usually play on."

Too Late

A professor at medical school asked a student how much of a certain drug should be administered to a patient and the young man replied, "Five grains."

A minute later he raised his hand. "Professor," he said, "I would like to change my answer to that question."

The professor looked at his watch and replied, "Never mind, young man, your patient has been dead for forty seconds."

He Did

Salesman: "I've been trying all week to see you; may I have an appointment?"

Big Businessman: "Make a date with my secretary."

Salesman: "I did, and we had a grand time, but I still want to see you."

Speaking Frankly

Novice, at bridge party: "You're an expert at bridge, Mr. Jones. How would you have played that last hand of mine?"

Mr. Jones: "Under an assumed name."

What a Voice

Singer: "How do you like my voice?"

Accompanist: "Lady, I've played the white keys. I've played the black keys. But you're the first one I ever saw that could sing in the cracks."

To the Point

An English cub reporter, reprimanded for relating too many details, and warned to be brief, turned in the following:

"A shooting affair occurred last night. Sir Dwight Hopeless, a guest at Lady Penmore's ball, complained of feeling ill, took his hat, his coat, his departure, no notice of friends, a taxi, a pistol from his pocket, and finally his life. Nice chap. Regrets and all that sort of thing."

He Had Seen Them

An artist painting in the country had a farmer spectator.

"Ah," said the artist, "perhaps you too are a lover of the beauties of nature. Have you seen the golden fingers of dawn spreading across the eastern sky, the red-stained, sulphurous islets floating in the lake of fire in the west, the ragged clouds at midnight blotting out the shuddering moon?"

"Nope," said the farmer, "not lately. I've been on the wagon for over a year."

Too Noisy

The three men who were cronies became convinced the world was making too many demands on their time and energy, so they packed up, gave up their jobs and went to a cabin in the North Woods. At the end of the first year, one remarked, "This quiet is enjoyable."

A year later the second remarked, "Yes."

At the end of the next year the third replied disgustedly, "If you two are going to keep on chattering, I'm going home."

Speed

Two men were flying East in a passenger plane, making the first air trip of their lives. The plane touched down at St. Louis and a little red truck sped out to its side to refuel it. The plane landed again at Cleveland and again a little red truck dashed up to it. The third stop was Albany and the same thing happened. One man looked at his watch and turned to his companion.

"This plane," he said, "makes wonderful time."

"Yes," said the other, "and that little red truck ain't doin' so bad either."

Smart Trader

"You got a good-looking hat, Bill."

"Yeah! Bought it five years ago, had it cleaned three times, changed it twice in restaurants—and it's still good as new."

254 THE TOASTMASTER'S AND SPEAKER'S HANDBOOK

Wonderful Man

The newlyweds were honeymooning at the seashore. As they walked arm in arm along the beach, the young groom looked poetically out to sea and eloquently cried out: "Roll on, thou deep and dark blue ocean—roll!" His bride gazed at the water a moment, then in hushed tones gasped, "Oh, Fred, you wonderful man! It's doing it."

Hard Worker

Foreman: "Hey, you! How come you're only carrying one sack? All the others are carrying two."

Worker: "Gee whiz, boss, guess the other guys are too lazy to make two trips like I do."

Real Entertainment

A salesman was passing through a small town and had several hours to while away. Seeing one of the natives, he inquired: "Any picture-show in town, my friend?"

"Nope, not one, stranger," was the answer.

"Any poolroom or bowling alley?"

"None of them, either," came the reply.

"What form of amusement have you here?" asked the salesman.

"Waal, come on down to the drugstore. Thar's a freshman home from the university."

We Had the Same Trouble

A little man walked to the box office, bought a ticket, and went in. A few minutes later he returned, bought another ticket and again went inside. Three times the same thing happened. By the fourth time the girl in the box office was completely perplexed and asked: "Why do you keep buying tickets to go into the theater?"

"It's not my fault," replied the little man. "They keep tearing them up every time I go inside."

Who Said That

The Army recently inducted a recruit of more than average literary education. On his first day at camp he was utterly exhausted after several hours of drilling.

"At ease," finally ordered the officer.

"How wonderful is death," muttered the recruit.

The officer turned instantly. "Who said that?" he demanded.

The culprit smiled weakly and replied: "Shelley, I believe, sir."

Truthful

Fisherman: "It was that long. . . . Never saw such a fish in my life."

Friend: "That I can believe."

No Splurging

Extract from a noncommissioned officer's letter to his wife: "I have now been made a corporal, which is my first step up in the Army's ladder of success. However, for the time being, please speak to the neighbors as usual and don't under any circumstances move to a larger house or buy a piano."

There's One Born Every Minute

P. T. Barnum, the great showman, once received a letter from a Vermonter offering him a cherry-colored cat for $600. Always on the lookout for a novelty for his show, Barnum sent the $600—after getting the man's solemn word that the creature was cherry colored. A crate arrived. Barnum opened it and a black cat jumped out. Around its neck was a ribbon and from the ribbon hung a note which read: "Up in Vermont our cherries are black."

To Whom It May Concern

A couple of Negro boys were crouched in a shell hole while a barrage whanged away over their heads. "Looka' here, Rastus," said one, "ain't you skeert?"

"Not me," boasted the other. "Ain't no shell gonna come along got my name on it."

"Me neither," says the first fellow. "I ain't worried about my name on no shell. What I *am* worried about is, maybe there's one marked 'To whom it may concern.' "

Too Tough

"Say, waiter, is this an incubator chicken? It tastes like it."
"I don't know, sir."
"It must be. Any chicken that has had a mother could never get as tough as this one."

Completely Lost

First Husband: "My wife finds my money wherever I hide it."

Second Husband: "My wife never finds mine. I put it in the basket with my undarned socks."

He Hot-Footed It

First Farmer: "I see by the paper your boy at Iowa is a very fast runner. It says he 'fairly burned up' the track during the race yesterday. I suppose you were there, and saw him do it."

Second Farmer: "I was there all right, but got there too late for to see the race. However, I did see the track, and there was nothing but cinders."

Minding His Business

First Traveler: "I see you have your arm in a sling. Broken?"

Second Traveler: "Yes, sir."

First: "Accident?"
Second: "No, I tried to pat myself on the back."
First: "What for?"
Second: "For minding my own business."

Information Please

Lady of the House: "Why don't you go to work? Don't you know that a rolling stone gathers no moss?"

Tramp: "Madam, not to evade your question at all, but merely to obtain information, may I ask what practical utility moss is to a man like me?"

You Can Say That Again

Farmer (*after the city boy had milked his first cow*): "Well, you learned something new today."

City Boy: "Yes, I learned that the man who says a cow gives milk is a liar."

Practice May Make Perfect

Husband: "I am going to discharge our chauffeur. Four times recently he almost killed me."

Wife: "Darling, give him another chance."

Backward in Her Homework

Visitor: "I must congratulate you on your daughter's brilliant paper on 'The Influence of Science on the Principles of Government.' "

Father: "Yes, and now I hope she will begin to study the influence of the vacuum cleaner on the carpet."

You Said It

"Women are not very strong physically."

"Perhaps not, but they can put the cap on a fruit jar so that it takes a man twenty minutes to take it off."

Agreeable

George: "I know my wife fooled me when we were engaged."

Robert: "Why, what do you mean?"

George: "Well, when I asked her to marry me, she said she was agreeable."

Notice in Advance

Prospective Father-in-Law: "Young man, can you support a family?"

Bridegroom-to-Be: "Well, no, sir. I was just planning to support your daughter. The rest of you will just have to shift for yourselves."

Missed Something

Boss: "You should have been here at nine o'clock."

New Stenographer: "Why? What happened?"

So We've Found

"What do you find best for cleaning windows?"

"I have tried lots of things, but I find my husband best."

Peace

Two women in a railway car argued about the window and at last called the porter as referee.

"If this window is open," one declared, "I shall catch cold and will die."

"If the window is shut," the other announced, "I shall certainly suffocate."

The two glared at each other. The porter was at a loss, but he welcomed the words of a man with a red nose who sat near. Said he: "First open the window. That will kill one. Next, shut it. That will kill the other. Then we can have peace."

Experience

"I guess my father must have been a pretty mischievous boy," said one youngster.

"Why?" inquired the other.

"Because he knows exactly what questions to ask when he wants to know what I have been doing."

Water Power

A delegate at a state convention had listened to a very long speech and as he saw the speaker reach for a glass of water he said to his neighbor, "That's the first windmill I have ever seen which ran by water."

Nonsupport

Dorothy Parker was bored by a talkative actress who hadn't had a part for years. "I simply can't think of leaving the theater," the woman gurgled. "I'm wedded to it."

"Then," retorted Miss Parker, "why not sue it for nonsupport?"

No Trouble

In a gay mood, a man telephoned a friend at two o'clock in the morning. "I do hope I haven't disturbed you," he said cheerily.

"Oh, no," the friend replied. "I had to get up to answer the telephone anyway."

They Do

Wife: "I think married men should wear something to show they're married."

Husband: "I do—this shiny suit."

Correct

The schoolteacher was taking her first golfing lesson. "Is the word spelled p-u-t or p-u-t-t?" she asked the instructor.

"P-u-t-t is correct," he replied. "Put means to place a thing where you want it. Putt means merely a vain attempt to do the same thing."

Truth in Advertising

Californian: "Now in my state we can grow a tree that size in about a year. How long did it take you to grow that one?"

Floridian: "Can't say for sure, but it wasn't there yesterday."

Honesty

Rastus (*throwing down four aces*): "Dar, guess I wins dis time, all right."

Sambo (*angrily*): "You play dis game honest; play it honest! I knows what cards I dealt you!"

Experience

Husband: "You're terribly extravagant. If anything should happen to me, you would probably have to beg."

Wife: "I'd get by. Look at all the experience I've had."

Modesty

She: "Handsome men are always conceited."
He: "Not always. I'm not."

Just a Pal

"He said you weren't fit to sleep with the pigs."

"And I suppose you pulled the old gag and said that I was."

"No, I stuck up for the pigs."

Busy

"Grandma, do you have to take all those different kinds of pills every day?"

"Yes, Betty. Yellow ones for my liver, pink ones for my stomach, black ones for my heart, orange ones for my nerves."

"Well, Grandma, what are the red ones for—to direct traffic?"

Notice to the Treasury

Brown: "So you took a five-hundred-dollar exemption on your income tax for the new bride?"

White: "Yes—and where you fill in your dependents I wrote, 'Watch this space!' "

Looking Ahead

Each time I pass a church,
I always pay a visit;
So when at last I'm carried in,
The Lord won't say, "Who is it?"

Small Business

Judge: "Now, John, did you have an assistant when you committed that burglary?"

John: "Naw, sir, boss. I never makes enough to hire a helper."

Tyro

Two Negro soldiers were on a transport going overseas. Standing on the deck they gazed out across the vast expanse of water.

"That's the mos' water I've eber seen in all my life," said one. "Did yo' eber see so much water?"

Said his companion: "Yo' ain't seen nothin' yet. That's jus' the top ob it."

The First 100 Years Are the Hardest

A curious tourist in the Ozarks inquired of an aged man sunning himself in front of a general store: "Just how old are you?"

Aged Man: "I'm jest a hundred."

Tourist: "Well, I doubt that you'll see another hundred."

Aged Man (*dryly*): "I ain't so sure about that. I'm stronger now than when I started my first hundred years."

Amateur Gardener

New Suburban Gardener: "I don't seem able to tell my garden plants from weeds. How do you distinguish between them?"

Old Suburban Gardener: "The only sure way is pull 'em out. If they come up again, they're weeds."

Considerate

Professor: "If there are any dumbbells in the room, please stand up."

A long pause, then a lone freshman stood up.

Professor: "What! Do you consider yourself a dumbbell?"

Freshman: "Well, not exactly that, sir, but I hate to see you standing all alone."

Bad Example

"Say, Pop, did you go to Sunday school when you were a little boy?"

"Yes, son—regularly."

"I'll bet it won't do me any good, either."

We Know the Railroad

A minister, traveling on one of those way-trains that stop at every station on the side line, was reading his Bible.

"Find anything about the railroad in that book?" asked the conductor, as he reached for the minister's ticket.

"Yes," replied the minister. "In the very first chapter it says that the Lord made every creeping thing."

An Economist

"I'm glad you're so impressed, dear, by all these explanations I have been giving you about banking and economics," remarked the young husband.

"Yes, darling. It seems wonderful that anybody could know as much as you do about money without having any."

Mistaken Identity

"Did my wife speak at the meeting yesterday?"

"I don't know your wife, but there was a tall, thin lady who rose and said she could not find words to express her feelings."

"That wasn't my wife."

He Knew

Lady (*to tramp*): "You would stand a better chance of getting a job if you would shave, cut your hair and clean yourself up."

Tramp (*to lady*): "Yes'm. I found that out."

Life

If a man runs after money, he's a materialist. If he keeps it, he's a capitalist. If he spends it, he's a playboy. If he doesn't get it, he lacks ambition. If he gets it without working, he's a parasite. If he gets it after a life of hard labor, he's a fool who got nothing out of life.

Slow Thinker

"I hadn't been talking to the fellow for more than five minutes when he called me a fool."

"What caused the delay?"

He Sits Loose

An old Negro down South was ninety-odd years of age and still in good health. Someone asked him how he kept so well at his time of life.

"Well, Captain Tom," he said, "when I works, I works hard, but when I sits, I sits loose."

Settling Down

Professor: "I won't begin today's lecture until the room settles down."

Voice from the rear: "Go home and sleep it off, old man."

Cautious

Rastus: "Where you goin', boy?"

Sambo: "I'se down to git myself some tuberculosis stamps."

Rastus: "What is dey? I ain't never heard tell of 'em."

Sambo: "Every year I gits myself fifty cents' worth of dem tuberculosis stamps and sticks dem on mah chest and I ain't never had tuberculosis yet."

Mistaken

A young woman boarded a crowded bus. A tired little man got up and gave her his seat. There was a moment of silence.

"I beg your pardon?" said the tired little man.

"I didn't say anything," rejoined the young woman.

"I'm sorry," said the little man. "I thought you said, 'Thank you.'"

More Vice Presidents

Office Boy: "I think I know what's wrong with this country."

Bank Executive: "What's that, son?"

Office Boy: "We are trying to run this country with only one vice president."

Discrimination

"I hear you have broken your engagement to Joe because your feelings toward him aren't the same. Are you going to return his ring?"

"Oh, no. My feelings toward the ring are the same as ever."

You're in the Army Now

The energetic sergeant was lecturing the new recruits:

"Here it is Monday morning and tomorrow will be Tuesday and the next day Wednesday—half the week gone and you guys don't know anything yet. Snap to!"

Modern Youth

Grandfather: "Isn't it time for a little boy to go to bed?"

Freddy (*eight years old*): "I do not know, grandfather. And it doesn't interest me, as I have no children."

Itemized Account

A Negro man doing a hauling job was told that he couldn't get his money until he submitted a statement. After much meditation he evolved the following bill:

"Three comes and three goes, at four bits a went, $3."

Acquitted

A seemingly stupid young fellow was being bullied in cross-examination. "Do you ever work?" demanded the attorney.

"Not much," the witness agreed.

"Have you ever earned as much as ten dollars in one week?"

"Ten dollars? Yeah. A couple of times."

"Is your father regularly employed?"

"Nope."

"Isn't it true that he's a worthless good-for-nothing, too?"

"I don't know about that," said the witness. "But you might ask him. He's sittin' there on the jury."

Thirty Days

Judge: "Was the rock as large as my fist?"

Defendant: "Yassuh, Jedge, it was dat big and maybe a little bigger."

Judge: "Was it as big as my two fists?"

Defendant: "Yassuh, Jedge, I 'spect it was bigger dan dat."

Judge: "Was it as large as my head?"

Defendant: "Jedge, it was as long, but I don't think it was as thick."

What's the Answer?

A woman when launching her first ship was a little nervous. She turned to the shipyard manager, standing beside her, and asked: "How hard do I have to hit to knock it into the water?"

Buyer or Seller

"You can take it as an elementary conception that when an article is sold it goes to the buyer," said Mr. Winter in the economics class.

"With the exception of coal," chirped the bright third-former.

"And why coal?" asked Mr. Winter.

"When that's bought, it goes to the cellar."

Manners

Herbert had been taught to rise when his mother came into a room, and to remain thus until she was seated or had left.

One day he had a friend with him when his mother arrived. He stood up, but his friend did not move, so Herbert asked him to do so.

A few minutes later his mother entered again, and the same procedure was gone through. When Herbert's mother entered for the third time, her son rose and the young guest asked, "I say, does your mother think she's the national anthem?"

Different

"I knew an artist who painted a cobweb so realistically that the maid spent several hours trying to get it down from the ceiling."

"I just don't believe it."

"Why not? Artists have been known to do such things."

"Yes, but not maids."

He Learnt Them

"Well, dear, and what did Mamma's little baby learn in school today?"

"I learnt two kids not to call me 'Mamma's little baby.'"

In Both Senses

Joseph Chitty, the famous English judge, was one day listening to a particularly uninteresting case. It dealt with household goods and agricultural implements. After talking about the implements until the court was nearly asleep, the lawyer remarked: "And now, my lord, I will address myself to the furniture."

"You have been doing that for an hour already," replied the learned judge.

Refreshed

A young author was introduced to a movie critic in the large city. The writer's first picture had just been shown on Broadway, and he immediately asked the critic what his opinion was.

"It was refreshing," returned the critic. "Very refreshing."

"Say, that's swell," beamed the young author. "Did you really find it so refreshing?"

"Absolutely," was the reply. "I felt like a new man when I woke up!"

Different Environment

Vacationist: "Any big men born here?"
Native: "Nope. Not very progressive 'round here; best we kin do is babies. Diff'rent in the city, I s'pose."

Too Much Character

"Did you do what I said an' ask the bank manager for a loan on the strength of your character?"
"Yes, an' he refused it on the strength of his."

Seeing Double

Second (*to boxer*): "Well, old man, I'm afraid you're licked now."
Boxer (*gazing dizzily across to the opposite corner*): "Yeah, I should have got him in the first round when he was alone."

Likes His Job

"It's not the work I enjoy," said the taxicab driver, "it's the people I run into."

Stewards

Dr. Ralph W. Sockman, pastor of Christ Church, New York City, tells the following interesting story:

We Americans, you know, when we start to think back to our basic philosophy of life come back to that foundation that is basically religious. Whatever you may say about the founders of this country, they had one overwhelming belief. They believed in the sovereignty of God. Rather whimsical proof of that came to my attention, perhaps to yours, out of a New Orleans law office. It seems that a New York law firm was trying to clear the title to a piece of property in New Orleans and it got the title back to 1803. That didn't satisfy the New York lawyer so he asked the New Orleans attorney to have the title cleared further back. The New Orleans attorney wrote him this letter: "Please be advised that in the year

1803 the United States of America acquired title to the Territory of Louisiana from the Republic of France by purchase, the Republic of France having first acquired title from the government of Spain by conquest, the government of Spain having originally acquired title by virtue of the discovery of Christopher Columbus, a Genoese sailor who, before setting out on his voyage of discovery, received the support of Queen Isabella of Spain, Queen Isabella having first secured the sanction of his Holiness, the Pope. The Pope is the Vicar of Jesus Christ; Jesus is the Son of God; God made Louisiana." I suppose that lawyer got it back about where it belongs. When we cut down through all these titles of property, all these labels of government, we come back to the basic proposition that everything we have came from God and we are stewards of it.

Next Time She Will Stand

Two glamour girls boarded a crowded streetcar, and one of them whispered to the other: "Watch me get a seat from a male passenger."

Pushing her way through the straphangers she turned her charms upon a gentleman who looked embarrassable. "My dear Mr. Brown," she gushed loudly, "fancy meeting you on the streetcar. Am I glad to see you! My, but I'm tired!"

The sedate gentleman looked up at the girl, whom he had never before seen, and as he rose said pleasantly, "Sit down, Bertha, my girl. It isn't often that I see you out on washday. No wonder you're tired. By the way, don't deliver the washing till Wednesday. My wife is going to the district attorney's office to see whether she can get your husband out of jail!"

Daffynition

Bachelor—A man who has been crossed in love. A married man is one who has been double-crossed.

Acceptance Speech

Best Acceptance Speech—Upon receiving a beautiful silver gift a famous baseball player picked it up and simply said, "Shore is pretty," and sat down.

He Followed Instructions

Then there's the rookie who took the sergeant's advice and put on a clean pair of socks every day. A week passed by. "Where are your shoes?" snarled the sergeant. "I can't get them on over seven pairs of socks," replied the rookie.—*Camp Blanding* (Florida) *Para Blasts.*

Speed

A famous minstrel man has related this story of a conversation he overheard in Fort Worth some years ago. Two Negro men were discussing the subject of speed.

Said one of the Negroes: "You claims you is fast! You says you's so fast folks calls you Speedy! Jest how fast is you, boy?"

"I'll tell you how fast I is," replied the other. "In my room dere's jes' an electric light, and it's twenty feet from ma baid. Come night time, I kin walk over to dat 'lectric light, turn it out, git into baid and be all covered up befo' de room gits dark."

Close Schedule

A Northern passenger on a small Mississippi River steamboat in the deep South was considerably perturbed when he heard the captain say his craft would be delayed some four or five hours, pending arrival of some expected cargo. He sought out the officer and expressed his regret that the craft would be late in arriving at New Orleans.

"Late?" said the captain. "Why I reckon we'll get in 'bout on time."

"But I just heard you say we'd be delayed here for four or five hours."

"Shucks," said the placid riverman, "we don't run on a schedule as close as all that."

Education

"A young lady who used to live next door to us," writes the editor of *The Postage Stamp*, "is out in Montana helping to instruct the Indians in grammar. We've heard from her recently, and she was pretty discouraged up until the other day. The only really loyal students she has are Mr. and Mrs. Bear-Don't-Walk. The others are continually bolting classes. She didn't think she was getting any place even with the dogged Bear-Don't-Walks, until she learned that this family had just applied to the Indian Agent to change its name to Bear-Doesn't-Walk."

Order in the Court

The *Houston* (Texas) *Press* style book admonishes reporters against the use of clichés and bromides. Among the examples is the word "bailiff."

"Don't write 'bailiff of the court.' What else can there be a bailiff of?"

"Hay," an office wag scrawled in with pencil.—*Editor & Publisher.*

His Problem

"My advice to you, Mr. Brown, is to go through the movements of driving without using the ball," said the golf instructor.

"My dear fellow," answered Mr. Brown, "that's precisely the trouble I'm trying to overcome!"

Sporting Chance

As a hunter, Irvin S. Cobb, the famous author, was not exactly a Daniel Boone.

One day Mr. Cobb went duck hunting. His guide rowed him to a likely spot and soon a flock of ducks settled on the water at a most convenient distance.

Cobb aimed his gun.

"You mustn't do that, Mr. Cobb," warned the guide.

"Do what?" said the mighty hunter.

"Shoot when the ducks are on the water. You must wait until they rise."

"Why?"

"You must give them a sporting chance."

"Sporting chance," laughed Cobb. "They always get a sporting chance when *I* shoot!"

The Easy Way

Dorothy: "I have a very literary boy friend. He recommended Einstein's *The Theory of Relativity* as a most interesting book."

Lou: "Excellent! And have you read it yet?"

Dorothy: "No, I'm waiting for it to come out in the movies, first."—*Pathfinder.*

Goldwyniana

Film producer Samuel Goldwyn usually succeeds in having his own way. Some time ago he and another producer got into an argument over the services of a well-known writer.

Goldwyn insisted that the writer belonged to him. The other claimed the scenarist. Finally, after hours of debate, the rival producer suggested that they submit the dispute to arbitration.

"All right," said Goldwyn. "I'll agree to arbitration. Nobody can say I'm not fair. But remember—no matter what the outcome he goes to work for me!"—*Milwaukee Journal.*

It Would Have Been Smarter

The gentleman left his country club slightly worse for wear. Turning into the main highway in his car he decided in his alcoholic daze that the safest procedure was to keep his eyes glued on the car ahead and follow it closely.

He did this for some time, and he was just congratulating himself when the car ahead suddenly stopped and he crashed into it.

The irate driver of the first car stuck his head out of his window and bellowed, "What's the big idea?"

"What's the big idea?" the other retorted. "Why didn't you stick out your hand?"

The first driver's eyes opened wide with astonishment. "I didn't think I had to do that in my own garage," he yelped.

Guessed Wrong

Judge: "I have been informed that you are six months behind in your alimony, Rastus. What have you to say?"

Rastus: "Ah knows it, Judge, but I jes' couldn't help it. Mah second wife ain't nowhere near as good a worker as Ah expected her to be!"

You Couldn't Fool Him

Store Manager: "What's your name?"
Applicant: "Scott."
Manager: "And your first name?"
Applicant: "Walter."
Manager (*smiling*): "That's a pretty well-known name."
Applicant (*proudly*): "It ought to be. I've been delivering groceries around here for two years now."

He Knew What He Liked

A man sat down at a lunch counter and ordered four poached eggs and chips, a dozen oysters, and a grilled steak. After wading through these he finished off with four doughnuts and two cups of coffee.

When the waiter had finished serving, he remarked: "You must enjoy your meals."

"Far from it," replied the diner. "As a matter of fact, I hate 'em—but I'm nuts about bicarbonate of soda."

Mistaken Identity

First Father: "What, your son is an undertaker? I thought you said your son was a doctor?"

Second Father: "No, I said he followed the medical profession."

Smile When You Say That

. . . Are you sure you had a muffler? . . . Those tables are reserved. . . . The apple pie is all gone. . . . I must have made a mistake in my addition. . . . Please read the guarantee more carefully. . . . I think you can get good tickets from the speculator down the street. . . . Let me see your tickets, please, a mistake has been made. . . . This space is reserved for guests. . . . Our contract is clear on that point. . . . Will you please spell your name again? . . . We are not responsible for hats and overcoats. . . . Who is this speaking, please? . . . Mr. Jones is in a conference this afternoon. . . .

Heritage

Father: "Don't you think our son gets his intelligence from me?"

Mother: "He must—I've still got mine."

Schoolteacher

A salesman stood in the hotel lobby reading a letter from his wife.

"Hang it," he exclaimed, "this is what I get for marrying a schoolteacher."

"What's the matter?" asked his friend.

"Here's what my wife has just written me: 'Dear Jack: I

notice that you have written me "Dearest Lucy." Now, either your grammar is bad, or else you are not a good husband. If I am the only Lucy you have, the "Dearest" is not correct; and if you have more than one Lucy, you've got something to explain when you get home.' "

A Bear for Punishment

Father: "Yes, son, I'm a self-made man."
Son: "Dad, that's what I like about you. You take the blame for everything."

Hardy Gurkhas

Two Gurkha soldiers, who had volunteered for service with India's sky troops, asked an N.C.O.:
"From what height are we supposed to jump?"
"Five hundred feet," was the reply.
"Nothing doing," they said, "it's too high. Can't we try from three hundred feet?"
The N.C.O. explained that from such a low height there was a danger of the parachutes not opening in time, and the Gurkhas broke into smiles.
"Oh, that's different," they said. "We get parachutes, do we?"

Thanks

Man (*to his wife*): "Do you know, dear, that the biggest idiot always marries the prettiest woman?"
Wife: "It is high time for you to hand me a compliment, but I must say you did it very nicely."

Both Right

Husband: "Darling did you ever stop to realize if you knew how to cook we'd be able to save some money?"
Wife: "Yes, and if you knew how to save money we could keep a cook."

A Reformer

Lilly: "Do you think Lucy will make Jim a good wife?"

Billy: "I don't know, but she'll make him a good husband if she gets the chance."

Smart Lad

"And what," asked the teacher, "do two ducks and a cow remind you of?"

"Quackers and milk," said the little boy.

Ah'll Say

"Doctah," said the wife of one of his patients, "Ah come to see if Rastus can have a slice of ham wid dat mustard plaster dat you told me to fix for him, 'count of it's a powerful strong prescription to take alone."

Brooklynese

Brooklyn teacher: "What is a stoic?"

Brooklyn youth: "De boid that brings de babies."

Easy Payments

Anent the case of borrowing and repaying money on the installment plan, there is the story about two Negroes, who stood in the alley at Birmingham listening to a terrible commotion going on in one of the shanties, on the porch of which hung the distinctive and truly Southern sign SLEEPERS WANTED.

From the outside, the slamming and banging of furniture plainly could be heard and there was an occasional shout, above the hubbub.

Another Negro man came along and inquired: "What's all the ruckus about?"

"Oh, that's just the white gennelmun come to collect one of them easy payments," was the response.—*Finance.*

Difficult to Get In

Into swanky St. Thomas Church walked a Negro man. After due inquiry, and some difficulty, he located the rector and said: "Sah, I'd like to join dis church."

The rector was in a dilemma. "My good man," he said, "where do you live?"

"I live in Harlem," was the reply.

"Then don't you think it would be wise to join a church in your own neighborhood?"

"Yes, sah, but I desires to join dis church."

The rector pondered. "My man," said he, "suppose you go home and pray over this important step."

The man agreed. The next day he appeared. "Rectah," he said, "I went home and done what you tole me. When I axed Him how could I get into St. Thomas' Church he say: 'Rastus, whaffo yo ax me how? Why, man, fo ten yeahs Ah been tryin' to get in dat church myself.'"

Working His Way

A haughty senior girl sniffed disdainfully as a tiny freshman cut in. "And just why did you have to cut in while I was dancing with a four-letter man?" she inquired nastily.

"I'm sorry, ma'am," said the frosh, "but I'm working my way through college, and your partner was waving a five-dollar bill at me."

Prepared

Old Gentleman: "You're an honest lad, but it was a ten-dollar bill I dropped, not ten ones."

Youngster: "I know, mister, but the last time I found a bill the man didn't have any change."

Not Easy

"When I went to work for you, didn't you say something about my getting a raise?"

"I did say that you would if you did your work well."

"I knew there was a catch in it somewhere."

He Knew Hospitals

Jimmy, six, youngest of eleven children, was taken to the hospital to see his father who was quite ill. Jimmy was quiet, almost reverent, until time came for him to leave. Then he tiptoed up to the bedside and whispered in his father's ear:
"Kin I see the baby now?"

Right

Auntie: "And what will you do, my little darling, when you grow up to be a great big girl?"
Child: "Reduce."

Yes, We Have None

Clerk: "No, madam, we haven't had any for a long time."
Manager (*overhearing*): "Oh, yes; we have it, madam. I will send to the warehouse and have some brought in for you." (*Aside to clerk*): "Never refuse anything. Send out for it."
As the lady went out laughing, the manager demanded: "What did she say?"
Clerk: "She said we haven't had any rain lately."

Speak Up

Judge: "Are you the defendant in this case?"
Negro: "No, suh. I'se got a lawyer to do my defendin'. I'se de gent'man what stole the chickens."

Real Mathematician

Constable (*to professor who had been run down*): "Did you chance to notice the number of the car, sir?"
Professor: "Well, not exactly, but I remember noticing that if it was doubled and then multiplied by itself, the square root of the product was the original number with the integers reversed."

Another Viewpoint

Rastus: "Have you ever thought what you would do if you had Henry Ford's income?"

Sambo: "No, but I have often wondered what he would do if he had mine."

G.I. Bride

John A. Straley tells the story about the two Irishmen who were standing in front of the kangaroo's cage in the Bronx zoo.

"Bejabers, Pat," Mike said, as he burst into tears. "Can yez read that there sign on the beast's cage?"

"Oi can thot," Pat replied. "It says 'A native of Australia.' But why are yez cryin?"

"You know my brother is with the American army in Australia," Mike sobbed. "We jist got a cable from him in Sydney, saying he's married one av thim."—*Finance.*

Empty-handed

Inviting a friend to his wedding anniversary, the man explained: "We're on the seventh, Apartment D; just touch the button with your elbow."

"And why should I use my elbow?"

"Well, for heaven's sake, you're not coming empty-handed, are you?"

Scotchman

Undertaker: "Are you one of the mourners?"

Scotchman: "I am, sir. The corpse owed me ten dollars."

Can You Spare a Dime?

"Buddy, couldja spare a dime?"

"No, but come along and I will buy your breakfast."

"Man, I've et three breakfasts now trying to get a dime!"

Yes, Dear—No, Dear

First Sergeant: "Stand up straight, throw your shoulders back and button up your coat."
Married Recruit (*absent-mindedly*): "Yes, dear."

Curiosity

Curious Lady: "Little boy, how is it that your mother's name is Jones and yours is Smith?"
Boy: "She got married again and I didn't."

He Should Know

Professor: "Here you see the skull of a chimpanzee, a very rare specimen. There are only two in the country—one is in the national museum and I have the other."

He Won't Eat It Either

Disgusted Diner: "You can't expect me to eat this stuff! Call the manager."
Waiter: "It's no use; he won't eat it either."

He Really Bugled

Two Negro soldiers were discussing the relative merits of their company buglers. Said one, "When dat boy of ouahs plays roll call, it sounds 'zactly like the Boston Symphony playin' *De Rosary.*"
The second Negro boy snorted.
"Brothah, you ain't got no bugler a-tall. When Snowball Jones wraps his lips aroun' dat bugle of his, an' plays mess call, I looks down at mah beans, an' I sez: 'Strawberries, behave. You is kickin' de whipped cream out of de plate.'"

He Did All Right

William H. Madden, raconteur of Irish stories, relates the tale of Mike O'Brien who had made his fortune in the construction business, despite the fact that Mike had never learned to read nor write. As was Mike's habit on a Sunday, he got out his boat and went fishing. During the afternoon, a storm swept over the lake, the boat overturned and poor Mike was drowned. One of Mike's friends came over to express his regrets to the widow.

"I hope, Mrs. O'Brien, that Mike left you well off."

"Indeed, he did," Mrs. O'Brien replied. "He left me forty-five thousand dollars in cash."

"Forty-five thousand!" his friend cried in astonishment. "Sure and he did all right by you."

"Didn't he do all right," said Mrs. O'Brien, "for a man who couldn't read, write nor swim."—*Finance.*

He Caught Big Fish

When President Cleveland's second child was born, the doctor asked the proud father to bring him a scale so that he could weigh the new offspring. Cleveland looked all over the house but could not find one. Finally he recalled that he had a scale in the cellar, which he used to weigh the fish he caught on his numerous trips. He fetched it, and when they placed the child upon it, they discovered that the new baby weighed 25 pounds.

Fifty-Fifty

Her Father: "Young man, how in the world do you expect to support my daughter when I can hardly manage it myself?"

Her Boy Friend: "Well, what would be the matter with our going fifty-fifty on it?"

That's Different

Mother: "Mrs. Smith says that one-half the world doesn't know how the other half lives."

Father: "Well, she shouldn't blame herself, dear; it isn't her fault."

Two-thirds for the Doctor

Admiral Dewey, hero of the Battle of Manila Bay, enjoyed splendid health. Once when he was complimented on his superb physique, he smiled and said, "I attribute my good condition to plenty of exercise and no banquets. One-third of what we eat, you know, enables us to live."

"In that case," he was asked, "what becomes of the other two-thirds?"

"Oh," replied the doughty admiral, "that enables the doctor to live."

Real Economy

"Why are you home so late, dear?"

"Well, I just missed the streetcar at one corner. Then I went around the corner to catch the bus, but I missed that, too. So I ran all the way home behind the streetcar, and saved the nickel fare."

"Why didn't you run behind the bus, and save a dime?"

Modern

"I am Brave Eagle," said the Indian chieftain, introducing himself to the paleface visitor. "This is my son, Fighting Bird."

"And here," he added, "is my grandson, DC-6."

The Missing Talent

A certain Negro preacher in Georgia failed to satisfy his flock and a committee from the congregation waited on him to request his resignation.

"Look here!" exclaimed the rejected shepherd indignantly. "What's de trouble wid mah preachin'? Don't I argufy?"

"You sho does, eldah," agreed the spokesman.

"Don't I 'sputify concerning de Scriptures?"

"You suttingly does."

"Den whut's wrong?" inquired the parson in profound bewilderment.

"Well, eldah," was the reply, "hit's dis way. You argufies and you 'sputifies, but you don't show wherein."

Sure Test

Jackson and his wife were doing a little fly hunting about the house.

"How many have you caught?" she asked after a while.

"Six," replied her husband. "Three males and three females."

"How absurd!" his wife sniffed. "How could you tell if they were males or females?"

"Easy, my dear," he retorted. "Three were on the apple pie and three were on the mirror."

Bluff

Two trucks met on a country road just wide enough for one. Truck driver No. 1, a scrawny, frail little man, leaned out of his cab.

"Turn out, you," he shouted. "If ya don't, I'll do to you what I did to the last guy who wouldn't turn out for me."

Two-hundred-pound, muscular driver No. 2, not caring for trouble, pulled out. As the other truck rumbled by, he yelled: "What'd ya do to that other guy?"

"Turned out for him," said No. 1.

Old Story to Married Men

"Dear," the little woman reported, "a man came yesterday gathering old clothes."

"Did you give him anything?" the husband inquired.

"Yes, Henry," she said. "I gave him that ten-year-old suit of yours and that dress I bought last month."

Mountain Climbing

On week-end leave, a soldier attended a movie at one of the Broadway houses. He was escorted by an usher who led him skyward on ramp after ramp to the floor level of the top balcony, where he stopped and pointed upward into the grayness. "You'll find a seat up there somewhere. This is as far as I go. Above this level, my nose bleeds."

Wrong Direction

Farmer: "You must be brave to come down in a hundred-mile gale like this in a parachute."

Soldier: "I didn't come down like this in a chute. I went up in a tent."

Mistaken Identity

Mrs. Clancy was returning from shopping in no pleasant humor. As she approached the door, she saw Mrs. Murphy, who occupied the street floor, sitting at her window.

"I say, Mrs. Murphy," she called out in deep sarcasm, "why don't ye take your ugly mug out of the window an' put your pet monkey in its place? That'd give the neighbors a change they'd like."

"Well now," Mrs. Murphy retorted, "it was only this mornin' that I did that very thing, an' the policeman came along an' when he saw the monkey he bowed and smiled an' said, 'Why, Mrs. Clancy, when did ye move downstairs?'"

Fortunate Break

Father: "Who broke that chair in the parlor last night?"

Daughter: "It just collapsed all of a sudden, Pop. But neither of us was hurt."

Modern Families

Two baby-sitters were discussing their infant charges. "Are you going to the dance tomorrow night?" one asked the other.

"I'm afraid not," she replied.

"What!" exclaimed the first. "I thought you were so fond of dancing?"

"I'd love to go," explained the conscientious sitter, "but to tell you the truth, I'm afraid to leave the baby with its mother!"

Good Description

Little Mary was walking in the garden. She happened to see a peacock, a bird she had never seen before. After gazing in silent admiration, she quickly ran into the house and cried out: "Oh, Granny, come and see! One of your chickens is in bloom!"

The Truth, the Whole Truth

A relief worker drove four miles into the country to take supplies to a deserving farmer. Before she left, she checked up on a rumor that had come to the welfare office: "We are told that you have been seen driving a car. How about it? You know help isn't given to people who own cars."

Promptly the farmer replied: "No, lady, I hain't got no car. I drive one once in a while when it is loaned to me."

"Who owns the car?" asked the worker.

"My brother-in-law's sister," he replied. "Sometimes she lets me drive it."

The explanation was satisfactory and the lady drove away. When she had gone the farmer chuckled: "She shore never figured out that my brother-in-law's sister is my wife."

Thought He Was Foreman

"Why did the foreman fire you?"

"Well, the foreman is the man who stands around and watches others work."

"Yes. But why did he fire you?"

"He got jealous of me. A lot of the fellows thought I was the foreman!"

A Little Later

"Sam, how long does you get in the jug for shootin' yo' wife?"

"Two weeks."

"Only two weeks for killin' yo' wife?"

"Yeah. Then I gets hung."

The Better Part

Once Clarence Darrow was visiting Brand Whitlock, then mayor of Toledo, when an admirer of the great lawyer burst into the office and asked Whitlock to introduce him.

"Ah, Mr. Darrow," gushed the intruder, "you have suffered a great deal in your life for being misunderstood, haven't you?"

Darrow smiled wryly and replied, "Yes, my friend, but I haven't suffered half as much as I would have if I had been understood."

British Version

At a party in London an American from the West was asked by a lovely English girl what part of the States he was from.

"Idaho," he told her.

"Isn't that interesting," she said. "You know, over here, we pronounce that Ohio."

Almost Heard It

Amos (after a narrow escape at a railroad crossing): "How come you blow yo' hawn? You oughta know it wouldn't do you no good."

Sambo: "Boy, dat wa'n't my hawn. Dat was Gabriel's."

Who Am I?

Of all nuisances, the one who runs up to you, grasps your hand and says, "You don't know me, do you?" is the worst.

Such a person once confronted William Howard Taft as he stood talking with a friend in Washington. He walked up and said, "How do you do, Mr. Taft; I'll bet you don't know me." Taft replied, "You win," and turned his broad back and walked away.

Worst Joke

Student: "Could one refer to the Venus de Milo as the girl who got the breaks?"

English Librarian: "Why not, may I awsk? It's an 'armless joke."

Vitamins

Little Betty concluded her evening prayer: "Lord, please, if you don't mind, from now on put the vitamins we need in pies, cakes and ice cream cones instead of spinach and cod liver oil."

How About Fog Lights?

Cowboy: "What kind of a saddle do you want—one with or without a horn?"

Dude: "Without a horn, I guess. There doesn't seem to be much traffic on these prairies."

No Bargain

A farmer was trying to sell a broken-winded horse to the Army, and was trotting him around for inspection. He stroked the animal's back and said to the Army buyer, "Hasn't he got a lovely coat?"

The Army man had noticed that the horse was touched in the wind, and answered, "Sure, his coat's all right, but I don't like his pants."

The Truth

The celebrated pianist Leopold Godowsky was once importuned by a father to pass judgment on his daughter's ability as a pianist. Godowsky, who had worked patiently but without success with the young woman through several lessons, sought to evade a direct reply. But the father was not to be put aside, and wrote demanding an utterly frank statement.

Godowsky laughed, reached for a piece of paper and wrote: "Your daughter is not without lack of talent, and she manages to play the simplest pieces with the greatest difficulty."

Difficult Choice

One day in the White House, President Coolidge was sitting with some of his political cronies, when some reference was made to the blunt style of oratory affected by Senator Jim Watson, of Indiana.

One of those present said: "Last week I heard Jim Watson speak before a group of constituents, and he said, 'Now I have given you all the facts, and you can vote for me or go to the devil.' "

Mr. Coolidge, who had been silently regarding the tips of his shoes, raised his eyes to the little group and with no particular emphasis remarked, "It was a difficult alternative."

Success

"If you get up earlier in the morning than your neighbor," said the town philosopher, "and work harder, and scheme more, and stick to your job more closely, and stay up later planning how to make more money than your neighbor, and burn the midnight oil more, planning how to get ahead of him while he's snoozing, not only will you leave more money when you die than he will, but you'll leave it much sooner."

Head of the Class

"How did Junior make out in his latest exams?"

"Oh, he's doing much better. He was almost on the top of the list of those who failed."

Diplomat

Father: "I hope you appreciate, young man, that in marrying my daughter you are getting a bighearted, generous girl."

Suitor: "I do, sir. And I trust she has acquired those fine qualities from her father."

Risky Undertaking

Bugler: "I'm entering the contest for the best bugler in camp. How do you think I'll come out?"

Corporal: "On a stretcher, probably."

Taking No Risk

Bill was just out of college, and got a job on the local staff of a newspaper. He listened intently to the city editor's instructions:

"Never write anything as a fact unless you are absolutely sure about it, or you'll get the paper in wrong. If you're not sure of an item being a fact use the words 'alleged,' 'reputed,' 'claimed,' 'rumored,' or 'it was said.' "

Bill kept repeating this instruction in his mind as he went on his first assignment, and this is the first story he turned in:

"It is rumored that a party was given yesterday by a number of reputed ladies. Mrs. Smith, it was said, was hostess, and the guests, it is alleged, with the exception of Mrs. Jones, who says she is fresh from Wheeling, were all local people. Mrs. Smith claims to be the wife of Joe Smith, rumored to be the president of an alleged bank."

Followed Instructions

"Where have you been, Johnnie?"

"Playing ball, Mother."

"I told you to beat the rug, didn't I?"

"No, ma'am, you told me to hang the rug on the line and then beat it."

Old Story But Still Good

He had opened a fish market and ordered a new sign painted, of which he was very proud. It read, FRESH FISH FOR SALE HERE.

"What did you put the word 'fresh' in for?" said his first customer. "You wouldn't sell them if they weren't fresh, would you?"

He painted out the word, leaving just FISH FOR SALE HERE.

"Why do you say 'here'?" asked his second customer. "You're not selling them anywhere else, are you?"

So he rubbed out the word "here."

"Why use 'for sale'?" asked the next customer. "You wouldn't have fish here unless they were for sale."

So he rubbed out everything but the word "Fish," remarking: "Well, nobody can find fault with that sign now, anyway."

A moment later another customer came in.

"I don't see what's the use of having that sign 'Fish' up there," said he, "when you can smell them a block away."

And that's how he went out of business.

Yes or No

Lawyer: "Now, sir, did you, or did you not, on the date in question, or at any other time, previously or subsequently say or even intimate to the defendant or anyone else, alone or with anyone, whether a friend or a mere acquaintance, or in fact, a stranger, that the statement imputed to you, whether

just or unjust, and denied by the plaintiff, was a matter of
no moment or otherwise? Answer me, yes or no."

Witness: "Yes or no what?"

Observation

Three-year-old Willie had taken his mother's powder puff
and was making himself up, as he'd seen her do. His five-
year-old sister came in, looked at him a moment, then took
the puff from Willie's hand. "Only ladies use powder; gentlemen wash themselves."

North and South

"What is the Mason-Dixon line?"

"It's the division between 'you all' and 'youse guys'!"

No Bids

First Shopper: "You seem to be busy."

Second Shopper: "Yes, I'm trying to get something for my
husband."

First Shopper: "Have you had any offers yet?"

Fast Thinker

Passenger: "Conductor, that fellow sitting opposite me is a
lunatic. He claims he is George Washington."

Conductor: "Be calm, lady; I'll take care of the matter.
(*Shouting*) Next station, Mount Vernon!"

Voice of Experience

Wife: "I think I hear burglars. Are you awake?"

Husband: "No!"

Psychology

A psychologist says that any girl can marry any man she
wants, if she repeats often enough to him these four words:
"You are so wonderful!"

Go Ahead

A junk shop near a railroad crossing carries a sign with this hint to motorists: "Go ahead; take a chance. We'll buy the car."

Mark Twain

A man once challenged Mark Twain to cite some passage from the Scriptures expressly forbidding polygamy.

"Certainly," replied the humorist. " 'No man can serve two masters.' "

Digging

When Rex Beach appeared as guest of honor at a writers' club he declined to make a speech, but agreed to answer any question asked by the club members.

"Tell me, Mr. Beach," said one young lady, "to what one thing do you attribute your success?"

The famous author considered the question briefly, and then replied: "I can best answer that by telling the story of a Swede in Alaska. He was owner of several rich mines, and all his friends wondered how he had managed to become so successful. One night one of their number asked him.

" 'Ay never tolt anybody before,' he replied, 'but Ay will tell you. Ay yust kept diggin' holes.' "

Discreet

The celebrated actor Maclyn Arbuckle was once a lawyer in a wild section of Texas, where the morning greeting was not "Fine morning, isn't it?" but "Wonder who gets it today."

Arbuckle was deeply inquisitive about the bad men of the section, and finally mustered up courage to corner the worst of their number and put him to a test.

"What would you do, Mr. Simmons," he timorously inquired, "if somebody called you a liar?"

Simmons scowled. "By word of mouth?"

"Yes," replied Arbuckle.

Simmons took out his Colt and regarded it lovingly. Then he looked at his questioner with a most terrifying expression. "How big a man?" he inquired.

Signs

Mother: "What makes you think your young man has matrimonial intentions?"

Daughter: "Well, when we were looking at Easter hats he tried to convince me I look better in a two ninety-eight model than one that cost fifteen dollars."

Never Told Him

Desperately in need of 50 cents, a husband finally got up enough courage to open his pay envelope before taking it to his wife. He hurried back to the cashier who had given him the envelope.

"You've given me ten dollars too much," he stammered.

The cashier counted the bills and coins, then replied impatiently: "It's quite correct. I suppose you've forgotten that you got a ten-dollar raise last month."

He placed his hand across his eyes, shrank into his collar and said faintly: "My wife never told me."

Home Economics

A Youngstown, Ohio, reporter had been fussing about the butter situation during the war, and finally decided to make some himself. He got a half pint of cream and went to work, shaking it seven and a half minutes in a jar. This was only the beginning. He gathered up the little ball of butter, "washed" it in ice water, salted it and looked upon it with love. It was pale. So he added some food coloring.

He also got some on his white shirt, ruining the shirt. Figuring his time, wear and tear on the shirt and other things, he had an eighth of a pound of butter which figures out at about $16.50 a pound. So he went out and bought a pound of oleo.—*Editor & Publisher.*

Not So Hard

A group of businessmen were discussing a certain tight-fisted banker. Every man present had suffered some unpleasant experience at the hands of this banker, and all save one offered fervent testimony concerning his unremitting toughness and hardheartedness.

"Haven't you something to say against that scamp?" the silent member was asked.

"No," was the reply. "I don't think he's so tough."

"He turned you down on a loan, didn't he?"

"Yes," replied the quiet one, "but he hesitated before he refused."

Second the Motion

It was the weekly meeting of a Negro club. At the end of the usual business, a loud voice yelled from the back of the hall: "Mistah Chayman, Ah makes a motion dat Sam Jackson am a low-down, sneaking, mis'rable chicken thief."

Down in front a little fellow leaped to his feet.

"Who makes dat motion dat Ah'm a low-down, sneakin' mis'rable chicken thief?"

A huge sour-faced Negro arose.

"Ah makes dat motion," he said.

"Mister Chayman," said Sam quickly, "Ah seconds dat motion."

Right Number

Customer: "Are these half dozen wedding rings all you have in stock? Why, you have a whole trayful of engagement rings over there!"

Jeweler: "Yes, sir. But it'll take that whole trayful of engagement rings to work off those half dozen wedding rings!"

Opposites

"They say people with opposite characteristics make the happiest marriages."

"Yes. That's why I'm looking for a girl with money."

We've Eaten That Sandwich

"This inn is historic. Almost everything here has its legend."

"Let's get them to tell us about this curious old ham sandwich. I'm sure it must have a quaint story attached."

Haircut

A professor was once accosted by a dirty little bootblack. "Shine, sir?" he asked.

The professor was disgusted by the dirt on the lad's face. "I don't want a shine, my lad," he said, "but if you will go and wash your face I'll give you a dime."

"Right, guv'nor," replied the boy, as he made his way to a neighboring fountain. Soon he returned, looking much cleaner.

"Well, my boy," said the professor, "you have earned your dime; here it is."

"I don't want your dime, guv'nor," replied the boy. "You hang on to it and git your hair cut."

Foir Away

There was a young girl in the choir
Whose voice went up hoir and hoir
　　Till one Sunday night
　　It went out of sight
And they found it next day in the spoir.

The Starting Point

Ramsay MacDonald, former prime minister of England, was discussing the possibility of lasting peace with another government official. The latter, an expert in foreign affairs, was unimpressed by the Prime Minister's idealistic viewpoint.

"The desire for peace does not necessarily insure it," he remarked somewhat cynically.

"Quite true," admitted Mr. MacDonald. "Neither does the desire for food satisfy your hunger, but at least it gets you started toward a restaurant."

Worst Moron Story

The moron dove into the swimming pool exclaiming, "Gee, I wish it was Wednesday."

"How come?" asked a bystander.

" 'Cause," said the moron, picking himself up, "they put water in the pool then."

Out She Goes

A deaf woman entered a church with an ear trumpet. Soon after she had seated herself, an usher tiptoed over and whispered, "One toot, and out you go."

We've Been There

Brown: "Did you fish with flies?"

Gray (back from camping holiday): "Fish with them? We fished with them, camped with them, ate with them, slept with them!"

Knew All the Answers

Caller: "Is the boss in?"

New Office Boy: "Are you a salesman, bill collector or a friend of his?"

"All three."

"He's in a business conference. He's out of town. Step in and see him."

Not Too Promising

Eugene Field was sometimes a little forgetful of his debts.

During his columnist days in Chicago, he was sought out by a visiting New York friend, from whom he had borrowed $25 some months before.

"Gene," the friend said, "I think you ought to clear up that old debt." And Field replied, "You're absolutely right; I'll do something about it tomorrow."

The next day, Field's column included mention of his friend's visit to Chicago. Then it revealed:

"He is in town to look after one of his permanent investments."

A Revised Memory

A Northern tourist was visiting the little cabin of an ancient Negro known as Uncle Mose, who lived in a small Virginia town, and who often entertained visitors with stories of the "War Between the States."

"I understand you remember seeing Lincoln," the visitor remarked.

Uncle Mose looked sheepish. "No, suh," he replied. "Ah used to 'member seeing Massa Linkum, but since Ah j'ined de church Ah doan' 'member seein' him no mo.' "

Domestic Scene

"Oh, Henry. You're just awful, and I'm sick of you. You sit there reading your old newspaper, not paying any attention to me. You don't love me any more."

"Nonsense, Isabel. I love you more than ever. I worship the ground you walk on. Your every wish is my command. I thrill at your proximity. Now for Pete's sake shut up and let me read the funnies."

Money Talks

The story is told that Winston Churchill hailed a cab in the West End and told the cabbie to drive him to BBC, where he was scheduled to make a speech to the world.

"Sorry, sir," said the driver. "Ye'll have to get yourself another cab. I can't go that far."

Mr. Churchill was somewhat surprised, and asked the cabbie why his field of operations was so limited.

"It hain't ordinarily, sir," apologized the driver, "but ye see, sir, Mr. Churchill is broadcasting in an hour, and I wants to get 'ome to 'ear 'im."

Mr. Churchill was so well pleased that he pulled out a pound note and handed it to the driver, who took one quick look at it and said: "Hop in, sir. To the devil with Mr. Churchill."

One Point of View

Life is cruel to men. When they are born, their mothers get the compliments and flowers. When they are married, their brides get the presents and publicity. And when they die, their wives get the insurance and winters in Florida.

Occasional Showers

"Daddy, don't they ever give showers for the groom?"

"No, son. There will be storms enough for him after the bride begins to reign."

No Interest

"What did the audience do when you told them you had never paid a dollar for a vote?" inquired the first politician.

"Some of them cheered, but the majority seemed to lose interest," replied the other.

Perfect Illustration

Dean: "What is density?"
Hansen: "I can't define it, but I can give an illustration."
Dean: "The illustration is good. Sit down."

New Idea

Husband (*the ingenious type*): "I've invented a new type of woman's handbag, dear."
Wife (*skeptically*): "What's new about it?"
Husband: "The zipper's at the bottom. Isn't that where everything usually is when you want it?"

Try, Try Again

"Mamma, what's a second-story man?"
"Your father is one, dear. If I don't believe his first story, he always has another one ready."

Nice Trick

The corporal was preparing to fingerprint a recruit.
"Wash your hands," he said.
"Both of them?" asked the recruit.
After a moment's hesitation, the corporal said: "No, just one. I want to see you do it."

Smart Girl

Employer to newly hired steno: "Now I hope you thoroughly understand the importance of punctuation?"
Steno: "Oh, yes, indeed. I always get to work on time."

• Quarantine

Old Lady: "Little boy, why aren't you in school instead of at this movie?"
Little Boy: "Well, you see, lady, I've got the measles."

Impressions

A Negro porter in a hotel was asked why rich men usually gave smaller tips than poor men.

"Well, suh," the porter answered, "the rich man don't want nobody t'know he's rich, and the po' man don't want nobody t'know he's po'."

It Works

"Sambo, how do you do your work so good and do it so fast?"

"Well, boss, Ah sticks de match ob enthusiasm to de fuse of energy an' jes' nacherly explodes, Ah does."

Careless Speech

Minister: "Well, Mose, how is your better half this morning?"

Mose: "She am done bettah, suh. But pahson, yo' is sho' careless wif yo' fractions."

Tall and Short

Detective: "You're looking for your cashier? Is he tall or short?"

Banker: "Both."

It's Essential

A small boy at the zoo asked why the giraffe had such a long neck.

"Well, you see," said the keeper gravely, "the giraffe's head is so far removed from his body that a long neck is absolutely necessary."

Pronunciation

First Freshman: "I hear you got thrown out of school for calling the dean a fish."

Second Frosh: "I didn't call him a fish. I just said, 'That's our dean,' real fast."

Idea

A Midwest manufacturer sent his son through his plant to improve efficiency and find ways to cut down portal-to-portal liability. After lengthy study, the son returned. "The plant is in pretty good shape," he declared. "My only suggestion is that you bank the curve near the time clock."

His Selection

Son: "Can I have any kind of sea food I like?"
Mother: "Yes, dear. What shall I order for you?"
Son: "Salt-water taffy."

At Sea

Two men, slightly inebriated, boarded a two-decker bus. There was a naval officer behind them. Tom went upstairs, leaving Bill to pay the fares. Bill turned to the officer and offered to pay two fares.

"My good man," said the scandalized officer, "I'm a naval officer, not a conductor."

"Hey, Tom," he shouted, "come on down. We're on a battleship."

Contented Composer

Beneath the gruff exterior of the great Johannes Brahms lurked a vast good humor that delighted his friends.

One day in his later years the composer encountered a friend whom he had not seen for several months, and confided in him: "While you were away I started many things, serenades, part songs and so on, but nothing would work out well. Then I thought: I am too old. I have worked long and diligently and have achieved enough. Here I have before me a carefree old age and can enjoy it in peace. I resolved to compose no more."

Brahms's friend regarded him with alarm and incredulity. "Compose no more!" he exclaimed.

The great composer smiled and added: "And that made me so happy, so contented, so delighted that all at once the writing began to go."

Modern Wage Earner On Vacation

He writes a picture postcard home: "Having a wonderful time and a half."

Must You Go?

There was once a young man who told his girl friend he'd never seen such dreamy eyes before. To which she replied, "You have never stayed so late before."

Kentucky Hills

An old man in the Kentucky hills was giving his summary of the atom bomb. "This here town will be the fust one that will be bombed one evening."

"Hardly," objected a visitor. "This town is a long way from the coast."

"Sure it'll be bombed," persisted the prophet. "It's the county seat, ain't it?"

Guilty

Judge: "Who was driving when you collided with that car?"

Drunk (*triumphantly*): "None of us. We were all in the back seat."

Often True

Toastmaster: "What is the hardest part of your work as a lecturer?"

Lecturer: "As a rule the hardest part of my work is waking up the audience after the man that introduces me has concluded his remarks."

Louder, Please

Voice over telephone: "Tommie Hagan will not be in school today."
Teacher: "Who is this speaking, please?"
Voice: "This is my father speaking."

Time to Leave

She: "My father takes things apart to see why they don't go."
He: "So what?"
She: "So you'd better go."

Thrift

She: "I can't make them out. They have no car, no piano, no radio, and she hasn't any jewelry, no furs."
He: "They probably have some money."

Expensive Tastes

A mountaineer coming to town saw for the first time a bunch of bananas.
"Want to try one?" asked a friend.
"No, I reckon not," said the man of the mountains. "I've got so many tastes now I can't satisfy, I don't reckon I'll take on more."

Responsible

Employer: "For this job, we need a responsible man."
Applicant: "I'm your man. In all my other jobs when anything went wrong, I was always held responsible."

It Makes a Difference

Mister (*exuberantly*): "A man is never older than he feels. Now this morning I feel as fresh as a two-year-old."

Missus (*sweetly*): "Horse or egg?"

Keep It Quiet

Farmer: "Let me tell you, my friend, that horse knows as much as I do."

Friend: "Well, don't tell anybody else; you might want to sell him someday."

What Every Renter Hopes For

Customer: "Young man, what do I get for my money if I rent this apartment?"

Salesman: "You get a home, on which we pay your taxes, your insurance, your water bill, buy your coal, fire your furnace and hot-water heater, furnish your window shades, gas stove, electric refrigerator, do your decorating and repairing, cut your grass, sweep your walks, clean your hall, pay the light bill for your garage, empty your garbage, fight your battles with the neighbors . . . and you ask me what do you get for your money!"

Customer: "Pardon me for being so stupid—where do I sign?"

Not a Bad Idea

Daughter: "Yes, I've graduated, but now I must inform myself in psychology, philology, bibli—"

Practical Mother: "Stop! I have arranged for you a thorough course in roastology, bakeology, stitchology, darnology, patchology and general domestic hustleology."

Keep the Change

A customer went into an expensive food store and asked the price of a peach.

"Fifteen cents," said the clerk.

The customer handed him 25 cents.

"Keep the change," he said. "I stepped on a grape as I came in."

Damaged

A man in a restaurant was having trouble cutting his steak. No matter how much he jabbed at it, he got no results. Finally he called the waiter. "You'll have to take this back and bring me another."

"Sorry, sir," said the waiter after closely examining the steak. "I can't take it back. You've bent it."

She Was a Star Pupil

A high-school girl seated next to a famous astronomer at a dinner party struck up a conversation asking, "What do you do in life?"

He replied, "I study astronomy."

"Dear me," said the young miss, "I finished astronomy last year."

Definition

Teacher: "What is the difference between caution and cowardice?"

Pupil: "Caution is when you're afraid and cowardice is when the other fellow's afraid."

Ample Evidence

At the age of sixteen the late Supreme Court Justice Louis Brandeis went to Europe with his parents, and while there attended school in Dresden.

Before admitting the prize student from Kentucky, the headmaster of the school demanded certificates of birth and vaccination. Young Brandeis did not have the certificates, but he did have a ready tongue.

"Why do you need the certificates?" he asked.

"As proof, of course," said the headmaster.

"To prove that I was vaccinated you have only to look at my arm," replied Brandeis, "and the fact that I am here to show you the arm should be ample proof that I was born."

He was admitted.—*Milwaukee Journal.*

He Understood

A man was giving some advice to his son. At the end of a rather stern lecture, he said: "Now, my boy, you understand perfectly what I mean?"

"Yes," replied the boy, "what it boils down to is this: If I do well it's because of heredity, and if I fail it's my own fault."

Difficult Choice

Lulu: "Last night my date asked me to marry him and make him happy."

Sue: "Which did you decide to do?"

Hard Work

Sandy was paying $7.50 weekly for board and lodging. One day his landlady said: "Sandy, I'm afraid I'll have to charge you a dollar a week more, you are such a good eater."

"For goodness' sake," cried Sandy, "dinna do that. I'm killing myself already trying to eat seven-fifty worth."

No Help

The great ocean liner rolled and pitched.

"Henry," faltered the young bride, "do you still love me?"

"More than ever, darling," was Henry's fervent answer.

Then there was an eloquent silence.

"Henry," she gasped, turning her pale, ghastly face away, "I thought that would make me feel better, but it doesn't."

Difficult Problem

A farmer was losing his temper trying to drive two mules into a field, when the parson came by.

"You are just the.man I want to see," said the farmer. "Tell me, how did Noah get these into the ark?"

Chauncey Depew

Once upon a time the mayor of a large city introduced Chauncey Depew by suggesting that he was like an automatic machine—"you put in a dinner and up comes a speech."

When Mr. Depew gained his feet, he suggested that the difference between his after-dinner speaking and the chairman's was that his honor the mayor "puts in a speech and up comes your dinner."

We're Revised Too

"I'm a self-made man."

"You're lucky. I'm the revised work of a wife and three daughters."

Appearance

"I need a holiday," said the cashier. "I'm not looking my best."

"Nonsense," said the boss.

"No, it isn't nonsense; the men are beginning to count their change."

Observation

"Sir," stormed the defense lawyer, "you have admitted you were seated on the right side of the passenger coach where you couldn't see an extra track. Will you please explain to this jury how you can swear the line was double-tracked?"

"Well," meekly answered the witness, "I could look across the aisle and through the coach windows. I saw a train whiz

by occasionally, and took it that there was either a track un- ·
der it or else this railroad had some mighty good railroaders."

Sneeze

I sneezed a sneeze into the air,
It fell to ground I knew not where
But hard and cold were the looks of those
In whose vicinity I snoze.

—*Commerce.*

Glad to Refund

A farmer had just made a purchase of a bushel of grass
seed.
"Is this seed guaranteed?"
"Guarantee the seed?" the merchant replied. "I should say
so. If that seed doesn't grow, bring it back and we'll refund
your money."

The Hammer

It's the only knocker in the world that does any good.
It keeps its head.
It doesn't fly off the handle.
It keeps pounding away.
It finds the point, then drives it home.
It looks at the other side, too, and thus often clinches the
matter.
It makes mistakes, but when it does, it starts all over.

Truth

Wife: "I've been asked for a reference for our last maid,
and I don't know exactly what to say. If I told the truth, I'd
say she was lazy, unpunctual and impertinent. Can you think
of anything favorable we could say?"
Husband: "You might say she's got a good appetite and
sleeps well."

All Grandparents Will Understand

Mother (*on phone*): "Daughter, dear, could Papa and I leave your kiddies with you and Bob tonight? We're invited out for the evening."

He Knew Better

They were out at sea—the ship was rolling and rocking something awful. One passenger got sick, and soon he was leaning over the rail. The captain came along and said: "Sorry, you cannot be sick here."

The passenger regarded the captain a moment and said, "Watch."

Winning Friends

Motor Cop: "Hey, you! Didn't you hear me say 'Pull over'?"

Driver: "Why, I thought you said, 'Good afternoon, Senator.'"

Motor Cop (*smiling*): "Isn't it a warm day today, Senator?"

Change This Story As You Wish

An advertisement appeared in the want ad columns reading as follows: "Wanted—Yale man or equivalent for position with a corporation." Someone asked a Harvard man what was meant by the words "or equivalent," and he said, "The equivalent would be two Princeton men or a Harvard man part time."

Prepared

Youth: "There's a very important question I've been wanting to ask you for days and days."

Girl: "Go right ahead. I've had the answer ready for months and months."

Scared

An Irishman was telling a friend of his narrow escape in France.

"The bullet went in me chest and came out me back," he said.

"But," protested his friend, "it would have gone through your heart and killed you."

"Me heart was in me mouth at the time."

Sad World

A shipwrecked sailor spent five years on a desert island. One day he was overjoyed to see a ship drop anchor in the bay. A small boat came ashore and an officer handed the sailor a bunch of newspapers.

"The captain suggests," he told the sailor, "that you read what's going on in the world and then let us know if you want to be rescued."

Go Easy

Mother: "Have you scolded Willie about the low marks on his report card?"

Father: "No. Every time I do he reminds me that he's an exemption on my income tax."

Description

"If you're looking for my husband, he's gone fishing. Just walk down to the bridge until you find a pole with a worm on each end."

Editor's Son

An editor had cause to admonish his son because of the lad's reluctance to attend school. "You must go every day and learn to be a great scholar," said the fond father, "otherwise you can never be an editor, you know. What would you do, for instance, if your magazine came out full of mistakes?"

"Father," was the reply, "I'd blame the printer."

And the father wept with joy, because he knew he had a successor for the editorial chair.—*Commerce.*

So Say We All

Wife: "There's an old-clothes man at the door."

Husband: "Tell him I can't afford to buy any."

Weighty Matter

In a small town where two brothers were engaged in the retail coal business a religious revival was held and one of the brothers got converted. He tried to persuade his partner to join the church. One day he asked: "Why can't you join the church like I did?"

"It's a fine thing for you to belong to the church," replied the other, "but if I join the church who'll weigh the coal?"

Poor Location

On a little service station away out on the edge of a Western desert there hangs a shingle bearing this strange legend: "Don't ask us for information. If we knew anything, we wouldn't be here."

Food for Thought

A young matron entered a grocery in one of our large cities. The counters were filled with gorgeous fruits and vegetables of every kind.

"How much are your watermelons?" she asked the grocer.

"Two dollars each," he replied.

"And your peaches?"

"Seventy-five cents a basket."

"And how much are those lovely cherries?"

"Eighty cents a pound."

The inquiring customer turned slowly away, saying: "Isn't it a shame to put them out here where people can see them!"

Honeymoon

Employee: "Please, sir, I'd like next week off if it's convenient."

Boss: "What's up?"

Employee: "My girl's going on her honeymoon and I'd like to go with her."

He Knew

The preacher was visiting a home and wanted to read a chapter from the Bible. The husband said to his little son:

"Bobby, go and get the Bible—you know, the big book we read so much."

So in a little while Bobby came in carrying the mail-order catalogue.

Salesman

A man went into a restaurant located near a depot. It was early in the morning. He sat down at one of the tables and near him sat a group of boys. A newsboy came in and yelled, "Paper! Paper!" One of the boys said, "We can't read and we don't enjoy the pictures." To which the newsboy replied, "Well, then, smell it. It's about half baloney anyway."

Advertising Pays

From an English grave marker: "Sacred to the memory of Jonathan Thompson, a pious Christian and affectionate husband. His disconsolate widow continues his grocery business at the old stand on Main Street and best prices in town."

This from a Maryland cemetery: "Here lies Jane Smith, wife of Thomas Smith, marble cutter. This monument erected by her husband. . . . Monuments of this same style are $250."
—The Presbyterian.

Tact

An Army sergeant had made an outstanding reputation for himself lecturing to enlisted men and noncommissioned officers on a certain subject. His captain called him in and said he had done such a splendid job they were going to ask him to lecture to a special group.

When he walked into the lecture room to appear before this group, he noticed there was not a man in the room who did not outrank him, and it was the biggest collection of brass hats he had ever seen.

In a moment of embarrassment, while he tried to think of an appropriate beginning, he said modestly, "There are thousands of men in the Army who know this subject much better than I do." He hesitated for a moment, and knew that was the wrong thing to say, because, after all, he had been selected because of his particular ability. Then he blurted out, "But I don't see any of them in this room."

The Awakening

Tom J. McKearnan, head of the famous Moffett Studios in Chicago, tells another of those ubiquitous bride and bridegroom stories.

The first evening, after the newlyweds came back from their honeymoon, the husband came home to find his bride studiously going through his bank books.

"Why, darling," he cried, "this leads me to believe you might have married me for my money."

"Don't be silly," the bride retorted. "I worship the very ground you walk on—and any other property you may acquire in the meantime."—*Finance.*

Cramming

Two little girls were discussing their families. "Why does your grandmother read the Bible so much?" asked one.

"I think," said the other little girl, "that she is cramming for her finals."—*Capper's Weekly.*

He Answered

Professor: "Why don't you answer me?"
Student: "I did, professor. I shook my head."
Professor: "But you don't expect me to hear it rattle way up here, do you?"

Convincing

Prosecutor: "Now tell the court how you came to take the car."
Defendant: "Well, the car was parked in front of the cemetery. So naturally I thought the owner was dead."

Inflation

Judge: "Why did you steal that fifty thousand dollars?"
Accused (*plaintively*): "I was hungry."

Good Reason

He: "I wonder why a girl can't catch a ball like a man?"
She: "Oh, a man is so much bigger and easier to catch."

Things Happened

"How was the wedding?" asked the preacher's wife.
"It was fine until I asked the bride if she would 'obey' and she said, 'Do you think I'm crazy?' The groom was in sort of a daze and mumbled, 'I do.' That's when things really began to happen," replied the preacher.

No Use Studying?

The teacher was talking about the law of gravity. "Sir Isaac Newton," she explained, "was looking at an apple tree and an apple fell to the ground. And from that he discovered gravitation. Wasn't that marvelous?"
"Yes," answered a boy in the last row scornfully, "but if he had been settin' lookin' at books, he wouldn't have discovered nothin'."

Not Real

Saleslady: "Isn't it a sweet doll? Lay it down and it closes its eyes and goes to sleep just like a real baby."

Mother: "Hmm, I can see you don't know real babies."

Why the Delay?

A merchant took out a fire-insurance policy and the same day his store burned to the ground. The insurance company suspected fraud, but couldn't prove anything. It had to content itself with writing the following letter:

"Dear Sir: You took out an insurance policy at 10 A.M. and your fire did not break out until 3:30 P.M. Will you kindly explain the delay?"

Appearance

"I notice you put your biggest apples on top. Why?" asked the cynical customer.

"For the same reason you comb your longest hairs over your bald spot," replied the grocer grimly.

An Idea

Mrs.: "Did you tell her that what I told you was in strict confidence?"

Miss: "Certainly not. I didn't want her to think it was important enough for her to repeat."

He'll Be Sorry

Judge (*in dentist's chair*): "Do you swear to pull the tooth, the whole tooth and nothing but the tooth?"

Expensive Information

"Daddy, if you will give me a dime, I'll tell you what the ice man said to Mamma."

"O.K., here's your dime."

"He said, 'Do you want any ice today, lady?' "

Too Cruel

"You naughty thing!" cried a little girl who saw a cat carrying a kitten by the nape of its neck. "You are not fit to be a mother! You're hardly fit to be a father."

It Seemed Like Yesterday

A Scot who had worn the same hat for 25 years decided with heavy heart to buy a new one. Going into the only shop in the neighborhood he said: "Well, here I am again."

Naturally

Teacher: "Can any bright pupil tell me why a man's hair turns gray quicker than his mustache?"

Pupil: "Sure, teacher. It's 'cause his hair has a twenty-year start on his mustache."

Too Close

"How close did it come to you?" asked the farmer, driving up to the tree where his hired man had taken shelter from an electrical storm.

"Well," stammered the hired man, still excited, "I don't know, but my pipe wasn't lit before."

Politeness

Customer: "Why is it I never get what I ask for here?"

Waiter: "Perhaps, madam, we are too polite."

Anxious

A blushing young woman handed the telegraph clerk a telegram containing only a name, address and one word—"Yes."

Wishing to be helpful, the clerk said: "You know, you can send nine more words for the same price."

"I know I can," replied the young woman, "but don't you think I'd look too eager if I said it ten times?"

Fundamentals

"You're the biggest dumbbell I've ever had the misfortune to employ in my coal yard! I can't teach you a thing."

"Well," said Mike, "I've larnt wan thing since I've been with you."

"Yes? And what's that?" asked the employer.

"That sixteen hundred pounds make a ton."

He kept his job.

They Wear Well

Billie proudly announced to his teacher: "We've got a new baby and it cost a hundred dollars."

"Goodness," the teacher replied. "Isn't that a lot of money for a tiny baby?"

"Yes, but think how long they last!"

Better or Worse

Business was a bit dull in town, so the carpet-sweeper salesman thought he'd try a rural neighborhood. When he began his sales talk the hillbilly interrupted with, "Don't waste your breath. I got a carpet sweeper."

The salesman was ready for his reply. "Good," he said. "Then I can make you a generous allowance on your old sweeper in part payment on a splendid new model."

The hillbilly seemed tempted, then shook his head. "No," he said, "I can't make that kind of a deal. After all, I took her for better or wuss."

A Second Thought

Junk Man: "Any beer bottles today, lady?"
Lady: "Do I look as though I drank beer, sir!"
Junk Man: "Any vinegar bottles today, lady?"

He Wasn't Selling Them

A house-hunter got off a train at a suburban station, and said to a boy standing near: "I'm looking for Mr. Brown's new block of brick houses. How far are they from here?"

"Twenty minutes' walk," said the boy.

"Twenty minutes!" exclaimed the prospective buyer. "Nonsense, the advertisement said five."

"Well," replied the boy, "you kin believe me or the advertisement, whichever you want. But I ain't trying to make no sale."

Forgetful

Private Jackson was on the carpet for the third time in as many days. The captain was very stern. "Did you call the sergeant a liar?" he demanded.

"I did, sir," admitted Jackson.

"And a louse?"

"Yes, sir."

"And did you also say he was a cockeyed, knock-kneed, dirty-tongued stooge?"

Jackson hesitated, then said regretfully, "No, sir. I forgot that."

Smile When You Say That

Hubby: "Darling, what's wrong? Why the bandage on your eye?"

Wife: "Don't be funny. This is my new hat."

The Real Test

"Was your uncle sensible until the last?"
"I won't know until his will is read tomorrow."

Biased

"Why don't you like girls?"
"They're too biased."

"Biased?"

"Yeh—buy us this, buy us that, until I'm broke."

An Early Settler

Bystander: "I observe that you treat that gentleman respectfully."

Grocer: "Yes, he's one of our early settlers."

Bystander: "Early settler! Why, he can't be more than thirty years old."

Grocer: "That may be true, but he pays his bills on the first of every month."

A Hard Life

The Navy cook had just prepared orders of fried eggs for a mob of sailors. Wearied by his efforts, he sat down, yawned, lit a black cigar and wrote a letter to his sweetheart.

"Darling," he began, "for the past three hours shells have been bursting all around me."

Juror Excused

A juryman asked the court to be excused, declaring: "I owe a man twenty-five dollars that I borrowed, and as he is leaving town today for some years I want to catch him before he gets to the train and pay him the money."

"You are excused," the judge announced in a cold voice. "I don't want anybody on the jury who can lie like you."

Sold Out

As the train pulled into the station, a traveler on the platform called to a boy and tossed him a coin. "Son," he said, "here's fifty cents. Get me a sandwich and get one for yourself."

Just as the train was pulling out, the boy returned to the platform where the passenger was waiting. "Here's your quarter, mister," he shouted. "They only had one sandwich."

Tired

A farmer drove into town to visit his doctor. "Doc," he said, "the first time you're out our way I wish you'd stop in and see my wife."

"Is she sick?"

"Not exactly."

"What's the trouble, then?"

"Well, yesterday morning she got up at the regular time, about four o'clock, milked the cows, got breakfast for the hands, done her housework, churned, and along about ten o'clock at night she said she felt a bit tired. I expect she needs a tonic or something."

To the Point

The cub reporter was told to cut his story to bare essentials. Following his orders he did so and produced one the next day:

"J. Smith looked up the elevator shaft to see if the car was on its way down. It was. Age 45."

Hard to Recognize

"Is this the laundry?" the irritated customer shouted into the telephone. "Well, you sent me a batch of very old handkerchiefs instead of my shirt."

"They ain't handkerchiefs," replied the laundry, "that's your shirt."

No Stopping

An ambitious young man asked a great merchant to reveal the secret of his success. "There is no secret," said the merchant. "Just jump at your opportunity."

"But," said the young man, "how can I tell when my opportunity is coming?"

"You can't," said the merchant. "You just have to keep jumping."

Inscribed

Little Herbert had bought Grandma a book for Christmas and wanted to write a suitable inscription on the flyleaf. He racked his brain, until suddenly he remembered that his father had a book with an inscription of which he was very proud. So Herbie decided to copy it.

You can imagine Grandma's surprise on Christmas morning when she opened her gift, a Bible, and found neatly inscribed the following phrase: "To Grandma, with the compliments of the Author."

Helpful Suggestion

"How did you lose your job at the dress shop, my dear?"

"Just because of something I said. After I had tried twenty dresses on a woman, she said, 'I think I'd look nicer in something flowing,' so I asked her why she didn't jump in the river."

Never Failed

Passenger: "You'll bring me down safely, won't you?"
Pilot: "I've never left anyone up there yet."

Smart Doctor

Woman: "Doctor, is it true that sleeping outdoors will cure insomnia?"

Doctor: "Perfectly true. But sleeping indoors will do the same thing."

Forever

"Eternity is so vast—who can comprehend it?" said the speaker.

"Perhaps," said the little man in the back row, "you never bought anything on the monthly payment plan."

What's Wrong with Hollywood

A Hollywood film actress was applying for a passport.
"Unmarried?" asked the clerk.
"Occasionally," replied the actress.

Smart Guy

A wise guy stepping up to a bus as it stopped the other morning said to the driver: "Well, Noah, you've got here. Is the Ark full?"
The motorman answered back: "Nope, we need one more monkey. Come on in."

To the Head of the Class

Harold had taken his first dancing lesson. When he returned home his mother asked him how he liked it. "Why, mother, it's easy," said Harold. "All you do is turn around and keep wiping your feet."

Experience

In a college town a student called at a boarding house to ask about rooms.
"What do you charge for your rooms?" he asked.
"Five dollars up," was the reply.
"But I'm a student," he said, thinking the price a little high.
"That being the case, the price is five dollars down," replied the landlady, who had had experience.

Saves Time

Older Woman: "I have my husband trained so he eats out of my hand."
Young Bride: "Saves a lot of dishwashing, doesn't it?"

Reasonable

Bridge Player: "Does your husband complain about getting his dinner so late?"

Other Bridge Player: "Oh, no. He just complains about having to get it."

Sounds Logical

Pat, a truck driver, stopped suddenly on the highway. The car behind crashed into the truck and its owner sued the Irishman.

"Why didn't you hold out your hand?" the judge asked Pat.

"Well," he said indignantly, "if you couldn't see the truck, how in hivin's name could he see my hand?"

Line Is Busy

Bill: "I haven't spoken to my wife in weeks!"

Sam: "Whassa matter? Mad at her?"

Bill: "Nope. I'm afraid to interrupt her!"

Father Knew

Her Father: "What? She's consented to marry you? Young man, you're the second-happiest man in the world.

Patience

Husband: "You will never succeed in making that dog obey you."

Wife: "Nonsense. It is only a matter of patience. I had a lot of trouble with you at first."

Worrying

"You sho' does look worried."

"Boy, I'se booked up solid on worrying. I'se got so many worries on my mind that if sumpin' happens to me today, Ah won't get time to worry about it foh two weeks."

Simple

First Aid Instructor: "How would you rescue a man from drowning?"

Eager Pupil: "That's easy. First you take the man out of the water, and then you take the water out of the man."

Fifty-Fifty

One of the boys who just got back from a Southern trip tells how he heard a couple of Negro fellows talking about a divorce one of them had just received.

"An' what about dat house you an' your woman got?" asked the friend of the lately liberated chap. "What you do wid dat, huh?"

"We splits it up—fifty-fifty."

"Divides yo' house? How you do dat?"

"Fifty-fifty. Ah takes de outside, she takes de inside."

He Fixed It

Husband: "When anything goes wrong around our house, I just get busy and fix it."

Wife: "Yeah? Since you fixed the clock the cuckoo backs out and asks: 'What time is it?' "

Trouble Sleeping

During a conversation with an old friend he hadn't seen for some time, a Florida farmer asked how he had been sleeping.

"I sleep good nights," he said, "and I sleep pretty good mornings, but afternoons I just seem to twist and turn."

High Price of Meat

Farmer: "You can't go wrong on this mare, sir. She's sound, gentle, a good worker and a fine saddle horse."

City Slicker: "What I want to know, is she tender?"

Sinks on Purpose

A Negro was asked if he wouldn't like to volunteer for sub-marine duty.

To this the gangling, good-natured boy replied: "No, suh. I don't want to get on no ship that sinks on purpose."

Income Tax

Some day a tax return may contain only three questions:
How much money have you got?
Where is it?
How soon can you get at it?

Best Years

They were having one of those dandy marital arguments and the little woman was getting to the tearful stage. "How can you talk to me like that," she wailed, "after I've given you the best years of my life?"

"Yeah?" returned the husband, unimpressed by her emotion. "And who made 'em the best years of your life?"

Boyhood Dream

Lawyer: "As a boy I always wanted to be a pirate."

Businessman: "You're lucky—not everyone gets to realize his boyhood ambition."

Stealing

Husband: "If a man steals—no matter what—he will live to regret it."

Wife: "You used to steal kisses."

Husband: "Well, you heard what I said."

Bought and Paid For

Joan, five, out to tea, was puzzled when she saw the family bow their heads for grace.

"What are you doing?" she said.

"Giving thanks for our daily bread," she was told. "Don't you give thanks at home, Joan?"

"No," said Joan, "we pay for our bread."

Misunderstood

Customer: "Give me a pound of those grapes. My husband is fond of them. Do you know if they have been sprayed with any kind of poison?"

Clerk: "No, ma'am; you'll have to get that at the drug-store."

Hired Him

Among the questions asked in the examination of an applicant for a place on the Washington police force was this one: "What would you do to disperse a crowd quickly and quietly?"

The answer: "I'd pass the hat."

Wrong Idea

She: "Did anyone ever tell you how wonderful you are?"

He: "No, I don't think anyone ever did."

She: "Then I'd like to know how and where you got the idea?"

Wrong Business

"I feel sure, my poor man," said the sympathetic old lady, visiting a prison, "it was poverty that brought you to this."

"No, ma'am, quite the contrary," returned the prisoner. "I happened to be coining money."

Special Service

"I ordered a dozen oranges, but you sent me only ten."

"Part of our special service, madam. Two were bad, so we threw them away for you."

Complete Information

The junior member of a firm of lawyers went several hundred miles to consult a client. When he arrived, he found he had forgotten his client's name. He telegraphed his partner, "What is our client's name?"

The answer came: "Jones, Joseph H. Yours is Kent, Jasper T."

Guilty

Conscientious Citizen: "I couldn't serve as a juror, Judge. One look at that fellow convinces me he's guilty."

Judge: "Quiet. That's the district attorney."

Married Life

Young Actor: "I've got a job at last, Father. It's a new play and I'm a man who has been married twenty years."

Father: "Splendid. That's a start anyway, my boy. Maybe some of these days they'll give you a 'speaking' part."

Cold

Two mountaineers were complaining about the cold. "Nearest I ever came to freezing," said one, "was when I was holding the lantern for my wife while she cut the kindling."

He Had the Answer

The teacher had forbidden the eating of candy and the chewing of gum during school time. One day she became suspicious of a lump in Jimmie's cheek.

"Jimmie, are you eating candy or are you chewing gum?" she asked.

"No, ma'am," replied Jimmie. "I'm just soaking a prune to eat at recess."

An Old One but Good

A Harvard man enlisted in the United States Army as a private. He had been in service only a few weeks when his captain posted a notice on the bulletin board. The Harvard man read it and sniffed.

"It is pretty hard," he told another soldier, "to take orders from a man who knows no better than to end a sentence with a preposition."

The captain overheard him. Next day the bulletin carried this notice: "There is in this company a certain amount of insubordination up with which I shall not put."

Good Observation

A city boy and a country lad were walking down a street. Coming toward them was a product of the beauty parlor—permanent wave, scarlet fingernails, drugstore complexion and gaudy lipstick.

"Now what do you think of that?" asked the city boy.

The farm boy looked carefully and observed: "Speaking as a farmer, I should say that it must have been mighty poor soil to require so much top-dressing."

In Texas

A Harvard professor, traveling deep in the heart of Texas, found himself seated next to a Texas cowboy and fell into conversation with him. The Texan confessed to eighty-seven years of age, whereupon the professor said: "To what do you attribute your remarkable longevity?"

The Texan thought a moment and answered gravely: "Well, I never stole a horse and I never called a man a liar to his face."

Salesman

Customer: "You don't seem quick at figures, my boy."

Newsie: "I'm out of practice, sir. Most people say, 'Keep the change.'"

Baseball

A country girl attended her first ball game. After watching the entire game she met one of the players. In her sweet little way she asked, "Why does the fellow behind the plate wear the muzzle when it's the one with the big stick in his hand that does all the growling?"

Penny and Dollar

The dollar, with his nose turned up scornfully, said to the penny: "Why, I am worth one hundred of you." "Yes," said the penny, "but even at that I am a good deal better than you. I go to Sunday school and church, both. You don't show up at either one."

Handle with Care

"Sorry to hear your engagement is broken off, old man."
"I'll get over it. But the worst blow was when she returned my ring marked 'Glass—Handle With Care.'"

Be Careful!

Bill: "How do you like this rainy weather?"
Joe: "It's terrible."
Bill: "And how's your wife?"
Joe: "Oh, about the same."

Of Course

Adam and Eve were naming the animals, when a hippopotamus strolled past.
"Well," said Adam, "what are we going to call it?"
Eve said, "Let's call it a hippopotamus."
"Why?" asked Adam.
"Well," said Eve, "it looks more like a hippopotamus than anything else so far."

Wanted a Good Job

Whistler had a French poodle of which he was very fond. One day the poodle had an infection of the throat, and Whistler had the audacity to send for the great throat specialist Mackenzie.

When Mackenzie saw that he had been called to treat a dog, he was incensed but said nothing. He prescribed, pocketed his fee and drove away.

The next day he sent hurriedly for Whistler. Whistler, thinking he had been summoned on some matter connected with his beloved dog, dropped his work and rushed to the home of Mackenzie.

On his arrival, the medical specialist said gravely, "How do you do, Mr. Whistler? I wanted to see you about having my front door painted."

Confidence

An old banker who pioneered in a small Western town was being interviewed about his career.

Interviewer: "How did you get started in banking?"

Old Banker: "It was simple. I put up a sign saying 'Bank.' A man came in and gave me one hundred dollars. Another came in with two hundred dollars. By that time my confidence reached such a point that I put in fifty dollars of my own money."

Answer: No More

He: "Dear, you must be more careful. The bank has just returned the last check you wrote."

She: "Darling, that's wonderful. What shall we buy with it this time?"

Not So Green a Buyer

A boy walked into a farmer's melon patch and asked the price of a fine big melon.

"That's forty cents," said the farmer.

"I have only four cents," the boy told him.

"Well," smiled the farmer and winked at his hired hand as he pointed to a very small and very green melon, "how about that one?"

"Fine. I'll take it," the boy said, "but don't cut it off the vine yet. I'll call for it in a week or so."

Attention, D.A.R.

They're telling of the Boston salesman who visited Texas and heard one particular Texan boasting about heroes of the Alamo who, almost alone, held off whole armies.

"I'll bet you never had anybody so brave around Boston," challenged the Texan.

"Did you ever hear of Paul Revere?" asked the Bostonian.

"Paul Revere?" said the Texan. "Isn't that the guy that ran for help?"

On the Up and Up

He was making his first ocean voyage and was in his cabin, groaning with seasickness.

"Shall I send you some dinner, sir?" the steward asked.

"No," was the reply. "Just throw it overboard and save me the trouble."

Good Mixture

An eminent painter was once asked what he mixed his colors with in order to produce so extraordinary an effect.

"I mix them with brains, sir," was his answer.

His Fault

Little Sue ran into the house crying as though her heart would break.

"What's wrong, dear?" asked her mother.

"My dolly—Billy broke it," she sobbed.

"How did he break it, dear?" asked Mother.

"I hit him on the head with it!"

He Remembered Him

Little six-year-old Jimmie was asked by his Sunday-school teacher: "And Jimmie, what are you going to give your little brother for Christmas this year?"

"I dunno," said Jimmie, "I gave him the measles last year."

Excitement

Willie to the circus went,
He thought it was immense;
His little heart went pitter-pat,
For the excitement was in tents.
                            —*Harvard Lampoon*

O.K., Yale, Tell It Your Way

Three young men from Yale, Princeton and Harvard were in a room when a lady entered. The Yale boy asked casually if someone ought not to give a chair to the lady; the Princeton lad slowly brought one; and the Harvard boy deliberately sat down in it.

Flashes of Silence

Sydney Smith said of Macaulay, "He once talked too much; but now he has occasional flashes of silence that make his conversation perfectly delightful."

Better Example

He was the young son of a bishop, and his mother was teaching him the meaning of courage.

"Suppose," she said, "there were ten boys in one bedroom, and nine got into bed at once, while the other knelt down to say his prayers. That boy would show true courage."

"Oh!" said the youngster. "I know something even more

courageous! Supposing there were ten bishops in one bedroom, and one got into bed without saying his prayers!"

Otherwise A Good Letter

Sam's wife cautioned him to control his temper in the letter he was about to write to a man who owed him for a diamond he had bought for his wife many months before.

"Be diplomatic, Sam," she warned. "Don't write notting dot might offend him."

"All right, Momma," he agreed.

Sam finished the letter and showed it to his wife for her approval.

"A verry, verry nize ledder," she admitted. "But, dollink, skunk ain't spelt vith two k's."

Lucky

Patient: "Man, what an awful bill just for one week's treatment."

Doctor: "My good fellow, if you knew what an interesting case yours was, and how strongly I was tempted to let it go to a post-mortem, you wouldn't grumble at a bill three times as large."

Curiosity

An insurance agent was filling out an application blank.

"Have you ever had appendicitis?" he asked the applicant.

"Well," he answered, "I was operated on, but I have never felt quite sure whether it was appendicitis or professional curiosity."

It's I

A Harvard man and a Yale man heard a knock at the door. The Yale man said: "Who's there?"

A voice said: "It's me."

The Harvard man, with a pained expression asked: "What is that oaf trying to say?"

Modern Toys

Mother (*examining toy*): "Isn't this rather complicated for a small child?"

Clerk: "It's an educational toy designed to adjust a child to live in the world today; any way he puts it together it's wrong."

Circus

When visitors came, Sonny, age five, took them to see the pigs in their electric fence enclosure, explaining, "When the piggies back into the 'lectric fence there'll be a short circus."

If He Had the Chance

The jury had been arguing for hours.

At last they straggled back, and the foreman, a mountaineer, expressed the opinion: "We don't think he did it," he said, "for we don't believe he was there; but we think he would have done it if he had had the chance."

Temptation

Grocer (*to boy standing near box of apples*): "Hey! Are you trying to take an apple?"

Boy: "No, I'm trying not to take one."

Recognized Him

Two farmers were sitting on the porch of the general store when a smart aleck drove up in a flashy convertible.

"Hey, you," yelled the smart aleck, "how long has this town been dead?"

"Can't be long," snapped back one of the natives. "You're the first buzzard we've seen."

Not So Backward

The mother went shopping with her small son. The grocer invited the boy to help himself to a handful of cherries. But the boy seemed backward.

"Don't you like cherries?" the grocer asked.

"Yes," said the boy.

The grocer put his hand in and dumped a generous portion into the little fellow's pocket, which he promptly held out. Afterward his mother asked him why he had not taken the cherries when first invited.

" 'Cause his hand was bigger'n mine," was the answer.

It Was a Tactless Laugh

"Have you ever laughed until you cried?"

"Yes, just last night I did."

"How?"

"Dad stepped on a tack. I laughed—he heard me—and then I cried."

Some Progress

The freshman class in trigonometry was reciting.

"And have you proved this proposition?" asked the professor.

"Well," said the freshman, "proved is a strong word, but I can say that I have rendered it highly probable."

Trouble

A little hillbilly watched a man at a tourist camp making use of a comb and a brush, a toothbrush, a nail file and a whisk broom.

"Say, mister," he finally queried, "are you always that much trouble to yourself?"

And a Closed Mind?

A politician is a person who approaches every subject with an open mouth.—*Adlai Stevenson, former governor of Illinois before the Executives' Club of Chicago, June 3, 1952.*

That's Different

Professor: "And whatever on earth made you write a paragraph like that?"
Student: "I quoted it from Dickens, sir."
Professor: "Beautiful lines, aren't they?"—*Dartmouth College Jack-O'-Lantern.*

Only God Above Him

Somebody once asked Professor Charles Townsend Copeland of Harvard why he lived on the top floor of Hollis Hall, in his small, dusty old rooms, and suggested that he move.

"No," said Copeland, "no, I shall always live on the top floor. It is the only place in Cambridge where God alone is above me." Then after a pause, "He's busy—but He's quiet."

INDEX

INDEX

A

Ability to speak, how to acquire, 33-34, 43, 45
Acquiring speaker's attitude, 50
Actors, quotations about, 194-195
Addison, Joseph, on humor, 29
Address
  of chairman, introducing speaker, 24, 25-27
  to chairman, 48
Advertisers, quotations about, 195
Age, quotations about, 195-197
Always have a message, 55-56
Anecdotes, how to use effectively, 29, 85-89
Announcements during program, 18
Anspach, Charles L., use of quotation in conclusion by, 83-84
Architects, quotations about, 197
Arrangement, ventilation, etc., of meeting room, 18-19
Artists, quotations about, 198-199
Astronomers, quotations about, 199
Attitude
  acquiring of speaker's, 50
  of responsibility in public speaking, 36-37
Audience
  conversing with, 52-53
  getting good will of, 20-21
  members of, are guests, 11
  physical well-being of, 18-19
  preparation for, 66
  presenting idea to, 56-57, 65
  treatment of, 11
Authors, quotations about, 199-200

B

Bankers, quotations about, 200-201
Barkley, Alben W.
  humorous introduction by, 78-79
  response by, 132
Beginner, vs. expert speaker, 41-42
Birthdays, special announcements of, 120-121
Body of speech, planning of, 79-81

Bradley, Dr. Preston, response by, 130
Breakfast, quotations about, 201-202
Brewster, Senator Owen, on introduction of himself as speaker, 23-24
Business
  and businessmen, quotations about, 202-203
  public speaking in, 35
Butler, Nicholas Murray, 6
Byrd, Admiral Richard E., response by, 128-129

C

Canham, Erwin D., on statement of topic, 77
Carlyle, Thomas, on books, 87
Carothers, Dr. Neil, response by, 134-135
Cause, for stage fright, 51
Chairman
  addressing, 48
  preparation for meeting, 31
  see also Toastmaster
Chess, T. Louis, introduction by, 108
Clergymen, quotations about, 203-205
Cleverness, in presentation and subject matter, 58-59, 61
Climax, use of, in telling anecdote, 88-89
Coleridge, Samuel Taylor, on epigrams, 29-30
Collins, Tom, response by, 126-127, 131
Commending the speaker, 21-22
Conclusion, of speech or talk, 81-82, 84
Consultation, value of, 67-68
Conversation
  with audience, 52-53
  and public speaking, 36, 44, 55-56
Conzelman, Jimmy, introduction by, 91-92

338

Index

341

Politicians, quotations about, 226
Power
    development of, through public speaking, 40, 46, 60
    of speech and expression, 60
Practice, expertness a matter of, 42-43
Preparation
    for meeting, 30-31
    vs. presentation of subject matter, 65-66
    various meanings, 63-64
Presentation, of ideas, 39-40
Preston, Keith, conclusion by, 86-87
Procedure, to become speaker, 43-44
Prochnow, Herbert V., excerpts from speeches by, 165-166
Profession, public speaking in, 35
Program
    announcements, entertainment and other parts of, 18
    brief opening comments, 18
    last-minute changes in, 28-29
    length, 12-13
    plan complete, 1-3, 18
    preparation of introductions in advance, 20
    subjects for, 3
Publicity
    for meeting, 8-10, 14
    for speaker, 8-10
Public speaking
    in business life, 35
    and conversation, 44, 55-56
    first steps to, 47-54
    instructions, 34
    motive for study of, 34-39
    responsibility in, 1-16, 36-37
    in social affairs, 36
    stage fright, 50-52
    training for, 33-40

Q

Questions
    asking of, 47
    expanding of, 48-49
Quotations
    for many occasions, 193-242
    use of, in conclusion, 83-84

R

Recitation, The Dissatisfied Golfer, 91-92
Reed, Philip D., introduction by, 119-120
Reflect, read, consult, 66

Remarks, offering of brief, 49
Remedy, for stage fright, 52
Reputation, quotations about, 232-235
Requirement, for speaking, 41
Response, illustrations of how, speakers to toastmasters, 125-138
Responsibility
    attitude toward, in conversation vs. public speaking, 36
    neglect of, and success, 37
    in public speaking, 36-37
        self-expression, 38
    of toastmaster, 1-16
Restatement, of chief points of speech, 82-83
Reward, in public speaking, 37-38, 45-46
Rockefeller, John D., restatement of chief points of speech by, 82-83
Rogers, W. B., as a chairman, 26
Roosevelt, Theodore, introduction to speech by, 76-77

S

Scholars, quotations about, 228-229
Scientists, quotations about, 228-229
Self-confidence, acquiring, 50
Self-expression, 38
Shakespeare, William, anecdote used by, 86
Short, Dewey, response by, 127
Sibley, Dr. Carroll, response by, 133-134
Skeleton of talk. See Plan
Snyder, Dr. Franklyn B.
    introduction of speech by, 111-113
    response by, 132-133
Social affairs, public speaking in, 36
Speaker
    ability, training, 33-40
    acquiring attitude of, 50
    commending of, 21-22
    after completion of talk, 25
    courtesies shown to, 7-8
    failure to arrive, 15-16
    good-natured "kidding" of, 22-24
    how and where to secure, 3-4
    impulse to become, 56-57
    after introduction, 24-25
    introduction of several, 25-27
    obligations to, 10-11
    presentation of ideas, 39-40
    publicity for, 8-10
    stage fright, cause and remedy, 50-52